# COMMON
# GRACE

*For Don and Gae Fleming –*
*our friends 'on the other side of the world'*

# COMMON GRACE

## LIFE AND FAITH
## IN CLASSIC LITERATURE

—— COMPILED BY: ——

# MARY BATCHELOR

*Common Grace: Life and Faith in Classic Literature*

This collection copyright © 2003 Mary Batchelor.

Original edition published in English under the title *The Lion Literature Collection on the Human and the Divine* by Lion Hudson plc, Oxford, England.

Copyright © Lion Hudson plc 2004

Cover Photo: ©Stockbyte Photography. Used with Permission.

Published by
Hendrickson Publishers, Inc.
P. O. Box 3473
Peabody, Massachusetts 01961-3473

ISBN 1-56563-603-1

*Printed in the United States of America*

*First Printing — October 2005*

**Library of Congress Cataloging-in-Publication Data**

Lion literature collection on the human and the divine.
    Common grace : life and faith in classic literature / compiled by Mary Batchelor.
        p. cm.
    Originally published: The Lion literature collection on the human and the divine. Oxford : Lion, 2003.
    Includes bibliographical references and index.
    ISBN 1-56563-603-1 (alk. paper)
    1. Faith—Literary collections. I. Batchelor, Mary. II. Title.
    PN6071.F17L56 2005
    808.8°'0382—dc22
                                                                    2005011141

# Contents

*Introduction*   12

*Thank You!*   14

Part One: The World We Live In   15

*Home*   16
New Testament Second Letter to the Corinthians   16
New Testament Gospel of John   16
J.R.R. Tolkien   17
Kenneth Grahame   18
C.S. Lewis   20
Charles Dickens   21
J.M. Coetzee   23

*Countryside and Animals*   25
Old Testament Book of Psalms   25
Old Testament Book of Psalms   25
Francis Kilvert   26
Dorothy Wordsworth   28
George MacDonald   30
Ellis Peters (Edith Pargeter)   31
Hans Christian Andersen   32
Aldous Huxley   34
Gilbert White   36
James Boswell   37
Charles Dickens   38
Rudyard Kipling   40
Robert Louis Stevenson   42
Hugh Lofting   44
Anna Sewell   46
Evelyn Waugh   48

*Food*   50
New Testament Gospel of John   50
New Testament Gospel of John   50
Kenneth Grahame   52
Doris Lessing   53
George Borrow   54
Samuel Pepys   56

Henry Handel Richardson (Ethel Robertson)  57
Charles Dickens  59
Lewis Carroll (Charles Dodgson)  61
Thomas Love Peacock  63
Walter Brueggemann  64

*The Church and its People*  66
New Testament Letter to the Ephesians  66
New Testament First Letter to Timothy  66
Alexander Pope  68
Francis Kilvert  70
Jonathan Swift  71
G.K. Chesterton  73
William Golding  75
Malcolm Muggeridge  77
Alan Bennett  79
P.D. James  81
J.B. Phillips  83
Iris Murdoch  85
Elizabeth Goudge  87

Part Two: Being Human  89

*Happiness, Laughter and Recreation*  90
Old Testament Book of Psalms  90
Old Testament Book of Ecclesiastes  90
William Law  91
William Cowper  92
G.K. Chesterton  93
Laurence Sterne  94
Iris Murdoch  96
Marcel Proust  97
Elizabeth Gaskell  98
Miguel de Cervantes  100
Izaak Walton  102
Thomas Hardy  103
Francis Kilvert  105
Charles Dickens  106
Kenneth Grahame  108

*Giving and Self-Giving*  110
New Testament Second Letter to the Corinthians  110

Elizabeth Gaskell   111
A.A. Milne   113
The Venerable Bede   115
Louisa May Alcott   116
Charles Dickens   118
John Foxe   120
O. Henry (William Sydney Porter)   122
Alan Paton   125

*Suffering*   127
Old Testament Book of Lamentations   127
Old Testament Book of Daniel   128
New Testament Second Letter to the Corinthians   130
Blaise Pascal   131
John Newton   132
Susan Howatch   134
Daniel Defoe   136
Thomas More   137
Charles Lamb   138
Eleanor Spence   140
Alexander Whyte   142

*Grief and Loss*   144
Old Testament Second Book of Samuel   144
Laurence Sterne   146
Charles Dickens   147
C.S. Lewis   149
Francis Kilvert   151
Susan Hill   152
William Shakespeare   154
Penelope Lively   155
Thomas Gray   157

*Human Love*   158
Old Testament Book of the Song of Songs   158
Dante Alighieri   159
George Eliot (Mary Ann Evans)   161
Aldous Huxley   162
George Bernard Shaw   164
Marcel Proust   166
Jane Austen   168
Fyodor Dostoevsky   170

Part Three: Knowing God   173

*The Cross and the Resurrection*   174
New Testament First Letter of Peter   174
New Testament First Letter to the Corinthians   174
C.S. Lewis   175
John Bunyan   177
Dorothy L. Sayers   179
Thomas à Kempis   181
William Penn   183
John Grisham   185
Malcolm Muggeridge   187
Leo Tolstoy   188
Piers Paul Read   190
John Irving   192

*Repentance, Forgiveness and Reconciliation*   194
New Testament Gospel of Luke   194
Aldous Huxley   196
G.K. Chesterton   197
Charles Dickens   199
John Bunyan   200
Les Murray   201
Herman Melville   202
Paul Scott   204

*Prayer and the Presence of God*   207
New Testament Gospel of Matthew   207
Old Testament Book of Genesis   208
William Law   209
John Donne   211
Leo Tolstoy   212
Teresa of Avila   214
Alexander Solzhenitsyn   216
Maya Angelou (Marguerite Johnson)   218
Teresa of Avila   219
Margery Kempe   220
Samuel Johnson   221

*Divine Love*   222
Old Testament Book of Hosea   222
New Testament First Letter of John   223
Julian of Norwich   224

William Langland   225
Simone Weil   226
Isak Dinesen (Karen Blixen)   227
*The Cloud of Unknowing*   229
Graham Greene   230

*Last Things*   232
New Testament Second Letter of Peter   232
New Testament Book of Revelation   233
John Donne   234
C.S. Lewis   236
John Bunyan   237
The Brothers Grimm   238
Richard Baxter   239


Part Four: Good and Evil   241

*Angels and Devils*   242
New Testament Gospel of Luke   242
New Testament First Letter of Peter   242
Beryl Bainbridge   243
John Bunyan   244
C.S. Lewis   246
Joseph Conrad   248
C.S. Lewis   250

*Goodness and Strivings for Goodness*   252
New Testament Letter to the Romans   252
Old Testament Book of Micah   252
Charles Lamb   253
Samuel Butler   254
Mark Twain (Samuel Langhorne Clemens)   255
Oscar Wilde   256
Melvyn Bragg   258
Jeremy Taylor   260
Anthony Trollope   261
Maya Angelou (Marguerite Johnson)   263
George Eliot (Mary Ann Evans)   266
Peter Ackroyd   268
Ellis Peters (Edith Pargeter)   269
Laura Ingalls Wilder   271
Geoffrey Chaucer   273

*Reaching Out to Others* 275
Old Testament Book of Amos 275
The Venerable Bede 277
Charles Kingsley 279
Harriet Beecher Stowe 280
Charles Dickens 282
George Orwell (Eric Arthur Blair) 283
Daniel Defoe 285
Elizabeth Gaskell 287
Lady Mary Wortley Montagu 289

*Foibles and Vices* 291
New Testament Letter to the Colossians 291
Jane Austen 292
Beatrix Potter 294
Samuel Pepys 295
Arnold Bennett 297
George Eliot (Mary Ann Evans) 299
Samuel Butler 301
William Langland 303
Rose Macaulay 305

*Truth and Pretence* 307
New Testament Gospel of John 307
New Testament First Letter of John 307
William Makepeace Thackeray 308
Lewis Carroll (Charles Dodgson) 310
Tom Wolfe 312
Beatrix Potter 314
Dorothy L. Sayers 316
T.S. Eliot 317

*War and Peace* 318
Old Testament Book of Micah 318
Old Testament First Book of Samuel 319
Wilfred Owen 320
Abraham Lincoln 321
Jonathan Swift 322
Sebastian Faulks 324
Winston Churchill 326
John Betjeman 328
Richard Baxter 330
Leo Tolstoy 331

Part Five: The Cycle of Life   333

*Birth, Childhood and Youth*   *334*
Old Testament Book of Psalms   334
New Testament Gospel of Luke   334
Tim Winton   335
E.M. Forster   337
L.P. Hartley   339
Maxim Gorky (Aleksei Maximovich Peshkov)   341
Daisy Ashford   343
Anton Chekhov   345
Kenneth Grahame   347
Dorothy L. Sayers   349
Dennis Potter   350

*Age*   *351*
Old Testament Book of Ecclesiastes   351
Barbara Pym   352
Muriel Spark   354
The Brothers Grimm   356
Ivan Turgenev   357
Margaret Forster   359
Christina Stead   361
Anne Tyler   363

*Death and Dying*   *364*
New Testament Book of Acts   364
Cuthbert, Abbot of Wearmouth and Jarrow   365
John Bunyan   367
Francis Bacon   369
James Boswell   370
John Updike   372
Peter Ackroyd   374
Evelyn Waugh   375
The Brothers Grimm   377
Muriel Spark   379
John Donne   381
Pope John XXIII (Angelo Roncalli)   382

*Author Biographies*   *384*
*Index of Authors*   *401*
*Index of Book Titles*   *403*
*Acknowledgements*   *406*

# Introduction

'If you believe in goodness and if you value the approval of God, fix your minds on whatever is true and honourable and just and pure and lovely and admirable' (Philippians 4). Paul's excellent advice has guided the compilation of this anthology.

My chief objective has been to aim for truth. A fictional story has as much if not more claim to be true as some accounts supposedly based on fact. Jesus used fiction in his parables, yet they are the embodiment of truth. Good writers of fiction portray the human condition truthfully and with integrity. Good literature does not glorify vice and undermine virtue – nor does it falsely idealize virtue. Instead it reflects the complexity of life and the conflicting demands of good and evil. It admits the self-gratification and also the pain caused by breaking God's commandments for right living. For example, Tolstoy's *Anna Karenina* and Galsworthy's *Forsyte Saga* both portray adultery and the deserting of marriage vows; Tolstoy with truth and complexity and Galsworthy, in my view, with false sentiment and half-truths. In *Crime and Punishment*, Dostoevsky uncovers the startling reality of mounting guilt and horror for a murderer who had expected no such consequences of his planned and reasoned brutality.

The Bible, supremely, tells a story as it is. Bible characters are depicted as real human beings, warts and all. Sometimes the author records the facts without moral comment and the reader is left to draw his or her own conclusions. Bible narratives are not for the prudish or faint-hearted. Think, for example, of Tamar, King David's daughter, incestuously raped by her half-brother, who then cruelly rejects her. He, for his crime, is brutally murdered by Tamar's brother Absalom, which in turn leads to a further trail of disaster. Some non-biblical extracts I have used also come from books not all readers might have the stomach for. But where an author throws light on the human condition with the clear ring of truth, I have decided to include something from their work. Good fiction rings true; it encourages us to exercise our moral judgement, leads to greater understanding of ourselves and of others, broadens our compassion and expands our knowledge of life and of human strength and frailty.

Extracts come from popular as well as so-called highbrow authors. John Grisham or Susan Howatch might not win top literary prizes but they are widely read by a huge cross-section of people, a fact that would disqualify them only in the eyes of literary snobs. These two authors tell stories that are irresistible page-turners – quite an achievement! Both also write from a standpoint of personal Christian conviction and values.

Books that had great influence in their own generation – and some that have stood the test of many centuries – are also represented. John Bunyan's *Pilgrim's Progress* is a winner on both these counts; William Law's *A Serious Call to a Devout and Holy Life* and Thomas à Kempis's *The Imitation of Christ* are two other such writings. I have also included some classic children's books and fairy stories, which speak truth in the guise of fantasy and are an important part of our earliest memories.

Personal taste has strongly influenced the selection. With such an enormous field to choose from, I naturally picked out books that have delighted me or have awakened my compassion or my conscience, and enlarged my own understanding of the mysteries of life and death. I also took the golden opportunity to embark on books that most of us know from their titles only and which I had always meant to read. But there are plenty of blameworthy omissions; in some cases I lacked space and in other instances extracts did not fall happily within the topics I finally selected as most fruitful. These neglected titles still stare reproachfully at me from overloaded bookshelves and I apologize to them and to my readers alike. So if you search the index in vain for inclusion of *your* favourites – or if some particularly appropriate author has been left out – I hope you will mentally slot it into its rightful place in the collection. Of course my excuse for the omission could well be, in Dr Johnson's words: 'Ignorance, madam, pure ignorance.'

Extracts in this volume are grouped under subject headings – with disparate authors sometimes making interesting bedfellows. The topics reflect, I hope, the main concerns of life and those which most reflect spiritual aspirations and needs. Amusing or satirical writings are sprinkled throughout rather than being put together in one section so that more serious topics can be leavened by laughter – or at least broad smiles.

I have so much enjoyed and benefited from making this collection. I hope and pray that laughter and tears, pleasure, enrichment and a growth in spiritual understanding and maturity will be the experience of readers too.

# Thank You!

Warm thanks to Morag Reeve, my editor, who has been unfailingly kind and wise in her comments, ready at hand but never obtrusive or overbearing. My thanks, too, to Jenni Dutton, with her colleague Sarah Hall, for excellent editing of the text. Many other people have helped in this project by their positive suggestions or unconscious comments. My thanks to them all.

My family – as always – has given unstinting support. My husband Alan, especially, has helped in very practical ways, taking on duties to give me time to write and listening patiently to endless talk about my hobby-horse of the moment. Our sons, Graham and Oliver, have listened, discussed, prayed and sent me books, renewing enthusiasm when my own waned. Our daughter, Pauline Shelton, now an Anglican priest, but previously a senior publishing editor, has given endless advice – technical, literary and spiritual. My thanks to them all and to their much-loved marriage partners.

Friends who are members of our church Home Group have been a constant support, by their genuine and continuing interest and prayers, as well as practical help, especially while I was recovering from surgery. Antony Beeley, a former French and Russian teacher, gave valuable advice in his special fields. David Saunders has kindly given excellent and much-needed help on the computer front in numerous emergencies. My deep gratitude to them all.

Professor Ronald Tamplin, poet and critic, gave warm support and advice on translations. Gae Fleming, in Australia, and some of her family, particularly her son Bruce, have recommended and sent me some of the books included from 'down under'.

My thanks to them all and many others but above all to God, the Spirit of truth, who has at all times been alongside to help. *Deo soli honor et gloria.*

*Mary Batchelor*

# PART ONE

# *THE WORLD WE LIVE IN*

# HOME

## A permanent home

We know that when this tent we live in – our body here on earth – is torn down, God will have a house in heaven for us to live in, a home he himself has made, which will last for ever... We know that as long as we are at home in the body we are away from the Lord's home. For our life is a matter of faith, not of sight. We are full of courage and would much prefer to leave our home in the body and be at home with the Lord. More than anything else, however, we want to please him, whether in our home here or there.

From 2 Corinthians 5

## Heaven is our home

*Before his death and resurrection, Jesus encouraged his followers with these words:*

Believe in God, and believe also in me. There are many rooms in my Father's house, and I am going to prepare a place for you. I would not tell you this if it were not so. And after I go and prepare a place for you, I will come back and take you to myself, so that you will be where I am.

From John 14

## J.R.R. Tolkien (1892–1973)

# *The hobbit's hole*

In a hole in the ground there lived a hobbit. Not a nasty, dirty, wet hole filled with the ends of worms and an oozy smell, nor yet a dry, bare, sandy hole with nothing in it to sit down on or to eat: it was a hobbit-hole, and that means comfort.

It had a perfectly round door like a porthole, painted green, with a shiny yellow brass knob in the exact middle. The door opened onto a tube-shaped hall like a tunnel: a very comfortable tunnel without smoke, with panelled walls, and floors tiled and carpeted, provided with polished chairs, and lots and lots of pegs for hats and coats – the hobbit was fond of visitors. The tunnel wound on and on, going fairly but not quite straight into the side of the hill – the Hill, as all the people for many miles round called it – and many little round doors opened out of it, first on one side and then on the other. No going upstairs for the hobbit: bedrooms, bathrooms, cellars, pantries (lots of these), wardrobes (he had whole rooms devoted to clothes), kitchens, dining-rooms, all were on the same floor, and indeed on the same passage. The best rooms were all on the left-hand side (going in), for these were the only ones to have windows, deep-set round windows looking over his garden, and meadows beyond, sloping down to the river.

From *The Hobbit*, 1937

Kenneth Grahame (1859–1932)

# *Home, sweet home*

The tunnel was close and airless, and the earthy smell was strong, and it seemed a long time to Rat ere the passage ended and he could stand erect and stretch and shake himself. The Mole struck a match, and by its light the Rat saw that they were standing in an open space, neatly swept and sanded underfoot, and directly facing them was Mole's little front door, with 'Mole End' painted, in Gothic lettering, over the bell-pull at the side.

Mole reached down a lantern from a nail on the wall and lit it, and the Rat, looking round him, saw that they were in a sort of forecourt. A garden-seat stood on one side of the door, and on the other, a roller; for the Mole, who was a tidy animal when at home, could not stand having his ground kicked up by other animals into little runs that ended in earth-heaps. On the walls hung wire baskets with ferns in them, alternating with brackets carrying plaster statuary – Garibaldi, and the infant Samuel, and Queen Victoria, and other heroes of modern Italy. Down one side of the forecourt ran a skittle-alley, with benches along it and little wooden tables marked with rings that hinted at beer-mugs. In the middle was a small round pond containing goldfish and surrounded by a cockle-shell border...

Mole's face beamed at the sight of all these objects so dear to him, and he hurried Rat through the door, lit a lamp in the hall, and took one glance round his old home. He saw the dust lying thick on everything, saw the cheerless, deserted look of the long-neglected house, and its narrow, meagre dimensions, its worn and shabby contents – and collapsed again on a hall chair, his nose in his paws. 'O, Ratty!' he cried dismally, 'why did I ever do it? Why did I ever bring you to this poor, cold little place, on a night like this, when you might have been at River Bank by this time, toasting your toes before a blazing fire, with all your own nice things about you!'

The Rat paid no heed to his doleful self-reproaches. He was running here and there, opening doors, inspecting rooms and cupboards, and lighting lamps and candles and sticking them up everywhere. 'What a capital little house this is!' he called out cheerily. 'So compact! So well-planned! Everything here and everything in its place! We'll make a jolly night of it. The first thing we want is a good fire; I'll see to that – I always know where to find things. So this is the parlour? Splendid! Your own idea, those little sleeping-bunks in the wall? Capital! Now, I'll fetch the wood and the coals, and you get a duster, Mole – you'll find one in the drawer of the kitchen table – and try and smarten things up. Bustle about, old chap!'

From *The Wind in the Willows*, 1908

C.S. Lewis (1898–1963)

# *Home for a faun*

Mr Tumnus turned suddenly aside as if he were going to walk straight into an unusually large rock, but at the last moment Lucy found that he was leading her into the entrance of a cave. As soon as they were inside she found herself blinking in the light of a wood fire. Then Mr Tumnus stooped and took a flaming piece of wood out of the fire with a neat little pair of tongs and lit a lamp. 'Now we shan't be long,' he said, and immediately put the kettle on.

Lucy thought she had never been in a nicer place. It was a little, dry, clean cave of reddish stone with a carpet on the floor and two little chairs ('one for me and one for a friend,' said Mr Tumnus) and a table and a dresser and a mantelpiece over the fire and above that a picture of an old faun with a grey beard. In one corner was a door which Lucy thought must lead to Mr Tumnus's bedroom, and on one wall was a shelf full of books. Lucy looked at these while he was setting out the tea things.

From *The Lion, the Witch and the Wardrobe*, 1950

## Charles Dickens (1812–70)

# *An Englishman's castle is his home*

*Mr Wemmick is clerk to Mr Jaggers, the London lawyer who is guardian to Pip after he enters upon his 'great expectations'. Pip meets Mr Wemmick when he goes regularly to collect his allowance, and one evening, he is invited to visit his home in Walworth:*

Wemmick's house was a little wooden cottage in the midst of plots of garden, and the top of it was cut out and painted like a battery mounted with guns.

'My own doing,' said Wemmick. 'Looks pretty; don't it?'

I highly commended it. I think it was the smallest house I ever saw; with the queerest gothic windows (by far the greater part of them sham) and a gothic door, almost too small to get in at.

'That's a real Flagstaff, you see,' said Wemmick, 'and on Sundays I run up a real flag. Then look here. After I have crossed this bridge, I hoist it up – so – and cut off the communication.'

The bridge was a plank, and it crossed a chasm about four feet wide and two deep. But it was very pleasant to see the pride with which he hoisted it up and made it fast; smiling as he did so, with a relish and not merely mechanically.

'At nine o'clock every night, Greenwich time,' said Wemmick, 'the gun fires. There he is, you see! And when you hear him go, I think you'll say he's a Stinger.'

The piece of ordinance referred to was mounted in a separate fortress, constructed of lattice-work. It was protected from the weather by an ingenious little tarpaulin contrivance in the nature of an umbrella.

'Then at the back,' said Wemmick, 'out of sight so as not to impede the idea of fortifications... there's a pig, and there are fowls and rabbits; then I knock together my own little frame, you see, and grow cucumbers; and you'll judge at supper what sort of salad I can raise. So, sir,' said Wemmick, smiling again, but seriously too, as he shook his head, 'If you can suppose the little place besieged, it would hold out the devil of a time in point of provisions.'...

Wemmick told me as he smoked a pipe that it had taken him a good many years to bring the property up to its present pitch of perfection.

'Is it your own, Mr Wemmick?'

'Oh yes,' said Wemmick, 'I have got hold of it, a bit at a time. It's a freehold, by George!'

'Is it indeed? I hope Mr Jaggers admires it?'

'Never seen it,' said Wemmick. 'Never heard of it... No; the office is one thing, and private life is another. When I go into the office, I leave the Castle behind me, and when I come into the Castle, I leave the office behind me. If it's not in any way disagreeable to you, you'll oblige me by doing the same. I don't wish it professionally spoken about.'

From *Great Expectations*, 1860–61

### J.M. Coetzee (b. 1940)

# *Coming home*

*In a South Africa torn by civil war, Michael K sets out to take his ailing mother back to her rural home, where her family had farmed. On the way she dies, leaving him alone in a brutal and dangerous world of roving armies. Michael is imprisoned but escapes, determined to live with dignity. Finally – still carrying her ashes – he arrives at his mother's birthplace:*

He explored the single-roomed cottages on the hillside behind the farmhouse. They were built of brick and mortar, with cement floors and iron roofs. It was not possible that they were half a century old. But a few yards away a little rectangle of weathered mudbrick stood out from the bare earth. Was this where his mother had been born, amid a garden of prickly pear? He fetched the box of ashes from the house, set it in the middle of the rectangle and sat down to wait. He did not know what he expected; whatever it was, it did not happen. A beetle scurried across the ground. The wind blew. There was a cardboard box standing in the sunlight on a patch of baked mud, nothing more. There was another step, apparently, that he had to take but could not yet imagine...

The time came to return his mother to the earth. He tried to dig a hole on the crest of the hill west of the dam, but an inch from the surface the spade met solid rock. So he moved to the edge of what had been cultivated land below the dam and dug a hole as deep as his elbow. He laid the packet of ash in the hole and dropped the first spadeful of earth on top of it. Then he had misgivings. He closed his eyes and concentrated, hoping that a voice would speak reassuring him that what he was doing was right – his mother's voice, if she still had a voice, or a voice belonging to no one in particular, or even his own voice as it sometimes spoke telling him what to do. But no voice came. So he extracted the packet from the hole, taking the responsibility on himself, and set about clearing a patch a few metres square in the middle of the field. There, bending low so that they would not be carried away by the wind, he distributed the fine grey flakes over the earth, afterwards turning the earth over spadeful by spadeful.

This was the beginning of his life as a cultivator. On a shelf in the shed he had found a packet of pumpkin seeds… he still had the mealie kernels; and on the pantry floor he had even picked up a solitary bean. In the space of a week he cleared the land near the dam and restored the system of furrows that irrigated it. Then he planted a small patch of pumpkins and a small patch of mealies; and some distance away on the river bank, where he would have to carry water to it, he planted his bean, so that if it grew it could climb into the thorn trees.

From *Life and Times of Michael K*, 1983

# COUNTRYSIDE AND ANIMALS

## 'The Lord God made them all'

*O come, let us sing to the Lord;*
*let us make a joyful noise to the rock of our salvation!*
*Let us come into his presence with thanksgiving;*
*let us make a joyful noise to him with songs of praise!*
*For the Lord is a great God,*
*and a great King above all gods.*
*In his hand are the depths of the earth;*
*the heights of the mountains are his also.*
*The sea is his, for he made it,*
*and the dry land, which his hands have formed.*

*O come, let us worship and bow down,*
*let us kneel before the Lord, our Maker!*

From Psalm 95

## All God's creatures

*Lord, you have made so many things!*
*How wisely you made them all!*
*The earth is filled with your creatures...*

*All of them depend on you*
*to give them food when they need it.*
*You give it to them, and they eat it;*
*you provide food and they are satisfied...*

*May the glory of the Lord last for ever!*
*May the Lord be happy with what he has made!*

From Psalm 104

Francis Kilvert (1840–79)

# Curious and wonderful life!

*The Reverend Francis Kilvert's clear observation and appreciation of the countryside and the people he encountered in his parishes have made what remained of his* Diary *a minor classic since its discovery and publication in 1938–40.*

*Tuesday 3 November 1874*

This morning between breakfast and luncheon I walked up to Bowood to see the beeches by way of the Cradle Bridge, Tytherton Stanley and Studley Hill. I went into Bowood Park by the Studley Gate and turned sharp left down a drive that brought me soon into the very heart and splendour of the beeches. As the sun shone through the roof of beech boughs overhead the very air seemed gold and scarlet and green and crimson in the deep places of the wood and the red leaves shone brilliant standing out against the splendid blue of the sky. A crowd of wood pigeons rose from the green and misty hollows of the plantation and flapped swiftly down the glades, the blue light glancing off their clapping wings. I went by the house down to the lakeside and crossed the water by the hatches above the cascade. From the other side of the water the lake shone as blue as the sky and beyond it rose from the water's edge the grand bank of sloping woods glowing with colours, scarlet, gold, orange and crimson and dark green. Two men were fishing on the further shore of an arm of the lake and across the water came the hoarse belling of a buck while a coot fluttered skimming along the surface of the lake with a loud cry and rippling splash.

To eye and ear it was a beautiful picture, the strange hoarse belling of the buck, the fluttering of the coot as she skimmed the water with her melancholy note, the cry of the swans across the lake, the clicking of the reels as the fishermen wound up or let out their lines, the soft murmur of the woods, the quiet rustle of the red and golden drifts of beech leaves, the rush of the waterfall, the light tread of the dappled herd of deer dark and dim glancing across the green glades from shadow into sunlight and rustling under the beeches, and the merry voices of the Marquis's children at play.

Why do I keep this voluminous journal? I can hardly tell. Partly because life seems to me such a curious and wonderful thing that it almost seems a pity that even such a humble and uneventful life as mine should pass altogether away without some such record as this, and partly too because I think the record may amuse and interest some who come after me.

From *Kilvert's Diary*, 1874

**Dorothy Wordsworth (1771–1855)**

# *Dancing daffodils*

*In her* Journal, *Dorothy described the daffodils that inspired her brother William's poem written two years later:*

*Thursday 15 April 1802*

It was a threatening misty morning – but mild. We set off after dinner from Eusemere – Mrs Clarkson went a short way with us but turned back. The wind was furious and we thought we must have returned. We first rested in the large Boat-house, then under a furze Bush opposite Mr Clarksons, saw the plough going in the field. The wind seized our breath, the Lake was rough. There was a boat by itself floating in the middle of the Bay below Water Millock – we rested again in the Water Millock lane. The hawthorns are black & green, the birches here & there greenish but there is yet more of purple to be seen on the Twigs. We got over into a field to avoid some cows – people working, a few primroses by the roadside, wood sorrel flowers, the anemone, scentless violets, strawberries, & that starry yellow flower which Mrs C calls pile wort. When we were in the woods beyond Gowbarrow park we saw a few daffodils close to the water side, we fancied that the lake had floated the seeds ashore & that the little colony had so sprung up – But as we went along there were more & yet more & at last under the boughs of the trees, we saw that there was a long belt of them along the shore, about the breadth of a country turnpike road. I never saw daffodils so beautiful they grew among the mossy stones about & about them, some rested their heads upon these stones as on a pillow for weariness & the rest tossed & reeled & danced & seemed as if they verily laughed with the wind that blew upon them over the Lake, they looked so gay ever glancing ever changing. The wind blew directly over the Lake to them. There was here & there a little knot & a few stragglers a few yards higher up but they were so few as not to disturb the simplicity & unity & life of that one busy highway. We rested again and again. The Bays were stormy & we heard the waves at different distances & in the middle of the water like the Sea – Rain came on, we were wet when we reached Luffs but we called in. Luckily all was chearless & gloomy so we faced the storm – we *must* have been wet if we had waited – put on dry clothes at Dobson's. I was kindly treated by a young woman, the Landlady looked sour but it is her way. She gave us a goodish supper, excellent ham and potatoes... William was sitting by a bright fire when I came downstairs he soon made his way to the Library piled up in a corner of the window... We had a glass of warm rum and water – we enjoyed ourselves and wished for Mary. It rained and blew when we went to bed. NB Deer in Gowbarrow park like skeletons.

From *The Grasmere Journals*, 1800–03

George MacDonald (1824–1905)

# *Nature and science?*

Human science is but the backward undoing of the tapestry-web of God's science, works with its back to him, and is always leaving him – his intent, that is, his perfected work – behind it, always going farther and farther away from the point where his work culminates in revelation...

Is oxygen and hydrogen the divine idea of water? Or has God put the two together only that man might separate and find them out? He allows his child to pull his toys to pieces: but were they made that he might pull them to pieces? He were a child not to be envied for whom his inglorious father would make toys to such an end! A school-examiner might see therein the best use of a toy, but not a father! Find for us what in the constitution of the two gases makes them fit and capable to be thus honoured in forming the lovely thing, and you will give us a revelation about more than water, namely about the God who made oxygen and hydrogen. There is no water in oxygen, no water in hydrogen; it comes bubbling fresh from the imagination of the living God, rushing from under the great white throne of the glacier. The very thought of it makes one gasp with an elemental joy no metaphysician can analyse. The water itself, that dances and sings, and slakes the wonderful thirst – symbol and picture of that draught for which the woman of Samaria made her prayer to Jesus – this lovely thing itself, whose very wetness is a delight to every inch of the human body in its embrace – this live thing, which, if I might, I would have running through my room, yea, babbling along my table – this water is its own self its own truth, and is therein a truth of God. Let him who would know the truth of the Maker, become sorely athirst, and drink of the brook by the way – then lift up his heart – not at that moment to the Maker of oxygen and hydrogen, but to the Inventor and Mediator of thirst and water, that man may foresee a little of what his soul may find in God.

From 'Truth in Unspoken Sermons', in *George MacDonald:
An Anthology: 365 Readings*, edited by C.S. Lewis, 1946

**Ellis Peters (Edith Pargeter) (1913–95)**

# Cadfael's herbarium in winter

*Brother Cadfael, one-time soldier and crusader, is in charge of*
*the herbarium in the twelfth-century Benedictine monastery at*
*Shrewsbury, during the turbulent times of King Stephen and the*
*Empress Maud.*

In the half-hour before High Mass at ten, Cadfael betook himself very thoughtfully to his workshop in the herb-gardens, to tend a few specifics he had brewing. The enclosure, thickly hedged and well-trimmed, was beginning now to look bleached and dry with the first moderate cold, all the leaves grown elderly and lean and brown, the tenderest plants withdrawing into the warmth of the earth; but the air still bore a lingering, aromatic fragrance composed of all the ghostly scents of summer, and inside the hut the spicy sweetness made the senses swim. Cadfael regularly took his ponderings there for privacy. He was so used to the drunken, heady air within that he barely noticed it, but at need he could distinguish every ingredient that contributed to it, and trace it to its source.

From *Monk's Hood*, 1980

### Hans Christian Andersen (1805–75)

# *Trees*

*Hans Andersen tells the story of a lonely painter, living in an attic room in a strange town. The Moon promises to tell him some of the scenes he has witnessed, so that the artist can paint them. On the seventh evening he tells him about some of the travellers who pass along a road by a forest:*

'Along the margin of the shore stretches a forest of firs and beeches, and fresh and fragrant is this wood; hundreds of nightingales visit it every spring. Close beside it is the sea, the ever-changing sea, and between the two is placed the broad high road. One carriage after another rolls over it; but I did not follow them, for my eye loves best to rest upon one point. A grave-mound stands there, and the sloe and blackberry grow luxuriantly among the stones. Here is true poetry in nature.

'And how do you think men appreciate this poetry? I will tell you what I heard there last evening and during the night.

'First, two rich landed proprietors came driving by. "Those are glorious trees!" said the first. "Certainly there are ten loads of firewood in each," observed the other: "it will be a hard winter, and last year we got fourteen dollars a load" – and they were gone. "The road here is wretched," observed another man who drove past. "That's the fault of those horrible trees," replied his neighbour; "there is no free current of air; the wind can only come from the sea" – and they were gone. The stage coach went rattling past. All the passengers were asleep at this beautiful spot. The postilion blew his horn, but he only thought, "I can play capitally. It sounds well here. I wonder if those in there like it?" – and the stage coach vanished. Then two young fellows came galloping up on horseback. There's youth and spirit in the blood here! thought I; and, indeed, they looked with a smile at the moss-grown hill and thick forest. "I should not dislike a walk here with the miller's Christine,' said one – and they flew past.

'The flowers scented the air; every breath of air was hushed: it seemed as if the sea were a part of the sky that stretched above the deep valley. A carriage rolled by. Six people were sitting in it. Four of them were asleep; the fifth was thinking of his new summer coat, which would suit him admirably; the sixth turned to the coachman and asked him if there were anything remarkable connected with yonder heap of stones. "No," replied the coachman, "it's only a heap of stones; but the trees are remarkable." "How so?" "Why, I'll tell you how they are very remarkable. You see, in winter, when the snow lies very deep, and has hidden the whole road so that nothing is to be seen, those trees serve me for a landmark. I steer by them, so as not to drive into the sea; and you see that is why the trees are remarkable."

'Now came a painter. He spoke not a word, but his eyes sparkled. He began to whistle. At this the nightingales sang louder than ever. "Hold your tongues!" he cried testily; and he made accurate notes of all the colours and transitions – blue, and lilac, and dark brown. "That will make a beautiful picture," he said. He took it in just as a mirror takes in a view; and as he worked he whistled a march of Rossini's. And last of all came a poor girl. She laid aside the burden she carried and sat down to rest by the grave-mound. Her pale handsome face was bent in a listening attitude towards the forest. Her eyes brightened, she gazed earnestly at the sea and the sky, her hands were folded, and I think she prayed, "Our Father." She herself could not understand the feeling that swept through her, but I know that this minute and the beautiful natural scene will live within her memory for years, far more vividly and more truly than the painter could portray it with his colours on paper. My rays followed her till the morning dawn kissed her brow.'

From 'The Seventh Evening', *The Complete
Fairy Tales of Hans Christian Andersen*, 1835–72

Aldous Huxley (1894–1963)

# 'Safe from books and botany'

*Published in 1932,* Brave New World *brilliantly satirises the optimism of scientists and philosophers of the time who were sure that scientific progress would mean improvement of the human lot. In this chillingly prophetic 'brave new world', pleasure is obligatory. Test-tube babies are designed – labelled from Alpha to Epsilon – to ensure that enough people are produced to do menial jobs as well as to excel academically.*

*Here, the Director instructs students and demonstrates his methods:*

INFANT NURSERIES. NEO-PAVLOVIAN CONDITIONING ROOMS announced the notice board.

The Director opened the door. They were in a large bare room, very bright and sunny; for the whole of the southern wall was a single window. Half a dozen nurses, trousered and jacketed in the regulation white viscose-linen uniform, their hair aseptically hidden under white caps, were engaged in setting out bowls of roses in a long row across the floor. Big bowls, packed tight with blossom...

The nurses stiffened to attention as the D.H.C. came in.

'Set out the books,' he said curtly.

In silence the nurses obeyed his command. Between the rose bowls the books were duly set out – a row of nursery quartos opened invitingly each at some gaily coloured image of beast or fish or bird.

'Now bring in the children.'

They hurried out of the room and returned in a minute or two, each pushing a kind of tall dumb-waiter laden, on all its four wire-netted shelves, with eight-month-old babies, all exactly alike... and all (since their caste was Delta) dressed in khaki.

'Put them down on the floor.'

The infants were unloaded.

'Now turn them so that they can see the flowers and books.'

Turned, the babies at once fell silent, then began to crawl towards those clusters of sleek colours, those shapes so gay and brilliant on the white pages... From the ranks of the crawling babies came little squeals of excitement, gurgles and twitterings of pleasure...

The swiftest crawlers were already at their goal. Small hands reached out uncertainly, touched, grasped, unpetalling the transfigured roses, crumpling the illuminated pages of the books. The Director waited until all were happily busy, Then, 'Watch carefully,' he said. And, lifting his hand, he gave the signal.

The Head Nurse, who was standing by a switchboard at the other end of the room, pressed down a little lever.

There was a violent explosion. Shriller and even shriller, a siren shrieked. Alarm bells maddeningly sounded.

The children started, screamed; their faces were distorted with terror.

'And now,' the Director shouted (for the noise was deafening), 'now we proceed to rub in the lesson with a mild electric shock.'

He waved his hand again, and the Head Nurse pressed a second lever. The screaming of the babies suddenly changed its tone. There was something desperate, almost insane, about the sharp spasmodic yelps to which they now gave utterance. Their little bodies twitched and stiffened as if to the tug of unseen wires...

'That's enough,' he signalled to the nurse.

The explosions ceased, the bells stopped ringing, the shriek of the siren died down from tone to tone into silence. The stiffly twitching bodies relaxed, and what had become the sob and yelp of infant maniacs broadened out once more into a normal howl of ordinary terror.

'Offer them the flowers and the books again.'

The nurses obeyed; but at the approach of the roses, at the mere sight of those gaily coloured images of pussy and cock-a-doodle-doo and baa-baa black sheep, the infants shrank away in horror; the volume of their howling suddenly increased.

'Observe,' said the Director triumphantly, 'observe.'

Books and loud noises, flowers and electric shocks – already in the infant mind these couples were compromisingly linked...

'They'll grow up with what the psychologists used to call an "instinctive" hatred of books and flowers. Reflexes unalterably conditioned. They'll be safe from books and botany all their lives.' The Director turned to his nurses. 'Take them away again.'

Still yelling, the khaki babies were loaded on their dumb-waiters and wheeled out, leaving behind them the smell of sour milk and a most welcome silence.

From *Brave New World*, 1932

Gilbert White (1720–93)

# Mother cat

*Selborne, 9 May 1776*

Dear Sir,
We have remarked in a former letter how much incongruous animals, in a lonely state, may be attached to each other from a spirit of sociality; in this it may not be amiss to recount a different motive which has been known to create as strange a fondness.

My friend had a little helpless leveret brought to him, which the servants fed with milk in a spoon, and about the same time his cat kittened and the young were dispatched and buried. The hare was soon lost, and supposed to be gone the way of most foundlings, to be killed by some dog or cat. However, in about a fortnight, as the master was sitting in his garden in the dusk of the evening, he observed his cat, with tail erect, trotting towards him, and calling with little short inward notes of complacency, such as they use towards their kittens, and something gambolling after, which proved to be the leveret that the cat had supported with her milk, and continued to support with great affection.

Thus was a graminiverous animal nurtured by a carniverous and predaceous one!

Why so cruel and sanguinary a beast as a cat, of the ferocious genus of *Felis*... should be affected with any tenderness towards an animal which is its natural prey, is not so easy to determine.

This strange affection probably was occasioned by that *desiderium*, those tender maternal feelings, which the loss of her kittens had awakened in her breast; and by the complacency and ease she derived to herself from procuring her teats to be drawn, which were too much distended with milk, till, from habit, she became as much delighted with the foundling as if it had been her real offspring.

This incident is no bad solution of that strange circumstance which grave historians as well as poets assert, of exposed children being sometimes nurtured by female wild beasts that probably had lost their young. For it is not one whit more marvellous that Romulus and Remus, in their infant state, should be nursed by a she-wolf, than that a poor little sucking leveret should be fostered and cherished by a bloody grimalkin.

From 'Letter LIX', *The Natural History of Selborne*, 1789

**James Boswell (1740–95)**

# Hodge

Johnson's love of little children, which he discovered upon all occasions…
was an undoubted proof of the real humanity and gentleness of his
disposition.

His uncommon kindness to his servants… was another unquestionable
evidence of what all, who were intimately acquainted with him, knew to be
true.

Nor would it be just, under this head, to omit the fondness which he
shewed for animals which he had taken under his protection. I never shall
forget the indulgence with which he treated Hodge, his cat: for whom he
himself used to go out and buy oysters, lest the servants, having that
trouble, should take a dislike to the poor creature. I am, unluckily, one of
those who have an antipathy to a cat, so that I am uneasy when in the
room with one; and I own, I frequently suffered a good deal from the
presence of this much satisfaction, while my friend, smiling and half-
whistling, rubbed down his back, and pulled him by the tail; and when I
observed he was a fine cat, saying, 'why yes, Sir, but I have had cats whom
I liked better than this'; and then, as if perceiving Hodge to be out of
countenance, adding, 'but he is a very fine cat, a very fine cat indeed.'

This reminds me of the ludicrous account which he gave Mr Langton,
of the despicable state of a young Gentleman of good family. 'Sir, when I
heard of him last, he was running about town shooting cats.' And then in
a sort of kindly reverie, he bethought himself of his own favourite cat, and
said, 'But Hodge shan't be shot; no, no, Hodge shall not be shot.'

From *The Life of Samuel Johnson*, 1791

## Charles Dickens (1812–70)

# *Bill Sikes's dog*

*Bill Sikes, housebreaker and accomplice of Fagin, had brutally murdered his girlfriend, Nancy. Horror-struck by the scene of carnage and the staring dead eyes of the girl, he fled London, accompanied, as always, by his vicious 'white-coated, red-eyed dog'.*

Suddenly, he took the desperate resolution of going back to London... He acted upon this resolution without delay, and choosing the least frequented roads, began his journey back, resolved to lie concealed within a short distance of the metropolis, and, entering it at dusk by a circuitous route, to proceed straight to that part of it which he had fixed on for his destination.

The dog, though – if any descriptions of him were out, it would not be forgotten that the dog was missing, and had probably gone with him. This might lead to his apprehension as he passed along the streets. He resolved to drown him, and walked on, looking about for a pond, picking up a heavy stone and tying it to his handkerchief as he went.

The animal looked up into his master's face while these preparations were making; and whether his instinct apprehended something of their purpose, or the robber's sidelong look at him was sterner than ordinary, skulked a little further in the rear than usual, and cowered as he came slowly along. When the master halted at the brink of a pool, and looked round to call him, he stopped outright.

'Do you hear me call? Come here!' cried Sikes.

The animal came up from the very force of habit; but as Sikes stooped to attach the handkerchief to his throat, he uttered a low growl and started back.

'Come back!' said the robber, stamping on the ground. The dog wagged his tail, but moved not. Sikes made a running noose, and called him again.

The dog advanced, retreated, paused an instant, turned, and scoured away at his hardest speed.

The man whistled again and again, and sat down and waited in the expectation that he would return. But no dog appeared, and at length he resumed his journey.

*Sikes made his way back to Fagin's London tenement overlooking Folly ditch, an inlet of the Thames. He planned to lower himself by a rope from the building, jump into the ditch and somehow escape:*

Roused into new strength and energy, and stimulated by the noise within the house which announced that an entrance had really been effected, he set his foot against the stack of chimneys, tightened one end of the rope tightly and firmly round it, and with the other made a strong running noose by the aid of his hands and teeth almost in a second. He could let himself down by the cord to within a less distance of the ground than his own height, and had his knife ready in his hand to cut it then and drop.

At the very instant when he brought the loop over his head previous to slipping it beneath his arm-pits... the murderer, looking behind him on the roof, threw his arms above his head and uttered a yell of terror.

'The eyes again!' he cried, in an unearthly screech.

Staggering as if struck by lightning, he lost his balance and tumbled over the parapet. The noose was at his neck. It ran up with his weight, tight as a bowstring, and swift as the arrow it speeds. He fell for five-and-thirty feet. There was a sudden jerk, a terrific convulsion of the limbs: and there he hung, with the open knife clenched in his stiffening hand...

A dog which had lain concealed till now, ran backwards and forwards on the parapet with a dismal howl, and collecting himself for a spring, jumped for the dead man's shoulders. Missing his aim, he fell into the ditch, turning completely over as he went, and striking his head against a stone, dashed out his brains.

From *Oliver Twist*, 1837–39

**Rudyard Kipling (1865–1936)**

# How the rhinoceros got his skin

Once upon a time, on an uninhabited island on the shores of the Red Sea, there lived a Parsee from whose hat the rays of the sun were reflected with more-than-oriental splendour. And the Parsee lived by the Red Sea with nothing but his hat and his knife and a cooking-stove of the kind that you must particularly never touch. And one day he took flour and water and currants and plums and sugar and things, and made himself one cake which was two feet across and three feet thick. It was indeed a Superior Comestible (*that's* magic) and he put it on the stove because *he* was allowed to cook on that stove, and he baked it and he baked it till it was all done brown and smelt most sentimental. But just as he was going to eat it there came down to the beach from the Altogether Uninhabited Interior one Rhinoceros with a horn on his nose, two piggy eyes, and few manners. In those days the Rhinoceros's skin fitted him quite tight. There were not wrinkles in it anywhere. He looked exactly like a Noah's Ark Rhinoceros, but of course much bigger. All the same, he had no manners then, and he has no manners now, and he never will have any manners. He said, 'How!' and the Parsee left that cake and climbed to the top of a palm tree with nothing on but his hat, from which the rays of the sun were always reflected in more-than-oriental splendour. And the Rhinoceros upset the oil-stove with his nose, and the cake rolled on the sand, and he spiked that cake on the horn of his nose, and he ate it, and he went away, waving his tail to the desolate and Exclusively Uninhabited Interior which abuts on the islands of Mazanderan, Socotra, and the Promontories of the Larger Equinox. Then the Parsee came down from his palm-tree and put the stove on its legs and recited the following *Sloka*, which, as you have not heard, I will now proceed to relate:

> *Them that takes cakes*
> *Which the Parsee-man bakes*
> *Makes dreadful mistakes.*

And there was a great deal more in that than you would think.

*Because*, five weeks later, there was a heat wave in the Red Sea, and everybody took off all the clothes they had. The Parsee took off his hat;

but the Rhinoceros took off his skin and carried it over his shoulder as he came down to the beach to bathe. In those days it buttoned underneath with three buttons and looked like a waterproof. He said nothing whatever about the Parsee's cake, because he had eaten it all; and he never had any manners, then, or since, or henceforward. He waddled straight into the water and blew bubbles through his nose, leaving his skin on the beach.

Presently the Parsee came by and found the skin, and he smiled one smile that ran all round his face two times. Then he danced three times round the skin and rubbed his hands. Then he went to his camp and filled his hat with cake-crumbs, for the Parsee never ate anything but cake, and never swept out his camp. He took that skin, and he rubbed that skin just as full of old, dry, stale, tickly cake-crumbs and some burned currants as ever it could *possibly* hold. Then he climbed to the top of his palm-tree and waited for the Rhinoceros to come out of the water and put it on.

And the Rhinoceros did. He buttoned it up with the three buttons, and it tickled like cake-crumbs in bed. Then he wanted to scratch, but that made it worse; and then he lay down on the sands and rolled and rolled and rolled, and every time he rolled the cake-crumbs tickled him worse and worse and worse. Then he ran to the palm-tree and rubbed and rubbed and rubbed himself against it. He rubbed so much and so hard that he rubbed his skin into a great fold over his shoulders, and another fold underneath, where the buttons used to be (but he rubbed the buttons off), and he rubbed some more folds over his legs. And it spoiled his temper, but it didn't make the least difference to the cake-crumbs. They were inside his skin and they tickled. So he went home, very angry indeed and horribly scratchy; and from that day to this every rhinoceros has great folds in his skin and a very bad temper, all on account of the cake-crumbs inside.

But the Parsee came down from his palm-tree, wearing his hat, from which the rays of the sun were reflected in more-than-oriental splendour, packed up his cooking-stove, and went away in the direction of Orotavo, Amygdala, the Upland Meadows of Anantarivo, and the Marshes of Sonaput.

From 'How the Rhinoceros Got His Skin', *Just So Stories*, 1902

Robert Louis Stevenson (1850–94)

# Cap'n Flint

*Jim Hawkins, son of the landlord of the Admiral Benbow, unwittingly takes the treasure chart from an old sailor and an expedition to Treasure Island is undertaken by the squire and the doctor, with Jim as cabin-boy. A seemingly kind old salt – Long John Silver – is taken on as cook. Jim describes him:*

All the crew respected and even obeyed him. He had a way of talking to each, and doing everybody some particular service. To me he was unweariedly kind; and always glad to see me in the galley, which he kept as clean as a new pin; the dishes hanging up burnished, and his parrot in a cage in one corner.

'Come away, Hawkins,' he would say, 'come and have a yarn with John. Nobody more welcome than yourself, my son. Sit you down and hear the news. Here's Cap'n Flint – I calls my parrot Cap'n Flint, after the famous buccaneer – here's Cap'n Flint predicting success to our v'yage. Wasn't you, cap'n?'

And the parrot would say, with great rapidity, 'Pieces of eight! pieces of eight! pieces of eight!' till you wondered that it was not out of breath, or till John threw his handkerchief over the cage.

'Now, that bird,' he would say, 'is, may be, two hundred years old, Hawkins – they lives for ever mostly; and if anybody's seen more wickedness, it must be the devil himself. She's sailed with England, the great Cap'n England, the pirate. She's been at Madagascar, and at Malabar, the Surinam, and Providence, and Portobello. She was at the fishing up of the wrecked Plate ships. It's there she learned "Pieces of eight," and little wonder; three hundred and fifty thousand of 'em, Hawkins! She was at the boarding of the Viceroy of the Indies, out at Goa, she was; and to look at her you would think she was a babby. But you smelt powder, didn't you, cap'n?'

'Stand by to go about,' the parrot would scream.

'Ah, she's a handsome craft, she is,' the cook would say, and give her sugar from his pocket, and then the bird would peck at the bars and swear straight on, passing belief for wickedness. 'There,' John would add, 'you can't touch pitch and not be mucked, lad. Here's this poor old innocent bird o'mine swearing blue fire, and none the wiser, you may lay to that. She would swear the same, in a manner of speaking, before chaplain.' And John would touch his forelock with a solemn way he had, that made me think he was the best of men.

From *Treasure Island*, 1883

Hugh Lofting (1886–1947)

# *John Doolittle MD*

Once upon a time, many years ago, when our grandfathers were little children – there was a doctor; and his name was Doolittle – John Doolittle MD... He lived in a little town called Puddleby-on-the-Marsh... The house he lived in, on the edge of the town, was quite small; but his garden was very large and had a wide lawn and stone seats and weeping-willows hanging over. His sister, Sarah Doolittle, was housekeeper for him; but the Doctor looked after the garden himself.

He was very fond of animals and kept many kinds of pets. Besides the gold-fish in the pond at the bottom of his garden, he had rabbits in the pantry, white mice in his piano, a squirrel in the linen-closet and a hedgehog in the cellar. He had a cow with a calf too, and an old lame horse – twenty-five years of age – and chickens, and pigeons, and two lambs, and many other animals. But his favourite pets were Dab-Dab the duck, Jip the dog, Gub-Gub the baby pig, Polynesia the parrot, and the owl Too-Too.

His sister used to grumble about all these animals and said they made the house untidy. And one day when an old woman with rheumatism came to see the Doctor, she sat on the hedgehog who was sleeping on the sofa, and never came to see him any more...

Then his sister, Sarah Doolittle, came to him and said:

'John, how can you expect patients to come and see you when you keep all these animals in the house? It's a fine doctor would have his parlour full of hedgehogs and mice! That's the fourth person these animals have driven away... We are getting poorer every day. If you go on like this, none of the best people will have you for a doctor.'

'But I like the animals better than the "best people",' said the Doctor.

'You are ridiculous,' said his sister, and walked out of the room.

So as time went on, the Doctor got more and more animals; and the people who came to see him got less and less. Till at last he had no one left – except the Cat's-meat-Man, who didn't mind any kind of animals. But the Cat's-meat-Man wasn't very rich, and he only got sick once a year – at Christmas – when he used to give the Doctor sixpence for a bottle of medicine.

Sixpence a year wasn't enough to live on – even in those days... It happened one day that the Doctor was sitting in his kitchen talking with the Cat's-meat-Man who had come to see him with a stomach-ache.

'Why don't you give up being a people's doctor, and be an animal doctor?' asked the Cat's-meat-Man... 'You know all about animals – much more than what these here vets do... And listen: you can make a lot of money doctoring animals. Do you know that? You see, I'd send all the old women who had sick cats or dogs to you. And if they didn't get ill fast enough, I could put something in the meat I sell 'em to make 'em bad, see?'

'Oh no,' said the Doctor quickly. 'You mustn't do that. That wouldn't be right.'

'Oh, I didn't mean real bad,' answered the Cat's-meat-Man. 'Just a little something to make them droopy-like was what I had reference to...'

When the Cat's-meat-Man had gone the parrot flew off the window on to the Doctor's table and said:

'That man's got sense. That's what you ought to do. Be an animal doctor... Now listen, Doctor, and I'll tell you something. Did you know that animals can talk?'...

All that afternoon, while it was raining, Polynesia sat on the kitchen table giving him bird words to put down in the book.

From *The Story of Doctor Doolittle*, 1920

Anna Sewell (1820–78)

# *Going for the doctor*

*One night Black Beauty is woken up to take John, the groom, to fetch the doctor at top speed, for his owner's wife is seriously ill. Squire Gordon tells John to rest the horse before riding him home. The horse tells his own story:*

The church clock struck three as we drew up at Doctor White's door. John rang the bell twice, and then knocked at the door like thunder. A window was thrown up, and Doctor White, in his nightcap, put his head out and said, 'What do you want?'

'Mrs Gordon is very ill, sir; master wants you to go at once, he thinks she will die if you cannot get there – here is a note.'

'Wait,' he said, 'I will come.'

He shut the window and was soon at the door.

'The worst of it is,' he said, 'that my horse had been out all day and is quite done up; my son has just been sent for, and he has taken the other. What is to be done? Can I have your horse?'

'He has come at a gallop all the way, sir, and I was to give him a rest here; but I think my master would not be against it if you think fit, sir.'

'All right,' he said, 'I will soon be ready.'

John stood by me and stroked my neck, I was very hot. The doctor came out with his riding whip.

'You need not take that, sir,' said John, 'Black Beauty will go till he drops; take care of him, sir, if you can; I should not like any harm to come to him.'

'No! no! John,' said the Doctor, 'I hope not,' and in a minute we had left John far behind.

I will not tell about our way back; the Doctor was a heavier man than John, and not so good a rider; however I did my very best…

Joe was at the lodge gate, my master was at the Hall door, for he had heard us coming. He spoke not a word; the doctor went into the house with him, and Joe led me to the stable. I was glad to get home, my legs shook under me, and I could only stand and pant. I had not a dry hair on my body, the water ran down my legs, and I steamed all over – Joe used to say, like a pot of fire. Poor Joe! he was young and small, and as yet he knew very little... but I am sure he did the very best he knew. He rubbed my legs and chest, but he did not put my warm cloth on me; he thought I was so hot I should not like it. Then he gave me a pail full of water to drink; it was cold and very good, and I drank it all; then he gave me some hay and some corn, and thinking he had done right, he went away. Soon I began to shake and tremble, and turned deadly cold, my legs ached, my loins ached, and my chest ached, and I felt sore all over. Oh! how I wished for my warm thick cloth as I stood and trembled. I wished for John, but he had eight miles to walk, so I lay down in my straw and tried to go to sleep. After a long while I heard John at the door; I gave a low moan, for I was in great pain. He was at my side in a moment, stooping down by me; I could not tell him how I felt; but he seemed to know it all; he covered me up with two or three warm cloths, and then ran to the house for some hot water; he made me some warm gruel, which I drank, and then I think I went to sleep.

John seemed to be very much put out. I heard him say to himself, over and over again, 'Stupid boy! stupid boy! no cloth put on, and I dare say the water was cold too; boys are no good;' but Joe was a good boy after all.

I was now very ill; a strong inflammation had attacked my lungs, and I could not draw my breath without pain. John nursed me night and day; he would get up two or three times in the night to come to me; my master, too, often came to see me. 'My poor Beauty,' he said one day, 'my good horse, you saved your mistress's life, Beauty! yes, you saved her life.'

From *Black Beauty*, 1877

**Evelyn Waugh (1903–66)**

# Death of a dog

*Dennis Barlow, whose contract with Megalopolitan Pictures in
Hollywood had run out, found work at Happier Hunting
Ground – a pet's cemetery. One evening he is summoned to the
home of Mr and Mrs Heinkel:*

A corpulent man came down the garden path to greet him…
'I am the Happier Hunting Ground,' said Dennis.
'Yes, come along in.'
Dennis opened the back of the wagon and took out an aluminium
container. 'Will this be large enough?'
'Plenty.'…
'This way,' said Mr Heinkel. 'In the pantry.'
The Sealyham lay on the draining-board beside the sink. Dennis lifted
it into the container.
'Perhaps you wouldn't mind taking a hand?'
Together he and Mr Heinkel carried their load to the wagon.
'Shall we discuss arrangements now, or would you prefer to call in the
morning?'
'I'm a pretty busy man mornings,' said Mr Heinkel. 'Come into the
study.'
There was a tray on the desk. They helped themselves to whisky.
'I have our brochure here setting out our service. Were you thinking of
interment or incineration?'
'Pardon me?'
'Buried or burned?'
'Burned, I guess.'
'I have some photographs here of various styles of urn.'
'The best will be good enough.'
'Would you require a niche in our columbarium or do you prefer to
keep the remains at home?'
'What you said first.'
'And the religious rites? We have a pastor who is always pleased to
assist.'
'Well, Mr –?'

'Barlow.'

'Mr Barlow, we're neither of us what you might call very church-going people, but I think on an occasion like this Mrs Heinkel would want all the comfort you can offer.'

'Our Grade A service includes several unique features. At the moment of committal, a white dove, symbolising the deceased's soul, is liberated over the crematorium.'

'Yes,' said Mr Heinkel, 'I reckon Mrs Heinkel would appreciate the dove.'

'And every anniversary a card of remembrance is mailed without further charge. It reads: *Your little Arthur is thinking of you in heaven today and wagging his tail.*'

'That's a very beautiful thought, Mr Barlow.'

'Then if you will just sign the order...'

From *The Loved One*, 1948

# FOOD

## Living bread

*After Jesus had fed over five thousand people with five small loaves and two fish, he told the complaining Jewish leaders:*

I myself am the living bread which came down from Heaven, and if anyone eats this bread he will live for ever. The bread which I will give is my own body and I shall give it for the life of the world.

From John 6

## Breakfast with Jesus

Jesus showed himself again to his disciples on the shore of Lake Tiberias, and he did it in this way. Simon Peter, Thomas (called the Twin), Nathanael from Cana of Galilee, the sons of Zebedee and two other disciples were together, when Simon Peter said,
  'I'm going fishing.'
  'All right,' they replied, 'we'll go with you.'
  So they went out and got into the boat and during the night caught nothing at all. But just as dawn began to break, Jesus stood there on the beach, although the disciples had no idea that it was Jesus.
  'Have you caught anything, lads?' Jesus called out to them.
  'No,' they replied.
  'Throw the net on the right side of the boat,' said Jesus, 'and you'll have a catch.'
  So they threw out the net and found that they were now not strong enough to pull it in because it was so full of fish! At this, the disciple that Jesus loved said to Peter, 'It is the Lord!'
  Hearing this, Peter slipped on his clothes, for he had been naked, and plunged into the sea. The other disciples followed in the boat, for they were only about a hundred yards from the shore, dragging in the net full of fish. When they had landed, they saw that a charcoal fire was burning,

with a fish placed on it, and some bread. Jesus said to them, 'Bring me some of the fish you've just caught.'

So Simon Peter got into the boat and hauled the net ashore full of large fish, one hundred and fifty-three altogether. But in spite of the large number the net was not torn.

Then Jesus said to them, 'Come and have your breakfast.'

None of the disciples dared to ask him who he was; they knew it was the Lord.

Jesus went and took the bread and gave it to them and gave them all fish as well. This was now the third time that Jesus showed himself to his disciples after his resurrection from the dead.

From John 21

Kenneth Grahame (1859–1932)

# The picnic hamper

*The Mole emerged from his underground home, leaving spring-cleaning behind him, and encountered the Water Rat, who invited him to a day out on the river. The Mole climbed into the boat and leaned back on the cushions:*

'*What* a day I'm having!' he said. 'Let us start at once!'

'Hold hard a minute, then!' said the Rat. He looped the painter through a ring in the landing-stage, climbed up into his hole above, and after a short interval reappeared staggering under a fat, wicker luncheon-basket.

'Shove that under your feet,' he observed to the Mole, as he passed it down into the boat. Then he untied the painter and took the sculls again.

'What's inside it?' asked the Mole, wriggling with curiosity.

'There's cold chicken inside it,' replied the Rat briefly; 'coldtonguecold hamcoldbeefpickledgherkinssaladfrenchrollscresssandwichespottedmeat gingerbeerlemonadesodawater –'

'O stop, stop,' cried the Mole in ecstasies: 'This is too much!'

'Do you really think so?' inquired the Rat seriously. 'It's only what I always take on these little excursions...'

The Mole never heard a word he was saying. Absorbed in the new life he was entering upon, intoxicated with the sparkle, the ripple, the scents and sounds and the sunlight, he trailed a paw in the water and dreamed long waking dreams.

From *The Wind in the Willows*, 1908

### Doris Lessing (b. 1919)

# *Food of the poor*

*In* The Diaries of Jane Somers, *the sophisticated, elegant Jane Somers befriends old Maudie, fiercely independent but living in squalor and poverty. She notices others like Maudie nearby and starts calling on Annie too.*

Annie talks of food a lot. Again I listen to details of meals eaten sixty, seventy years ago. The family lived in Holborn, in a now demolished tenement that had stone stairs and two lavatories, one for one side of the building, one for the other... The father was a labourer. He drank. He was continually losing his job. Three children, Annie the oldest. In hard times, which were frequent, the children would run down to the shops for six eggs, sixpence; for yesterday's stale bread, kept for the poor by the German bakers. For the liquid from boiling sheep's heads, given away free to the poor; they brought back a jug of this, the mother made dumplings, and that is what they ate for supper. They got sixpennyworth of scraps from the butcher and made stew. Enormous boiled puddings full of fruit, with sugar sprinkled on, were used to stay appetites – just as Maudie remembered. When they were flush, the family had the best of everything in the food line, for the father went up to the auctions on a Saturday night, when the meat was sold that would spoil, and came back with a large sirloin for half a crown, or a leg of mutton. They ate eels and potatoes and parsley sauce, brought from the eel shop in a basin, or a thick pea soup with potatoes in it. They got their milk from an old woman who had a cow. The cow had its head sticking out over the door in a shed in the back yard, and went moo when the children came in. The old woman sold buttermilk and butter and cream.

The family bought 'specks' from the greengrocer: apples that had a brown spot on them; or yesterday's greens. Just as good as new, they were, and sometimes no money asked at all, just given away.

At the baker's, if they bought that day's bread, the German woman would always give the children a makeweight, cakes from yesterday. And in the market a man made sweets standing at a stall under a canopy, boiling toffee over a flame, and then spread it with coconut or walnuts or hazelnuts, and he always gave the children the little crushed splinters from when he broke up the toffee with his little hammer.

From *The Diaries of Jane Somers*, 1984

## George Borrow (1803–81)

# *Rabbits and figs*

*George Borrow spent the years from 1835 to 1840 in Spain and Portugal, distributing tracts and copies of the Bible from an old carpet bag, on behalf of the Bible Society, for whom he worked as a translator. He described these years as 'the most happy of my existence'; he gives a lively account of his experiences in* The Bible in Spain:

We continued discoursing until we arrived at Pegoens.

Pegoens consists of about two or three houses and an inn; there is likewise a species of barrack, where half-a-dozen soldiers are stationed. In the whole of Portugal there is no place of worse reputation, and the inn is nicknamed *Estalagem de Ladrones* or the hostelry of thieves; for it is there that the banditti of the wilderness, which extends around it on every side for leagues, are in the habit of coming and spending the money, the fruits of their criminal daring; there they dance and sing, eat fricasseed rabbits and olives, and drink the muddy but strong wine of the Alemtejo. An enormous fire, fed by the trunk of a cork tree, was blazing in a niche on the left hand on entering the spacious kitchen. Close by it, seething, were several large jars, which emitted no disagreeable odour, and reminded me that I had not broken my fast, although it was now nearly one o'clock, and I had ridden five leagues. Several wild-looking men, who if they were not banditti might easily be mistaken for such, were seated on logs about the fire. I asked them some unimportant questions, to which they replied with readiness and civility, and one of them, who said he could read, accepted a tract which I offered him.

My new friend, who had been bespeaking dinner, or rather breakfast, now, with great civility, invited me to partake of it, and at the same time introduced me to the officer who accompanied him, and who was his brother, and also spoke English, though not so well as himself. I found I had become acquainted with Don Geronimo Joze D'Azveto, secretary to the government at Evora; his brother belonged to a regiment of hussars, whose headquarters were at Evora, but which had outlying parties along the road, – for example, the place where we were stopping.

Rabbits at Pegoens seem to be a standard article of food, being produced in abundance on the moors around. We had one fried, the gravy of which was delicious, and afterwards a roasted one, which was brought up on a dish entire; the hostess, having washed her hands, proceeded to tear the animal to pieces, which having accomplished, she poured over the fragments a sweet sauce. I ate heartily of both dishes, particularly of the last; owing, perhaps, to the novel and curious way it was served up. Excellent figs, from the Algarves, and apples concluded our repast; which we ate in a little side-room with a mud floor, which sent such a piercing chill into my system, as prevented me from deriving that pleasure from my fare and my most agreeable companions that I should have otherwise experienced.

From *The Bible in Spain*, 1843

## Samuel Pepys (1633–1703)

# *Mr Pepys entertains*

*13 January 1663*

So my poor wife rose by 5 a-clock in the morning, before day, and went to market and bought fowle and many other things for dinner – with which I was highly pleased. And the chine of beef was done also before 6 a-clock... Things being put in order and the cooke come, I went to the office, where we sat till noon; and then broke up and I home, whither by and by comes Dr Clerke and his lady, his sister and a she-cosen, and Mr Pierce and his wife, which was all my guest[s]. I had for them, after oysters – at first course, a hash of rabbits and lamb, and a rare chine of beef; next a great dish of roasted fowl, cost me about 30*s*; and a tart; and then fruit and cheese. My dinner was noble and enough. I had my house mighty clean and neat, my room below with a good fire in it – my dining-room above, and my chamber being made a withdrawing-chamber, and my wife's a good fire also. I find my new table very proper, and will hold nine or ten people well, but eight with great room. After dinner, the women to cards in my wife's chamber, and the Doctor [and] Mr Pierce in mine, because the dining-room smokes unless I keep a good charcole fire, which I was not then provided with. At night to supper; had a good sack-posset and cold meat and sent my guests away about ten a-clock at night – both them and myself highly pleased with our management of this day. And indeed, their company was very fine, and Mrs Clerke a very witty, fine lady, though a little conceited and proud. So weary to bed. I believe this day's feast will cost me near 5 *l*.

An entry from Pepys's diary, 1663

### Henry Handel Richardson (Ethel Robertson) (1870–1946)

# *Midnight feast*

*Young Trixie – en route for her first term at boarding-school – is staying the night with seventeen-year-old Alice, but she can't sleep. Alice hears her sigh loudly:*

'What's the matter, child? Aren't you asleep yet?'
'No, I simply can't.'
Alice sat up in bed, and shook her hair back from her face.
'You're over-excited. Try a drink of water.'
'I have. I've drunk it all up.'
'Then you must be hungry.'
'Well, yes, I am perhaps… a little.'
'Come on, then, let's forage.' And throwing back the sheet, the elder girl slid her feet to the floor.

One tall white figure, one short, they opened the door and stepped out on the verandah. Here it was almost as bright as day; for the moon hung like a round cheese in the sky, and drenched everything with its light…

Turning a corner, they stepped off the verandah and took a few steps on hard pebbly ground. Inside the pantry, which was a large outhouse, there were sharp contrasts of bluish-white moonlight and black shadows.

Swiftly Alice skimmed the familiar shelves. 'Here's lemon-cheesecakes… and jam tarts… and gingersnaps… and pound cake. But I can't start you on these, or you'd be sick.' And cutting a round off a home-made loaf, she spread it thickly with dairy butter, topped with a layer of quince jelly. 'There, that's more wholesome.'

Oh, had anything ever tasted so delicious?… as this slice eaten at dead of night. Perched on an empty, upturned kerosene-tin, the young girl munched and munched, holding her empty hand outspread below, lest the quivering jelly glide over the crust's edge.

Alice took a cheesecake and sat down on a lidded basket. 'I say, *did* you hear Father? Oh, Trix, wouldn't it be positively awful if one discovered *afterwards* that one had married a man who snored?'

The muncher made no answer; the indelicacy of the question stunned her… Hastily squeezing down her last titbit – she felt it travel, overlarge, the full length of her gullet – she licked her jellied fingers clean…

'But come!' cried Alice... 'to bed and to sleep with you, young woman, or we shall never get you up in time for the morning coach. Help yourself to a couple of cheesecakes, we can eat them as we go.'

Tartlets in hand, back they stole along the moon-blanched verandah; back past the row of dark windows... guided by a moon, which, riding at the top of the sky, had shrunk to the size of a pippin.

From 'Conversation in a Pantry', *The End of a Childhood and Other Stories*, 1934

**Charles Dickens (1812–70)**

# The shops on Christmas Day

The poulterers' shops were still half open, and the fruiterers were radiant in their glory. There were great, round, pot-bellied baskets of chestnuts, shaped like the waistcoats of jolly old gentlemen, lolling at the doors, and tumbling out into the street in their apoplectic opulence. There were ruddy, brown-faced, broad-girthed Spanish Onions, shining in the fatness of their growth like Spanish Friars; and winking from their shelves in wanton slyness at the girls as they went by, and glancing demurely at the hung-up mistletoe. There were pears and apples, clustered high in blooming pyramids; there were bunches of grapes, made, in the shopkeepers' benevolence, to dangle from conspicuous hooks, that people's mouths might water gratis as they passed; there were piles of filberts, mossy and brown, recalling, in their fragrance, ancient walks among the woods, and pleasant shufflings ankle deep through withered leaves; there were Norfolk Biffins, squab and swarthy, setting off the yellow of the oranges and lemons, and, in the great compactness of their juicy persons, urgently entreating and beseeching to be carried home in paper bags and eaten after dinner...

The Grocers'! oh the Grocers'! nearly closed, with perhaps two shutters down, or one; but through those gaps such glimpses! It was not alone that the scales descending on the counter made a merry sound, or that the twine and roller parted company so briskly, or that the canisters were rattled up and down like juggling tricks, or even that the blended scents of tea and coffee were so grateful to the nose, or even that the raisins were so plentiful and rare, the almonds so extremely white, the sticks of cinnamon so long and straight, the other spices so delicious, the candied fruits so caked and spotted with molten sugar as to make the coldest lookers-on feel faint and subsequently bilious. Nor was it that the figs were moist and pulpy, or that the French plums blushed in modest tartness from their highly decorated boxes, or that everything was good to eat and in its Christmas dress: but the customers were all so hurried and so eager in the hopeful promise of the day, that they tumbled up against each other at the door, crashing their wicker baskets wildly, and left their purchases on the counter, and came running back to fetch them, and committed hundreds of the like mistakes, in the best humour possible...

But soon the steeples called good people all, to church and chapel, and away they came, flocking through the streets in their best clothes, and with their gayest faces.

From *A Christmas Carol,* 1843

**Lewis Carroll (Charles Dodgson) (1832–98)**

# A mad tea-party

There was a table set out under a tree in front of the house, and the March Hare and the Hatter were having tea at it; a Dormouse was sitting between them, fast asleep, and the other two were using it as a cushion, resting their elbows on it, and talking over its head. 'Very uncomfortable for the Dormouse,' thought Alice; 'only, as it's asleep, I suppose it doesn't mind.'

The table was a large one, but the three were all crowded at one corner of it. 'No room! No room!' they cried out when they saw Alice coming. 'There's *plenty* of room!' said Alice indignantly, and she sat down in a large armchair at one end of the table.

'Have some wine,' the March Hare said in an encouraging tone.

Alice looked all round the table, but there was nothing on it but tea. 'I don't see any wine,' she remarked.

'There isn't any,' said the March Hare.

'Then it wasn't very civil of you to offer it,' said Alice angrily.

'It wasn't very civil of you to sit down without being invited,' said the March Hare.

'I didn't know it was *your* table,' said Alice; 'it's laid for a great many more than three.'...

The Hatter was the first to break the silence. 'What day of the month is it?' he said, turning to Alice: he had taken his watch out of his pocket, and was looking at it uneasily, shaking it every now and then, and holding it to his ear.

Alice considered a little, and then said, 'The fourth.'

'Two days wrong,' sighed the Hatter. 'I told you butter wouldn't suit the works!' he added, looking angrily at the March Hare.

'It was the *best* butter,' the March Hare meekly replied.

'Yes, but some crumbs must have got in as well,' the Hatter grumbled: 'you shouldn't have put it in with the bread knife.'

The March Hare took the watch and looked at it gloomily: then he dipped it into his cup of tea, and looked at it again: but he could think of nothing better to say than his first remark, 'It was the *best* butter, you know.'...

'The Dormouse is asleep again,' said the Hatter, and he poured a little hot tea upon its nose...

The Dormouse slowly opened his eyes. 'I wasn't asleep,' he said, in a hoarse, feeble voice: 'I heard every word you fellows were saying.'

'Tell us a story!' said the March Hare.

'Yes, please do!' pleaded Alice.

'And be quick about it,' added the Hatter, 'or you'll be asleep again before it's done.'

'Once upon a time there were three little sisters,' the Dormouse began in a great hurry; 'and their names were Elsie, Lacie, and Tillie; and they lived at the bottom of a well –'

'What did they live on?' asked Alice, who always took great interest in questions of eating and drinking.

'They lived on treacle,' said the Dormouse, after thinking for a minute or two.

'They couldn't have done that, you know,' Alice gently remarked; 'they'd have been ill.'

'So they were,' said the Dormouse; '*very* ill.'

Alice tried a little to fancy to herself what such an extraordinary way of living would be like, but it puzzled her too much, so she went on: 'But why did they live at the bottom of the well?'

'Take some more tea,' the March Hare said to Alice, very earnestly.

'I've had nothing yet,' Alice replied in an offended tone, 'so I can't take more.'

'You mean you can't take *less*,' said the Hatter: 'it's very easy to take *more* than nothing.'…

Alice did not quite know what to say to this: so she helped herself to some tea and bread-and-butter, and then turned to the Dormouse, and repeated her question. 'Why did they live at the bottom of a well?'

The Dormouse again took a minute or two to think about it, and then said, 'It was a treacle-well.'

From *Alice's Adventures in Wonderland*, 1865

Thomas Love Peacock (1785–1866)

# Food – academically speaking

'Palestine soup!' said the Reverend Doctor Opimian, dining with his friend Squire Gryll; 'a curiously complicated misnomer. We have an excellent old vegetable, the artichoke, of which we eat the head; we have another, of subsequent introduction, of which we eat the root, and which we also call artichoke, because it resembles the first in flavour, although, *me judice*, a very inferior affair. This last is a species of the helianthus, or sunflower genus of the *Syngenesia frustranea* class of plants. It is therefore a girasol, or turn-to-the-sun. From the girasol we have made Jerusalem, and from the Jerusalem artichoke we make Palestine soup...'

*Miss Gryll*: 'You and my uncle, doctor, get up a discussion on everything that presents itself... You have run half round the world *à propos* of the soup. What say you of the fish?'

*The Reverend Dr Opimian*: 'Premising that this is a remarkably fine slice of salmon, there is much to be said about fish; but not in the way of misnomers. Their names are single and simple. Perch, sole, cod, eel, carp, char, skate, tench, trout, brill, bream, pike, and many others, plain monosyllables: salmon, dory, turbot, gudgeon, lobster, whitebait, grayling, haddock, mullet, herring, oyster, sturgeon, flounder, turtle, plain dissyllables; only two trisyllables worth naming, anchovy and mackerel; unless anyone should be disposed to stand up for halibut, which, for my part, I have excommunicated.'

From *Gryll Grange*, 1860–61

## Walter Brueggemann (b. 1933)

# *What you eat is what you get!*

*Better is a dinner of vegetables where love is*
*than a fatted ox and hatred with it.*
Proverbs 15:17

What you eat is what you get! At the first table is gravy and roast beef and rice. This is the main course, but there have been preliminary courses... and there will be a rich dessert and nuts and fruit and claret. At the centre, between soup and nuts, is roast beef, large, rare slices – call it fatted ox. You can kill a fatted ox for a special party. But these people have it every night. Every night – extravagance and satiation, and with it pressure and anxiety. They have eaten this way so long they do not regard their eating as conspicuous consumption. They simply enjoy fatted ox. They can afford it... so why not?

In describing the scene, the wisdom teacher construes what else goes with such eating... imagines that such a diet bespeaks busyness and overextendedness, drivenness, restlessness, and anxiety. To have such food, you have to keep at things all the time – drive, drive, drive, great second effort – and then be satiated. After a while, such extravagance is not very special, not even noticed, and not much appreciated.

Worse than that, it takes two incomes to maintain the menu and everything that goes with it: two incomes, a busy schedule, a crowded social calendar, long hours (not just for roast beef, but all the things along with it, of social expectation and entertaining), stopping at the store, rushing home, fixing, too many evening meetings, cook it, eat it, three phone calls, a good dinner with little time to eat it. The kids just home from soccer and off to band, what a waste, too much on edge... Maybe roast beef need not lead to all of that. The wisdom teacher summarizes his view:

Fatted ox and strife with it.

The roast beef becomes a cipher for excessive, luxurious living, the social requirements and tensions, excessive preoccupation with things that lead to tension, quarrelling, fear, and hate...

What you eat is what you get. There is another table set for us. Not much on it, only greens, call it herbs. Just simple vegetables, a little bread, plain wine, quiet, simplicity, no leftovers, no fuss. Call it health food, but don't romanticize. Call it poor people's food. A dinner of herbs – greens – is a virtue once, but every night makes it seem like an unending Lent.

It is all we can afford. Well, that is because you do not work very hard or very much and are not productive. You could work in the afternoons and afford some meat regularly. But a choice has been made: work less, more time to do what we want. More time for each other... We arrive at supper unrushed, without great food. We eat slowly or it will be over too soon, not much food. But time for what there is. Maybe the neighbours will be there... sharing and laughing and listening – and peace... We finish, nourished, not excessively full, but hunger done, and healing comes. It is not just the food, because the difference between spinach and beef does not amount to much, except that the two epitomize a whole range of choices for people and things, for ease or drivenness, for sufficiency and satiation, for listening and bickering, contentment gained not by consuming but by communion...

Spinach breeds love no more than beef yields hate. The proverb only imagines two ways in the world, one that moves from well-being to caring, the other that moves from franticness to having and gaining the whole world and finishing supper with a diminished soul. Soulless food causes loss of soul.

Taken from a sermon preached by Walter Brueggemann at
Columbia Theological Seminary, published in *The Threat of Life:
Sermons on Pain, Power and Weakness*, edited by Charles L. Campbell, 1996

# THE CHURCH AND ITS PEOPLE

## Christ and the church

Christ loved the church and gave his life for it. He made the church holy by the power of his word, and he made it pure by washing it with water. Christ did this so that he would have a glorious and holy church, without faults or spots or wrinkles or any other flaws.

*From Ephesians 5*

## Belonging to God's family

First of all, I ask you to pray for everyone. Ask God to help and bless them all, and tell God how thankful you are for each of them. Pray for kings and others in power, so that we may live quiet and peaceful lives as we worship and honour God. This kind of prayer is good, and it pleases God our Saviour. God wants everyone to be saved and to know the whole truth, which is,

> *There is only one God,*
> *and Christ Jesus*
> *    is the only one*
> *who can bring us*
> *    to God.*
> *Jesus was truly human,*
> *and he gave himself*
> *    to rescue all of us...*

I want everyone everywhere to lift innocent hands towards heaven and pray, without being angry or arguing with each other...

It is true that anyone who desires to be a church official wants to be something worthwhile. That's why officials must have a good reputation and be faithful in marriage. They must be self-controlled, sensible, well-behaved, friendly to strangers, and able to teach. They must not be heavy drinkers or troublemakers. Instead, they must be kind and gentle and not love money.

Church officials must be in control of their own families, and they must see that their children are obedient and always respectful. If they don't know how to control their own families, how can they care for God's people?

They must not be new followers of the Lord. If they are, they might become proud and be doomed along with the devil. Finally, they must be well respected by people who are not followers. Then they won't be trapped and disgraced by the devil...

I hope to visit you soon. But I am writing these instructions, so that if I am delayed, you will know how everyone who belongs to God's family ought to behave. After all, the church of the living God is the strong foundation of truth.

From 1 Timothy 2, 3

Alexander Pope (1688–1744)

# Church unity

*Pope was brought up – and remained in – the Roman Catholic Church in spite of attempts by the bishop of Rochester to 'convert' him to Anglicanism. In this letter to the bishop, he shows loyalty with tolerance in an age when religious feelings ran high.*

*To the Bishop of Rochester, 20 November 1717*

My Lord,
I am truly obliged by your kind condolence on my father's death, and the desire you express that I should improve this incident to my advantage. I know your Lordship's friendship to me is so extensive, that you include in that wish both my spiritual and my temporal advantage; and it is what I owe to that friendship, to open my mind unreservedly to you on this head... Whether the change would be to my spiritual advantage, God only knows: this I know, that I mean as well in the religion I now profess, as I can possibly ever do in another. Can a man, who thinks so, justify a change, even if he thought both equally good? To such an one, the part of *joining* with any one body of Christians might perhaps be easy, but I think it would not be so, to *renounce* the other.

Your Lordship has formerly advised me to read the best controversies between the churches. Shall I tell you a secret? I did so at fourteen years old, for I loved reading, and my father had no other books; there was a collection of all that had been written on both sides in the reign of King James the Second. I warmed my head with them, and the consequence was that I found myself a Papist and a Protestant by turns, according to the last book I read. I am afraid most seekers are in the same case, and when they stop, they are not so properly converted as outwitted. You see how little glory you would gain by my conversion. And after all, I verily believe your Lordship and I are of the same religion, if we were thoroughly understood by one another; and that all honest and reasonable Christians would be so, if they did but talk enough together every day, and had nothing to do together, but to serve God, and live in peace with their neighbour.

As to the *temporal* side of the question, I can have no dispute with you; it is certain, all the beneficial circumstances of life, and all the shining ones, lie on the part you would invite me to. But, if I could bring myself to fancy, what I think you do not fancy, that I have any talents for active life, I want health for it; and besides, it is a real truth, I have less inclination (if possible) than ability. Contemplative life is not only my scene, but it is my habit too. I begun my life, where most people end theirs, with a disrelish of all that the world calls ambition. I do not know why it is called so, for to me it always seemed to be rather *stooping* than *climbing*. I will tell you my political and religious sentiments in a few words. In my politics, I think no further than how to preserve the peace of my life, in any government under which I live; nor in my religion, than to preserve the peace of my conscience in any church with which I communicate. I hope all churches and all governments are so far of God, as they are rightly understood, and rightly administered: and where they are, or may be wrong, I leave it to God alone to mend or reform them; which whenever he does, it must be by greater instruments than I am...

Believe me, with infinite obligation and sincere thanks, ever yours &c.

Letter to the bishop of Rochester, 1717

Francis Kilvert (1840–79)

# *Water for the font*

*Thursday 30 April 1874*

The vicar of Fordington told us of the state of things in his parish when he first came to it nearly half a century ago. No man had ever been known to receive the Holy Communion except the parson, the clerk and the sexton. There were 16 women communicants and most of them went away when he refused to pay them for coming. They had been accustomed there at some place in the neighbourhood to pass the cup to each other with a nod of the head. At one church there were two male communicants. When the cup was given to the first he touched his forelock and said, 'Here's your good health, Sir.' The other said, 'Here's the good health of our Lord Jesus Christ.'

One day there was a christening and no water in the Font. 'Water, Sir!' said the clerk in astonishment. 'The last parson never used no water. He spit into his hand.'

From *Kilvert's Diary*, 1874

**Jonathan Swift (1667–1745)**

# Argument against abolishing Christianity in England

*Swift has the reputation of being the greatest prose satirist in English literature. In this article, he lampoons both the church and its opponents.*

I am very sensible how much the gentlemen of wit and pleasure are apt to murmur, and be choked at the sight of so many daggled-tail parsons, who happen to fall in their way and offend their eyes; but, at the same time, these wise reformers do not consider what an advantage and felicity it is for great wits to be always provided with objects of scorn and contempt, in order to exercise and improve their talents, and divert their spleen from falling on each other or on themselves; especially when all this may be done without the least imaginable danger to their persons.

And to urge another argument of a parallel nature: if Christianity were once abolished, how could the freethinkers, the strong reasoners, and the men of profound learning, be able to find another subject, so calculated in all points, whereon to display their abilities? What wonderful productions of wit should we be deprived of from those whose genius, by continual practice, has been wholly turned upon raillery and invective against religion, and would therefore never be able to shine or distinguish themselves upon any other subject? We are daily complaining of the great decline of wit among us, and would we take away the greatest, perhaps the only, topic we have left?...

If, notwithstanding all I have said, it still be thought necessary to have a bill brought in for repealing Christianity, I would humbly offer an amendment, that instead of the word Christianity, may be put religion in general, which, I conceive, will much better answer all the good ends proposed by the projectors of it. For as long as we leave in being a God and his providence, with all the necessary consequences which curious and inquisitive men will be apt to draw from such premises, we do not strike at the root of the evil, though we should ever so effectually annihilate the present scheme of the gospel: for of what use is freedom of thought, if it will not produce freedom of action? Which is the sole end,

how remote soever in appearance, of all objections against Christianity...
I think nothing can be more manifest than that the quarrel is not against
any particular points of hard digestion in the Christian system, but
against religion in general; which, by laying restraints on human nature,
is supposed the great enemy to the freedom of thought and action...

To conclude: whatever some may think of the great advantages to trade
by this favourite scheme, I do very much apprehend that, in six months
time after the act is passed for the extirpation of the gospel, the Bank and
East-India stock may fall at least one *per cent*. And since that is fifty times
more than ever the wisdom of our age thought fit to venture for the
preservation of Christianity, there is no reason we should be at so great a
loss, merely for the sake of destroying it.

From *An Argument Against Abolishing Christianity*, 1708

## G.K. Chesterton (1874–1936)

# *The danger of climbing too high*

The Innocence of Father Brown *was the first collection of short detective stories featuring the little priest.*

*In* The Hammer of God, *Father Brown – his case solved – runs up the winding steps of the church and calls his suspect, the Reverend Wilfred Bohun, to follow:*

This church was hewn out of ancient and silent stone, bearded with old fungoids and stained with the nests of birds. And yet, when they saw it from below, it sprang like a fountain at the stars; and when they saw it, as now, from above, it poured like a cataract into a voiceless pit. For these two men on the tower were left alone with the most terrible aspect of the Gothic: the monstrous foreshortening and disproportion, the dizzy perspectives, the glimpses of great things small and small things great; a topsy-turvydom of stone in the mid-air. Details of stone, enormous by their proximity, were relieved against a pattern of fields and farms, pygmy in their distance. A carved bird or beast at a corner seemed like some vast walking or flying dragon wasting the pastures or villages below. The whole atmosphere was dizzy and dangerous, as if men were upheld in air amid the gyrating wings of colossal genii; and the whole of that old church, as tall and rich as a cathedral, seemed to sit upon the sunlit country like a cloudburst.

'I think there is something rather dangerous about standing on these high places even to pray,' said Father Brown. 'Heights were made to be looked at, not to be looked from.'

'Do you mean that one may fall over?' asked Wilfred.

'I mean that one's soul may fall if one's body doesn't,' said the other priest.

'I scarcely understand you,' remarked Bohun indistinctly.

'Look at that blacksmith, for instance,' went on Father Brown calmly; 'a good man, but not a Christian – hard, imperious, unforgiving. Well, his Scotch religion was made up by men who prayed on hills and high crags, and learnt to look down on the world more than to look up at heaven. Humility is the mother of giants. One sees great things from the valley; only small things from the peak... I knew a man who began by worshipping God with others before the altar, but who grew fond of high and lonely places to pray from, corners or niches in the belfry or the spire. And once in one of those dizzy places, where the whole world seemed to turn under him like a wheel, his brain turned also, and he fancied he was God. So that though he was a good man, he committed a great crime.'

From *The Innocence of Father Brown*, 1911

## William Golding (1911–93)

# *Sabbath service on board ship*

Rites of Passage *recounts a nineteenth-century voyage from England to Australia, mainly through the letters of Mr Talbot, young and self-assured, who is on his way to take up administrative office in the colony. The disturbing and shocking events of the voyage cause him to reach his destination a humbler and wiser man. Other passengers include some ladies and Colley, a timid clergyman, bullied by the fiercely anti-clerical captain. It is the 'Sabbath':*

I attended the service our little cleric was allowed to perform. I was disgusted by it. Just previous to the service I saw Miss Brocklebank and her face was fairly plastered with red and white!... Yet later I found I had underestimated both her judgement and her experience. For when it was time for the service the candles of the saloon irradiated her face, took from it the damaging years, while what had been paint now appeared a magical youth and beauty! She looked at me. Scarcely had I recovered from the shock of having this battery play on me when I discovered... Mr Summers had... allowed in, to share our devotions with us, a number of the more respectable emigrants... I was recovering from this invasion when there entered to us – we standing in respect – five feet nothing of parson complete with surplice, cap of maintenance perched on a round wig, long gown, boots with iron-shod heels – together with a mingled air of diffidence, piety, triumph and complacency...

He knows of my consequence. At times it was difficult to determine whether he was addressing Edmund Talbot or the Almighty. He was theatrical as Miss Brocklebank. The habit of respect for the clerical office was all that prevented me from breaking into indignant laughter. Among the respectable emigrants that attended was the poor, pale girl, carried devotedly by strong arms and placed in a seat behind us. I have learned that she suffered a miscarriage in our first *blow* and her awful pallor was in contrast with the manufactured allure of La Brocklebank... I set aside the sound of pacing steps from above our heads where Mr Prettiman demonstrated his anticlericalism as noisily on the afterdeck as possible. I omit the trampings and shouts at the changing of the watch... with as much rowdiness as can be procured among skylarking sailors. I think only of the gently swaying saloon, the pale girl and the farce that was played out before her! For no sooner did Mr Colley catch sight of Miss Brocklebank than he could not take his eyes off her... Her eyes never left his face but when they were turned to heaven. Her lips were always parted in breathless ecstasy except when they opened and closed swiftly with a passionate 'Amen!' Indeed there was one moment when a sanctimonious remark in the course of his address from Mr Colley, followed by an 'Amen!' from Miss Brocklebank was underlined, as it were... by a resounding fart from that wind-machine Mr Brocklebank, so as to set most of the congregation sniggering like schoolboys on their benches.

However much I attempted to detach myself from the performance I was made deeply ashamed by it... We had a handful of the common people with us. It is possible they had entered the after part of the ship in much the same spirit as those visitors who declare they wish to view your lordship's Canalettos but who are really there to see if they can how the nobility live. But I think it more probable that they had come in a spirit of simple devotion. Certainly that poor, pale girl could have no other object than to find the comforts of religion.

From *Rites of Passage*, 1980

## Malcolm Muggeridge (1903–90)

# Dr Barnes et al

*C.P. Scott (1846–1932) was Muggeridge's controversial literary editor at the* Manchester Guardian; *Hewlitt Johnson (1874–1966), known as the 'Red Dean', had strong communist leanings and championed Marxist policies. Alec Vidler (1899–1991), Christian priest and writer, was Muggeridge's lifelong friend.*

When I was working on the *Manchester Guardian*, I met Dr Barnes, a friend of C.P. Scott. Clergymen, in my experience, tend to get holier and holier-looking as they move farther and farther away from their faith; rather in the same way that a womaniser gets more ethereal looking the more women he seduces. It must be some kind of inner adjustment mechanics, like a thermostat. There never was a more deaconal dean than Dr Hewlitt Johnson when, in his gaiters and with a large cross adorning his waistcoat, he sat beaming beatifically among his church's foremost enemies. Dr Barnes's rig was also elegantly clerical, and he had a gentle, purring, exaggeratedly meek manner of addressing one. At the time I met him he was much exercised about a new telescope which had just been developed. Telescopes, he seemed to imply, were getting so powerful that before long they'd be looking into heaven itself. Then all doubts would be set at rest, and science and religion come together in one blessed consummation. When Scott died, Barnes conducted his funeral service in Manchester Cathedral. In the course of his address on that occasion he remarked that some might consider it strange that he, an Anglican bishop, should be presiding over the obsequies of a distinguished Unitarian in an Anglican cathedral; but to him it seemed the most natural thing in the world, since Scott, like himself, had been a puzzled theist. This appeared in *The Times* report as 'puzzled atheist'. It confirmed my feeling that misprints, like the foolishness of men, are the wisdom of God. Alec, though mixed up in the controversy with his Bishop... was still, I felt, essentially uninvolved. He has an enviable capacity for being able thus to withdraw into some deep inward serenity of his own, and in that sanctuary, totally private and impregnable; there able to meet his God and work out the relationship between them. Without understanding precisely how this happens, or the terms arrived at, a third person can still draw strength from the resultant serenity. I regard Alec as one of the great Christians of our time, even though – perhaps because – I should have the greatest difficulty in defining just where he stands in the different theological disputes which have accompanied the steady erosion of Christian faith. To me he has been like a rock where there is always shelter, however fierce the hurricane. A lifelong comfort.

From *The Green Stick*, volume 1 of *Chronicles of Wasted Time*, 1972

**Alan Bennett (b. 1934)**

# Keeping up appearances

*Susan, the vicar's wife, is an alcoholic. In one of Bennett's television* Talking Heads, *she reminisces about the bishop's visit as she polishes a candlestick in the side-chapel:*

We were discussing the ordination of women. The bishop asked me what I thought. Should women take the services? So long as it doesn't have to be me, I want to say, they can be taken by a trained gorilla. 'Oh yes,' Geoffrey chips in, 'Susan's all in favour. She's keener than I am, aren't you, darling?' 'More sprouts anybody?' I said.

On the young side for a bishop, but he's been a prominent sportsman at university so that would explain it. Boxing or rugby. Broken nose at some stage anyway. One of the 'Christianity is common sense' brigade. Hobby's bricklaying apparently and refers to me throughout as 'Mrs Vicar'. Wants beer with his lunch and Geoffrey says he'll join him so this leaves me with the wine. Geoffrey's all over him because the rumour is he's shopping around for a new Archdeacon. Asks Geoff how outgoing I am. Actually says that. 'How outgoing is Mrs Vicar?' Mr Vicar jumps in with a quick rundown of my accomplishments and an outline of my punishing schedule. On a typical day, apparently, I kick off by changing the wheel on the Fiesta, then hasten to the bedside of a dying pensioner, after which, having done the altar flowers and dispensed warmth and appreciation to sundry parishioners en route, I top off a thrill-packed morning by taking round Meals on Wheels... somehow – 'and this to me is the miracle,' says Geoffrey – 'somehow managing to rustle up a delicious lunch in the interim,' the miracle somewhat belied by the flabby lasagna we are currently embarked on. 'The ladies,' says the bishop. 'Where would we be without them?'

Disaster strikes as I'm doling out the tinned peaches: the jug into which I've decanted the Carnation milk gets knocked over, possibly by me. Geoffrey, for whom turning the other cheek is part of the job, claims it caught his elbow and his lordship takes the same line, insisting he gets doused in Carnation milk practically every day of his life. Still, when I get a dishcloth and sponge off his gaiters I catch him giving me a funny look. It's Mary Magdalene and the Nivea cream all over again. After lunch Geoffrey's supposed to be taking him on a tour of the parish but while we're having a cup of instant he claps his hand to his temple because he's suddenly remembered he's supposed to be in Keighley blessing a steam engine.

From 'Bed Among the Lentils', *Talking Heads*, televised 1988

## P.D. James (b. 1920)

# *The suspect in church*

*In an interview on BBC Radio 4, P.D. James agreed that her books are always sparked off by a place. She herself is an avid viewer of churches and A Taste for Death was conceived on a visit to a church at Jericho, Oxford; for the purposes of her book she has transposed it from Oxford to London.*

The afternoon was so dark now that it could have been night, the sky thick and furred as a blanket, the air heavy to breathe and with the sharp metallic taste of the coming storm. Just as he turned the corner and saw the church, it broke. The air and sky glittered with the first flash of lightning, then almost at once there came the crack of thunder. Two large drops stained the pavement in front of him and the rain sheeted down. He ran into the shelter of the church porch, laughing aloud. Even the weather was on his side...

Gently he turned the great iron handle of the door. It was unlocked, slightly ajar. But he had expected to find it open. With part of his mind he believed that churches, buildings of sanctuary and superstition, were always left open for their worshippers. But nothing could surprise him, nothing could go wrong. The door squeaked as he closed it behind him and stepped into the sweet-smelling quietness.

The church was larger than he had imagined, so cold that he shuddered and so still that he thought for a second that he heard an animal panting before he realized that it was his own breath. There was no artificial light except for a single chandelier and a lamp in a small side chapel, where a crimson glow stained the air. Two rows of candles burning before the statue of the Madonna gusted in the draught from the closing door... The box containing the button was at the west end of the church in front of the iron ornamental grille. But he didn't hurry. He moved into the middle of the nave facing the altar and spread his arms wide as if to take possession of the vast emptiness, the holiness, the sweet-smelling air. In front of him the mosaics of the apse gleamed richly gold and turning to look up at the clerestory he could see in the half-light the ranks of painted figures, one-dimensional, harmlessly sentimental as cut-outs from a child's picture book. The rainwater ran down his hair to wash over his

face, and he laughed as he tasted its sweetness on his tongue. A small pool
gathered at his feet. Then slowly, almost ceremoniously, he paced down
the nave to the candleholder in front of the grille.

There was a padlock on the box, but it was only small, and the box itself
more fragile than he had expected. He inserted the chisel under the lid
and heaved. At first it resisted, and then he could hear the gentle splinter
of the wood and the gap widened. He gave one more heave and suddenly
the padlock sprang apart with a crack so loud that it echoed through the
church like a pistol shot. Almost at once it was answered by a crack of
thunder. The gods, he thought, are applauding me.

And then he was aware of a dark shadow moving up to him and heard
a voice, quietly untroubled, gently authoritative.

'If you're looking for the button, my son, you've come too late. The
police have found it.'

From *A Taste for Death*, 1986

### J.B. Phillips (1906–82)

# Christian escapism

*In* Your God is Too Small, *J.B. Phillips reasons that many people today reject God because they have failed to form an adult image of him that is big enough to meet the questions and demands of life. In this extract he describes those he dubs 'bosom-flyers':*

The critics of the Christian religion have often contended that a religious faith is a form of psychological 'escapism'. A man, they say, finding the problems and demands of adult life too much for him will attempt to return to the comfort and dependence of childhood by picturing for himself a loving parent, whom he calls God. It must be admitted that there is a good deal of ammunition ready to hand for such an attack, and the first verse of a well-known and well-loved hymn provides an obvious example –

*Jesu, Lover of my soul,*
  *Let me to thy bosom fly,*
*While the nearer waters roll,*
  *While the tempest still is high:*
*Hide me, O my Saviour, hide,*
  *Till the storms of life be past:*
*Safe into the haven guide,*
  *O receive my soul at last.*

Here, if the words are taken at their face value, is sheer escapism, a deliberate desire to be hidden safe away until the storm and stress of life are over, and no explaining away by lovers of the hymn can alter its plain sense. It can hardly be denied that if this is true Christianity then the charge of 'escapism', of emotional immaturity and childish regression, must be frankly conceded. But although this 'God of escape' is quite common the true Christian course is set in a very different direction. No one would accuse its Founder of immaturity in insight, thought, teaching or conduct, and the history of the Christian Church provides thousands of examples of timid half-developed personalities who have not only found in their faith what psychologists call integration, but have coped with difficulties and dangers in a way that makes any gibe of 'escapism' plainly ridiculous.

Yet is there in Christianity a legitimate element of what the inimical might call escapism?

The authentic Christian tradition... show[s] that throughout the ages heroic men and women have found in God their 'refuge' as well as their 'strength'... It has been well said by several modern psychologists that it is not the outward storms and stresses of life that defeat and disrupt personality, but its inner conflicts and miseries. If a man is happy and stable at heart, he can normally cope, even with zest, with difficulties that lie outside his personality...

Now Christians maintain that it is precisely this secure centre which faith in God provides. The genuine Christian can and does venture out into all kinds of exacting and even perilous activities, but all the time he knows that he has a completely stable and unchanging centre of operations to which he can return for strength, refreshment and recuperation. In that sense he does 'escape' to God, though he does not avoid the duties or burdens of life. His very 'escape' fits him for the day-to-day engagement with life's strains and difficulties...

Today the gibe is that the message of Christianity attracts only the psychologically immature. Even if the charge were true, the answer to it would be that those who know they are at sixes and sevens with themselves are more likely to respond to a gospel offering psychological integration (among other things), than those who feel perfectly competent and well adjusted. Nevertheless the true Christian does not long *remain* either immature or in internal conflict. It is only if he becomes 'fixed' with the inadequate god of escape that he exhibits the pathetic figure of the perpetual bosom-flyer.

From *Your God is Too Small*, 1952

### Iris Murdoch (1919–99)

# *Bishop talk*

*In* The Bell, *a lay community, housed near an enclosed order of nuns, prepares for the arrival of a new bell, to replace the legendary one, long lost. Iris Murdoch describes the motley members of the community, with their complex relationships; brooding gently over them all is the presence of the wise, loving abbess, whose holiness is compassionate and practical. The bishop, who arrives to consecrate the new bell, is very different:*

The Rolls Royce came onto the terrace with the dignified condescension of a very large car moving slowly. It stopped at the foot of the steps, quite near to the bell… The Bishop, who had apparently been driving himself, got out of the car with an affable leisureliness of the great personage who knows that whenever and wherever he arrives he is immediately the centre of the scene. He was a big portly man with frizzy hair and rimless glasses, dressed in a plain black cassock and purple stock. His large fleshy face turned slowly, glowing with friendliness. He pulled a stick out of the car on which he leaned lightly while shaking hands with Mrs Mark, James, and Noel, and then with Dora, whom he was anxious not to exclude, although she was hovering uncertainly in the background. Dora decided he took her for one of the maids.

'Well, here I am!' said the Bishop. 'I hope I'm not late? My charming chauffeur has abandoned me – a lady, I hasten to say – and also my secretary. The exigencies of motherhood call her to a higher task. She has three children to look after, and that is not counting myself! So at much wear and tear to my own nerves and those of my fellow motorists I have driven myself to Imber!'

'We're so glad you've managed to come, sir,' said James, beaming. 'We know how busy you are. It means a lot to us to have you at our little ceremony.'

'Well, I think it's all most exciting,' said the Bishop. 'And is this exhibit A?' He pointed with his stick to the white ribbony mound of the bell.

'Yes,' said Mrs Mark, blushing with excitement. 'We just thought we'd deck it up a little.'

'Very pretty too,' said the Bishop. 'You are Mrs Strafford I believe? And you are Mr Meade?' he said to James. 'I've heard so much about you from the Abbess, bless her.'

'Oh no,' said James. 'I'm James Tayper Pace.'

'Ah!' said the Bishop. 'You are the man who is so sorely missed in Stepney! I was there only a few weeks ago at the opening of a new youth centre, and your name was often taken in vain. Or rather, not in vain. What an absurd expression that is, to be sure! Your name was mentioned, most fruitfully I've no doubt, and with positively devout enthusiasm!'

It was James's turn to blush. He said, 'We ought to have introduced ourselves. I'm afraid we make you a very poor reception committee, sir. This is indeed Mrs Strafford. This is Mrs Greenfield. Michael Meade is just coming across the grass with Dr Greenfield. And I'm afraid I don't know this gentleman.'

'Noel Spens, from the office of the *Daily Record*,' said Noel. 'I'm afraid I'm what they call a reporter.'

'Why, splendid!' said the Bishop. 'I hoped some gentleman of the press might be present. Did you say the *Daily Record*? You must excuse me, I'm such a deaf old codger now, practically incommunicado on this side. May I ask if you were put on my track by my old crony Holroyd? I believe he now edits your distinguished rag.'

'That's correct,' said Noel. 'Mr Holroyd got wind of this picturesque ceremony and sent me along. He sends you his greetings, sir.'

'An excellent fellow,' said the Bishop, 'in the best traditions of British journalism. I have always thought the church was foolish to shun publicity. What we need is more publicity, of the right kind, of course. Perhaps I may say of *this* kind. What's that? No, I won't eat anything now, thank you. I'll just have the good old English cup of tea, if I may. Since my trip to America I value it more than ever. Then we might proceed to our little service, if the clans have mustered? And have the feasting afterwards. I see a board or two groaning with goodies in there.'

From *The Bell*, 1958

## Elizabeth Goudge (1900–84)

# *A village service*

*The Little White Horse won the Carnegie Medal for the most outstanding contribution to children's literature in 1946. The setting is an English West Country village, a few hundred years ago, where Maria, with her governess, Miss Heliotrope, and her dog, Wiggins, go to live in the manor house of Moonacre with Maria's cousin, Sir Benjamin Merryweather. On Sunday they go to church:*

The church was as lovely inside as it was outside, with beautiful soaring pillars like the trunks of trees and arches that sprang upwards like a shout of joy to meet the grand upward curve of the vaulted roof. The windows glowed with the deep rich colours of very old stained glass, and the sun shining through them painted the flag-stones below with all the colours of the rainbow.

To the left of the chancel steps was a tall pulpit, and to the right was a very old small stone chantry, with a small doorway, through which Maria could just make out the figure of a knight in armour lying upon his tomb. At sight of him her heart missed a beat, because she knew, without being told, that the chantry was a Merryweather shrine and that he was her ancestor.

Under the east window there was a simple stone altar, spread with a clean white linen cloth, and upon the altar step below was a great earthenware pitcher, filled with the first catkins and branches of glorious golden gorse. Though, of course, ladylike behaviour forbade the turning of her head to look, Maria was aware, from the sounds of scraping of chairs, the muffled voices, and the soft tuning of strings, that over the western doorway there was a gallery, and that the village choir, with the fiddles and cellos and Digweed's double bass, had already arrived.

And in the boxed-in wooden pews many worshippers were gathered, the bonnets of the women and the bare heads of the men just visible to Maria as she passed. Presently, when the villagers they had seen outside had come in also, the church would be quite full.

From *The Little White Horse*, 1946

# PART TWO

# BEING HUMAN

# HAPPINESS, LAUGHTER AND RECREATION

## Safety and re-creation

*The Lord is my shepherd; I shall not want.*
*He maketh me to lie down in green pastures: he leadeth me beside the still*
*waters.*
*He restoreth my soul: he leadeth me in the paths of righteousness for his*
*name's sake.*
*Yea, though I walk through the valley of the shadow of death, I will fear*
*no evil: for thou art with me; thy rod and thy staff they comfort me.*
*Thou preparest a table before me in the presence of mine enemies: thou*
*anointest my head with oil; my cup runneth over.*
*Surely goodness and mercy shall follow me all the days of my life: and*
*I will dwell in the house of the Lord for ever.*

From Psalm 23

## Enjoy yourself!

What do people really get for all their hard work? I have thought about this in connection with the various kinds of work God has given people to do. God has made everything beautiful for its own time. He has planted eternity in the human heart, but even so, people cannot see the whole scope of God's work from beginning to end. So I concluded that there is nothing better for people than to be happy, and to enjoy themselves as long as they can. And people should eat and drink and enjoy the fruits of their labour, for these are gifts from God.

From Ecclesiastes 3

**William Law (1686–1761)**

# The secret of true happiness

Would you know him who is the greatest saint in the world? It is not he who prays most or fasts most; it is not he who gives most alms, but it is he who is always thankful to God, who receives everything as an instance of God's goodness and has a heart always ready to praise God for it.

If anyone would tell you the shortest, surest way to all happiness and perfection, he must tell you to make a rule to thank and praise God for everything that happens to you. Whatever seeming calamity happens to you, if you thank and praise God for it, you turn it into a blessing. Could you therefore work miracles you could not do more for yourself than by this thankful spirit; it turns all that it touches into happiness.

From *A Serious Call to a Devout and Holy Life*, 1729

William Cowper (1731–1800)

# *Happiness recalled*

*12 October 1785*

My dear Cousin – It is no new thing with you to give pleasure. But I will venture to say that you do not often give more than you gave me this morning. When I came down to breakfast and found upon the table a letter franked by my uncle, and when opening that frank I found that it contained a letter from you, I said within myself – 'This is just as it should be. We are all grown young again, and the days that I thought I should see no more are actually returned.' You perceive, therefore, that you judged well when you conjectured that a line from you would not be disagreeable to me. It could not be otherwise than, as in fact it proved, a most agreeable surprise, for I can truly boast of an affection for you that neither years nor interrupted intercourse have at all abated. I need only recollect how much I valued you once, and with how much cause, immediately to feel a revival of the same value; if that can be said to revive which at the most has only been dormant for want of employment. But I slander it when I say that it has slept. A thousand times I have recollected a thousand scenes, in which our two selves have formed the whole of the drama, with the greatest pleasure; at times, too, when I had no reason to suppose that I should ever hear from you again. I have laughed with you at the Arabian Nights' Entertainment, which afforded us, as you well know, a fund of merriment that deserves never to be forgot. I have walked with you to Netley Abbey, and have scrambled with you over hedges in every direction; and many other feats we have performed together upon the field of my remembrance, and all within these few years. Should I say within this twelvemonth I should not transgress the truth. The hours that I have spent with you were among the pleasantest of my former days, and are therefore chronicled in my mind so deeply as to fear no erasure...

My dear cousin, dejection of spirits, which I suppose may have prevented many a man from becoming an author, made me one. I find constant employment necessary, and therefore take care to be constantly employed... composition, especially of verse, absorbs me wholly...

Adieu, my beloved cousin, I shall not always be thus nimble in reply, but shall always have great pleasure in answering you when I can.

Yours, my dear friend and cousin.

W.C.

Letter from Cowper to Lady Hesketh, 1785

### G.K. Chesterton (1874–1936)

# *Letting happiness happen*

Most of the inconveniences that make men swear or women cry are really sentimental or imaginative inconveniences – things altogether of the mind. For instance, we often hear grown-up people complaining of having to hang about a railway station and wait for a train. Did you ever hear a small boy complain of having to hang about a railway station and wait for a train? No; for to him to be inside a railway station is to be inside a cavern of wonder and a palace of poetical pleasures... I myself am of little boys' habit in this matter. They also serve who only stand and wait for the two fifteen. Their meditations may be full of rich and fruitful things. Many of the most purple hours of my life have been passed at Clapham Junction... You can safely apply the test to almost every one of the things that are currently talked of as the typical nuisance of daily life.

For instance, there is a current impression that it is unpleasant to have to run after one's hat. Why should it be unpleasant to the well-ordered and pious mind? Not merely because it is running, and running exhausts one. The same people run much faster in games and sports. The same people run much more eagerly after an uninteresting little leather ball than they will after a nice silk hat. There is an idea that it is humiliating to run after one's hat; and when people say that it is humiliating they mean that it is comic. It certainly is comic; but man is a very comic creature, and most of the things he does are comic – eating, for example. And the most comic things of all are exactly the things that are most worth doing – such as making love. A man running after a hat is not half so ridiculous as a man running after a wife.

Now a man could, if he felt rightly in the matter, run after his hat with the manliest ardour and the most sacred joy... When last I saw an old gentleman running after his hat in Hyde Park, I told him that a heart so benevolent as his ought to be filled with peace and thanks at the thought of how much unaffected pleasure his every gesture and bodily attitude were at that moment giving to the crowd.

'On Running After One's Hat', *All Things Considered*, 1908

Laurence Sterne (1713–68)

# Dr Slop arrives

*Tristram Shandy tells his life story – with many interruptions and diversions – from the moment of conception.*
*When Tristram Shandy's mother goes into labour, his father sends the servant, Obadiah, with all haste to fetch Dr Slop:*

Imagine to yourself a little squat, uncourtly figure of a Doctor Slop, of about four feet and a half perpendicular height, with a breadth of back, and a sesquipedality of belly, which might have done honour to a sergeant in the horse-guards...

Imagine such a one, – for such, I say, were the outlines of Dr Slop's figure, coming slowly along, foot by foot, waddling thro' the dirt upon the vertebrae of a little diminutive pony, of a pretty colour – but of strength, – alack! – scarce able to have made an amble of it, under such a fardel, had the roads been in an ambling condition. – They were not. – Imagine to yourself, Obadiah mounted upon a strong monster of a coach-horse, pricked into a full gallop, and making all practicable speed the adverse way...

What then do you think must the terror and hydrophobia of Dr Slop have been, when you read (which you are just going to do) that he was advancing thus warily along towards Shandy-Hall, and had approached to within sixty yards of it, and within five yards of a sudden turn, made by an acute angle of the garden-wall, – and in the dirtiest part of a dirty lane, – when Obadiah and his coach-horse turned the corner, rapid, furious, – pop, – full upon him! – Nothing, I think, in nature, can be supposed more terrible than such a rencounter, – so imprompt! so ill-prepared to stand the shock of it as Dr Slop was.

What could Dr Slop do? – he crossed himself... he had better have kept hold of the pummel – He had so; nay, as it happened, he had better have done nothing at all; for in crossing himself he let go his whip, – and in attempting to save his whip betwixt his knee and his saddle's skirt, as it slipped, he lost his stirrup, – in losing which he lost his seat; – and in the multitude of all these losses (which, by the bye, shews what little advantage there is in crossing) the unfortunate doctor lost his presence of mind. So that without waiting for Obadiah's onset, he left his pony to its destiny, tumbling off it diagonally, something in the stile and manner of a pack of wool, and without any other consequence of the fall, save that of being left (as it would have been) with the broadest part of him sunk about twelve inches deep in the mire.

From *Tristram Shandy*, 1759

## Iris Murdoch (1919–99)

# *Moment of knowing*

Dora had been in the National Gallery a thousand times and the pictures were almost as familiar to her as her own face. Passing between them now, as through a well-loved grove, she felt a calm descending on her. She wandered a little, watching with compassion the poor visitors armed with guide books who were peering anxiously at the masterpieces. Dora did not need to peer. She could look, as one can at last when one knows a great thing very well, confronting it with a dignity which it has itself conferred. She felt that the pictures belonged to her, and reflected ruefully that they were about the only thing that did...

Dora stopped at last in front of Gainsborough's picture of his two daughters. These children step through a wood hand in hand, their garments shimmering, their eyes serious and dark, their two pale heads, round full buds, like yet unlike.

Dora was always moved by the pictures. Today she was moved, but in a new way. She marvelled, with a kind of gratitude, that they were all still here, and her heart was filled with love for the pictures, their authority, their marvellous generosity, their splendour...

The pictures were something real outside herself, which spoke to her kindly and yet in sovereign tones, something superior and good whose presence destroyed the dreary trance-like solipsism of her earlier mood. When the world had seemed to be subjective it had seemed to be without interest or value. But now there was something else in it after all.

These thoughts, not clearly articulated, flitted through Dora's mind. She had never thought about the pictures in this way before; nor did she draw now any very explicit moral. Yet she felt that she had had a revelation. She looked at the radiant, sombre, tender, powerful canvas of Gainsborough and felt a sudden desire to go down on her knees before it, embracing it, shedding tears.

Dora looked anxiously about her, wondering if anyone had noticed her transports. Although she had not actually prostrated herself, her face must have looked unusually ecstatic, and the tears were in fact starting into her eyes. She found that she was alone in the room, and smiled, restored to a more calm enjoyment of her wisdom. She gave a last look at the painting, still smiling... Then she turned and began to leave the building.

From *The Bell*, 1958

**Marcel Proust (1871–1922)**

# Place names in the imagination

Words present to us little pictures of things, lucid and normal, like the pictures that are hung on the walls of schoolrooms to give children an illustration of what is meant by a carpenter's bench, a bird, an anthill; things chosen as typical of everything else of the same sort. But names present to us – of persons and towns which they accustom us to regard as individual, as unique, like persons – a confused picture, which draws from the names, from the brightness or darkness of their sound, the colour in which it is uniformly painted, like one of those posters, entirely blue or entirely red, in which, on account of the limitations imposed by the process used in their reproduction, or by a whim on the designer's part, are blue or red not only the sky and the sea, but the ships and the church and the people in the streets. The name of Parma, one of the towns that I most longed to visit, after reading the *Chartreuse*, seeming to me compact and glossy, violet-tinted, soft, and that bore no relation to the houses in any other part of Italy, since I could imagine it only by the aid of that heavy syllable of the name of Parma, in which no breath of air stirred, and of all that I had made it assume of Stendhalian sweetness and the reflected hue of violets. And when I thought of Florence, it was of a town miraculously embalmed, and flower-like, since it was called the City of the Lilies, and its Cathedral, Our Lady of the Flower...

Doubtless, if, at that time, I had paid more attention to what was in my mind when I pronounced the words 'going to Florence, to Parma, to Pisa, to Venice', I should have realised that what I saw was in no sense a town, but something as different from anything I knew, as delicious as might be for a human race whose whole existence had passed in a series of late winter afternoons, that inconceivable marvel, a morning in spring. These images, unreal, fixed, always alike, filling all my nights and days, differentiated this period of my life from those which had gone before it (and might easily have been confused with it by an observer who saw things only from without, that is to say, who saw nothing), as in an opera a fresh melody introduces a novel atmosphere which one could never have suspected if one had done no more than read the libretto, still less if one had remained outside the theatre, counting only the minutes as they passed.

From *Swann's Way*, 1922, translated by C.K. Scott-Moncrieff from *Du côté de chez Swann*, 1913; volume 1 of *Remembrance of Things Past*

## Elizabeth Gaskell (1810–65)

# *The cat and the lace*

*In* Cranford *Mrs Gaskell describes life in a provincial town in northern England and the genteel poor who lived there. Real goodness is portrayed as well as the vanities and hypocrisies of small-town communities.*

*Mrs Jamieson had warned her friends that they were not fine enough to be invited to meet her aristocratic sister-in-law, Lady Glenmire, when she came to stay. But eventually they are invited and attend:*

As a proof of how thoroughly we had forgotten that we were in the presence of one who might have sat down to tea with a coronet, instead of a cap, on her head, Mrs Forrester related a curious little fact to Lady Glenmire – an anecdote known to the circle of her intimate friends, but of which even Mrs Jamieson was not aware. It related to some fine old lace, the sole relic of better days, which Lady Glenmire was admiring on Mrs Forrester's collar.

'Yes,' said that lady, 'such lace cannot be got now for either love or money; made by the nuns abroad, they tell me. They say that they can't make it now even there. But perhaps they can now they've passed the Catholic Emancipation Bill. I should not wonder. But, in the meantime, I treasure up my lace very much. I daren't even trust the washing of it to my maid' (the little charity school-girl I have mentioned before, but who sounded well as 'my maid'). 'I always wash it myself. And once it had a narrow escape. Of course, your ladyship knows that such lace must never be starched or ironed. Some people wash it in sugar and water, and some in coffee, to make it the right yellow colour; but I myself have a very good receipt for washing it in milk, which stiffens it enough, and gives it a very good creamy colour. Well, ma'am, I had tacked it together (and the beauty of this fine lace is that, when it is wet, it goes into a very little space), and put it to soak in milk, when, unfortunately, I left the room; on my return, I found pussy on the table, looking very like a thief, but gulping very uncomfortably, as if she was half-choked with something she wanted to swallow and could not. And would you believe it? At first I pitied her, and said, 'Poor pussy! poor pussy!' till, all at once, I looked and saw the cup of milk empty – cleaned out! 'You naughty cat!' said I, and I believe I was provoked enough to give her a slap, which did no good, but only helped the lace down, just as one slaps a choking child on the back. I could have cried, I was so vexed; but I determined I would not give the lace up without a struggle for it. I hoped the lace might disagree with her, at any rate; but it would have been too much for Job, if he had seen, as I did, that cat come in, quite placid and purring, not a quarter of an hour after, and almost expecting to be stroked… then a thought struck me; and I rang the bell for my maid, and sent her to Mr Hoggins, with my compliments, and would he be kind enough to lend me one of his top-boots for an hour? I did not think there was anything odd in the message; but Jenny said the young men in the surgery laughed as if they would be ill at my wanting a top-boot. When it came, Jenny and I put pussy in, with her forefeet straight down, so that they were fastened, and could not scratch, and we gave her a teaspoonful of currant-jelly in which (your ladyship must excuse me) I had mixed some tartar emetic. I shall never forget how anxious I was for the next half-hour. I took pussy to my own room, and spread a clean towel on the floor. I could have kissed her when she returned the lace to sight, very much as it had gone down. Jenny had boiling water ready, and we soaked it and soaked it, and spread it on a lavender-bush in the sun before I could touch it again, even to put it in milk. But now your ladyship would never guess that it had been in pussy's inside.'

From *Cranford*, 1853

## Miguel de Cervantes (Saavedra) (1547–1616)

# *Windmills in his head*

*Don Quixote, a poor gentleman whose senses are turned by obsessive reading about the chivalrous deeds of knights, determines to do heroic deeds in the world. He saddles his thin old horse, whom he names Rozinante, finds some old, rusty armour and takes the country bumpkin Sancho Pança for his esquire. Then he sets out looking for adventures:*

As they were thus discoursing, they discovered some thirty or forty windmills that are in that plain; and as soon as the knight had spied them... 'Look yonder, friend Sancho, there are at least thirty outrageous giants, whom I intend to encounter; and, having deprived them of life, we will begin to enrich ourselves with their spoils: for they are lawful prize; and the extirpation of that cursed brood will be an acceptable service to Heaven.' 'What giants?' quoth Sancho Pança. 'Those whom thou seest yonder,' answered Don Quixote, 'with their long-extended arms.'... 'Pray, look better, sir,' quoth Sancho, 'those things yonder are no giants, but windmills, and the arms you fancy, are their sails, which, being whirled about with the wind, make the mill go.'... 'I tell thee they are giants; and therefore, if thou art afraid, go aside and say thy prayers, for I am resolved to engage in a dreadful, unequal combat against them all.' This said, he clapped spurs to his horse Rozinante, without giving ear to his squire Sancho, who bawled out to him, and assured him that they were windmills, and no giants. But... he did not so much as hear his squire's outcry, nor was he sensible of what they were, although he was already very near them... 'Stand, cowards,' cried he as loud as he could; 'stand your ground, ignoble creatures, and fly not basely from a single knight, who dares encounter you all.' At the same time the wind rising, the mill-sails began to move, which, when Don Quixote spied, 'Base miscreants,' cried he, 'though you move more arms than the giant Briareus, you shall pay for your arrogance.'... Covering himself with his shield, and couching his lance, he rushed with Rozinante's utmost speed upon the first windmill he could come at, and, running his lance into the sail, the wind whirled about with such swiftness, that the rapidity of the motion presently broke the lance into shivers, and hurled away both knight and horse along with it, till down he fell, rolling a good way off in the field. Sancho Pança ran as fast as his ass could drive to help his master, whom he found lying, and not able to stir, such a blow he and Rozinante had received. 'Mercy on me!' cried Sancho, 'did I not give your worship fair warning? Did I not tell you they were windmills, and that nobody could think otherwise, unless he had also windmills in his head?'

From *Don Quixote*, 1605

## Izaak Walton (1593–1683)

# *The pleasant life of an angler*

*'Piscator', the fisherman, argues the case for his sport being superior to those of his two companions – the hunter and falconer:*

No life, my honest scholar, no life so pleasant as the life of a well-governed angler, for when the lawyer is swallowed up with business, and the statesman is preventing or contriving plots, then we sit on cowslip banks, hear the birds sing, and possess ourselves in as much quietness as these silent silver streams, which we now see glide so quietly by us. Indeed, my good scholar, we may say of angling, as Dr Boteler said of strawberries, 'Doubtless God could have made a better berry; but doubtless God never did;' and so (if I might be judge) 'God never did make a more calm, quiet, innocent recreation than angling.'

I'll tell you, scholar, when I sat last on this primrose bank, and looked down these meadows, I thought of them, as Charles the emperor did of the city of Florence, 'That they were too pleasant to be looked on, but only on holidays.'

From *The Compleat Angler*, 1653

### Thomas Hardy (1840–1928)

# *Preparations for the party*

*At Christmas, the Deweys were busy preparing for a party.*
*Reuben Dewey made his living as a tranter – or occasional*
*carrier.*

During the afternoon unusual activity was seen to prevail about the
precincts of tranter Dewey's house. The flagstone floor was swept of dust,
and a sprinkling of the finest yellow sand from the innermost stratum of
the adjoining sand-pit lightly scattered thereupon. Then were produced
large knives and forks, which had been shrouded in darkness and grease
since the last occasion of the kind… The key was left in the tap of the
cider-barrel, instead of being carried in a pocket. And finally the tranter
had to stand up in the room and let his wife wheel him round like a
turnstile, to see if anything discreditable was visible in his appearance.

'Stand still till I've been for the scissors,' said Mrs Dewey.

The tranter stood as still as a sentinel at the challenge.

The only repairs necessary were a trimming of one or two whiskers that
had extended beyond the general contour of the mass; a like trimming of
a slightly frayed edge visible on his shirt-collar; and a final tug at a grey
hair – to all of which operations he submitted in resigned silence, except
the last, which produced a mild 'Come, come, Ann,' by way of
expostulation.

'Really, Reuben, 'tis quite a disgrace to see such a man,' said Mrs
Dewey, with the severity justifiable in a long-tried companion, giving him
another turn round, and picking several of Smiler's hairs from the
shoulder of his coat. Reuben's thoughts seemed engaged elsewhere, and he
yawned. 'And the collar of your coat is a shame to behold – so plastered
with dirt, or dust, or grease, or something. Why, wherever could you have
got it?'

''Tis my warm nater in summer-time, I suppose. I always did get in such
a heat when I bustle about.'

'Ay, the Deweys always were such a coarse-skinned family… If the sun
only shines out a minute, there be you all streaming in the face – I
never see!'

'If I be hot week-days, I must be hot Sundays.'…

'You never did look so well in a pair o' trousers as in them,' she continued in the same unimpassioned voice... 'Such a cheap pair as 'twas too. As big as any man could wish to have, and lined inside, and double-lined in the lower parts, and an extra piece of stiffening at the bottom. And 'tis a nice high cut that comes right up under your arm-pits, and there's enough turned down inside the seams to make half a pair more...'

The guests had all assembled and [at ten o'clock] the sound of a fiddle tuning was heard from the inner pantry.

'That's Dick,' said the tranter. 'That lad's crazy for a jig.'

'Dick! Now I cannot – really, I cannot have any dancing at all till Christmas-day is out,' said old William emphatically. 'When the clock ha' done striking twelve, dance as much as ye like.'

'Well, I must say there's reason in that, William,' said Mrs Penny. 'If you do have a party on Christmas-night, 'tis only fair and honourable to the sky-folk to have it a sit-still party. Jigging parties may be all very well on the Devil's holidays; but a jigging party looks suspicious now. O yes; stop till the clock strikes, young folk – so say I.'

It happened that some warm mead accidentally got into Mr Spinks's head about this time.

'Dancing,' he said, 'is a most strengthening, livening and courting movement, specially with a little beverage added! And dancing is good. But why disturb what is ordained, Richard and Reuben, and the company zhinerally? Why, I ask, as far as that do go?'

'Then nothing till after twelve,' said William.

From *Under the Greenwood Tree*, 1872

**Francis Kilvert (1840–79)**

# Football on Sunday

*Wednesday, 21 October 1874*

John Hatherell said he remembered playing football with the men on Sunday evenings when he was a big boy and the Reverend Samuel Ashe, the Rector, trying to stop the Sunday football playing. He would get hold of the ball and whip his knife into the bladder, but there was another bladder blown the next minute. 'Well,' said the Rector in despair, 'it must go on.'

From *Kilvert's Diary*, 1874

## Charles Dickens (1812–70)

# *Trying out the slide*

*The members of the Pickwick Club spent Christmas with their
friend Mr Wardle at Dingley Dell. The gentry skated on the
frozen lake, then the servants – Sam Weller and the fat boy –
made a slide and took turns on it:*

It was a good long slide, and there was something in the motion which Mr
Pickwick, who was very cold with standing still, could not help envying.

'It looks a nice warm exercise, that, doesn't it?' he inquired of Wardle...

'Ah, it does indeed,' replied Wardle. 'Do you slide?'

'I used to do so, on the gutters, when I was a boy,' replied Mr Pickwick.

'Try it now,' said Wardle.

'Oh, do, please, Mr Pickwick,' cried all the ladies.

'I should be very happy to afford you any amusement,' replied Mr
Pickwick, 'but I haven't done such a thing these thirty years.'

'Pooh! Pooh! Nonsense!' said Wardle, dragging off his skates with the
impetuosity which characterised all his proceedings. 'Here; I'll keep you
company; come along!' And away went the good-tempered old fellow
down the slide, with a rapidity which came very close to Mr Weller and
beat the fat boy all to nothing.

Mr Pickwick paused, considered, pulled off his gloves and put them in
his hat, took two or three short runs, baulked himself as often, and at last
took another run and went slowly and gravely down the slide, with his
feet about a yard and a quarter apart, amidst the gratified shouts of all the
spectators.

'Keep the pot a-bilin', sir!' said Sam; and down went Wardle again, and
then Mr Pickwick, and then Sam, and then Mr Winkle, and then Mr Bob
Sawyer, and then the fat boy, and then Mr Snodgrass, following closely
upon each other's heels and running after each other with as much
eagerness as if their future prospects in life depended upon their
expedition.

It was the most intensely interesting thing to observe the manner in
which Mr Pickwick performed his share in the ceremony; to watch the
torture of anxiety with which he viewed the person behind, gaining upon
him at the imminent hazard of tripping him up... to contemplate the

playful smile which mantled on his face when he had accomplished the distance, and the eagerness with which he turned round when he had done so and ran after his predecessor, his black gaiters tripping pleasantly through the snow, and his eyes beaming cheerfulness and gladness through his spectacles. And when he was knocked down (which happened, upon the average, every third round), it was the most invigorating sight that can possibly be imagined to behold him gather up his hat, gloves, and handkerchief with a glowing countenance, and resume his station in the rank with an ardour and enthusiasm that nothing could abate.

From *The Pickwick Papers*, 1836

Kenneth Grahame (1859–1932)

# Messing about in boats

*The Mole had forsaken his spring-cleaning and emerged into the
sunshine and the world above. When he arrived at a river, he
caught sight of the Water Rat, at the entrance of his riverbank
hole:*

'Hello, Mole!' said the Water Rat.

'Hello, Rat!' said the Mole.

'Would you like to come over?' inquired the Rat presently.

'Oh, it's all very well to *talk*,' said the Mole, rather pettishly, he being
new to a river and riverside life and its ways.

The Rat said nothing, but stooped and unfastened a rope and hauled
on it; then lightly stepped into a little boat which the Mole had not
observed. It was painted blue outside and white within, and was just the
size for two animals; and the Mole's heart went out to it at once, even
though he did not yet fully understand its uses.

The Rat sculled smartly across and made fast. Then he held up his fore-
paw as the Mole stepped gingerly down. 'Lean on that!' he said. 'Now
then, step lively!' and the Mole, to his surprise and rapture found himself
actually seated in the stern of a real boat.

'This has been a wonderful day!' said he, as the Rat shoved off and took
to the sculls again. 'Do you know, I've never been in a boat before in all
my life.'

'What?' cried the Rat open-mouthed: 'Never been in a – you never –
well, I – what have you been doing, then?'

'Is it so nice as all that?' asked the Mole shyly, though he was quite
prepared to believe it as he leant back in his seat and surveyed the
cushions, the rowlocks, and all the fascinating fittings, and felt the boat
sway lightly under him.

'Nice? It's the *only* thing,' said the Water Rat solemnly, as he leant
forward for his stroke. 'Believe me, my young friend, there is *nothing* –
absolutely nothing – half so much worth doing as simply messing about
in boats. Simply messing,' he went on dreamily: 'messing – about – in –
boats; messing –'

'Look ahead, Rat!' cried the Mole suddenly.

It was too late. The boat struck the bank full tilt. The dreamer, the joyous oarsman, lay on his back at the bottom of the boat, his heels in the air.

'– about in boats – or *with* boats,' the Rat went on composedly, picking himself up with a pleasant laugh. 'In or out of 'em, it doesn't matter. Nothing seems really to matter, that's the charm of it. Whether you get away or whether you don't... you're always busy, and you never do anything in particular; and when you've done it, there's always something else to do, and you can do it if you like, but you'd much better not...'

From *The Wind in the Willows*, 1908

# GIVING AND SELF-GIVING

## Give generously – give cheerfully!

*Paul the apostle made a collection of money from the Gentile churches to give to the Jewish church in Jerusalem, which was desperately poor. In this letter, he encourages the Christians in Corinth to give all they can to the fund.*

I really don't need to write to you about this gift for the Christians in Jerusalem. For I know how eager you are to help... But I want it to be a willing gift, not one given under pressure.

Remember this – a farmer who plants only a few seeds will get a small crop. But the one who plants generously will get a generous crop. You must each make up your own mind as to how much you should give. Don't give reluctantly or in response to pressure. For God loves the person who gives cheerfully. And God will generously provide all you need. Then you will always have everything you need and plenty left over to share with others.

As the Scriptures say:

*Godly people give generously to the poor.*
*Their good deeds will never be forgotten.*

For God is the one who gives seed to the farmer and then bread to eat. In the same way, he will give you many opportunities to do good, and he will provide a great harvest of generosity in you.

Yes, you will be enriched so that you can give even more generously. And when we take those gifts to those who need them, they will break out in thanksgiving to God. So two good things will happen – the needs of the Christians in Jerusalem will be met, and they will joyfully express their thanksgiving to God. You will be glorifying God through your generous gifts. For your generosity to them will prove that you are obedient to the Good News of Christ. And they will pray for you with deep affection because of the wonderful grace of God shown through you.

Thank God for his Son – a gift too wonderful for words!

From 2 Corinthians 9

### Elizabeth Gaskell (1810–65)

# *Costly giving*

*Miss Matty's small resources were all invested in the Town and County Bank; one morning she received a letter asking her to attend a shareholders' meeting. By the same post a letter from her father warned Mary (the narrator) of a rumour that the bank might fail.*

*Mary and Miss Matty go shopping; it is market day:*

We began to talk of Miss Matty's new silk gown... Miss Matty anticipated the sight of the glossy folds with as much delight as if the five sovereigns, set apart for the purchase, could buy all the silks in the shop...

If a happy sea-green could be met with, the gown was to be sea-green: if not, she inclined to maize, and I to silver-grey... We were to... select the silk, and then clamber up the iron corkscrew stairs that led into what was once a loft, though now a fashion show-room... The silks were unrolled in good truth. By this time the shop was pretty well filled, for it was Cranford market-day and many of the farmers and country people from the neighbourhood round came in... One honest-looking man... made his way up to the counter at which we stood, and boldly asked to look at a shawl or two... It soon became a question with me, whether he or Miss Matty would keep their shopmen the longest time. He thought each shawl more beautiful than the last; and, as for Miss Matty, she smiled and sighed over each fresh bale that was brought out.

And now... our attention was called off to our neighbour. He had chosen a shawl of about thirty shillings' value; and his face looked broadly happy... He had tugged a leathern purse out of his breeches pocket, and had offered a five-pound note in payment... and it was just at this point that he attracted our notice. The shopman was examining the note with a puzzled, doubtful air.

'Town and County Bank! I am not sure, sir, but I believe we have received a warning against notes issued by this bank only this morning... I'm afraid I must trouble you for payment in cash, or in a note of a different bank.'

I never saw a man's countenance fall so suddenly into dismay and bewilderment...

'Dang it!' said he, striking his fist down on the table, 'the chap talks as if notes and gold were to be had for the picking up.'

Miss Matty had forgotten her silk gown...

'Let me see it,' said she quietly to the shopman, gently taking it out of his hand...

'This lilac silk will just match the ribbons in your new cap, I believe,' I continued... But Miss Matty put on the soft dignified manner peculiar to her, rarely used but which became her so well, and laying her hand gently on mine, she said –

'Never mind the silks for a few minutes, dear. I don't understand you, sir,' turning now to the shopman... 'Is this a forged note?'

'Oh, no, ma'am. It is a true note of its kind; but you see, ma'am, it is a joint-stock bank, and there are reports out that it is likely to break.'

But Mr Dobson... was turning the note absently over in his fingers...

'It's hard upon a poor man,' said he, 'as earns every farthing by the sweat of his brow. However, there's no help for it. You must take back your shawl, my man; Lizzie must go on with her cloak for a while. And yon figs for the little ones – I promised them to 'em – I'll take them; but the bacco, and the other things' –

'I will give you five sovereigns for your note, my good man,' said Miss Matty...

The shopman whispered a word or two across the table to Miss Matty. She looked at him with a dubious air.

'Perhaps so,' said she. 'But I don't pretend to understand business... only I would rather exchange my gold for the note, if you please,' turning to the farmer; 'and then you can take your wife the shawl...'

The man looked at her with silent gratitude – too awkward to put his thanks into words...

'I'm loth to make another one lose instead of me, if it is a loss. But, you see, five pounds is a deal of money to a man with a family; and, as you say, ten to one in a day or two the note will be as good as gold again.'

'No hope of that, my friend,' said the shopman.

'The more reason why I should take it,' said Miss Matty quietly. She pushed her sovereigns towards the man, who slowly laid his note down in exchange. 'Thank you. I will wait a day or two before I purchase any of these silks; perhaps you will then have a greater choice. My dear, will you come upstairs?'

From *Cranford*, 1853

## A.A. Milne (1882–1956)

# *Birthday presents*

*When Pooh Bear discovered that it was Eeyore's birthday he hurried home to find him a present. There he met Piglet:*

The first thing Pooh did was to go to the cupboard to see if he had quite a small jar of honey left; and he had, so he took it down.

'I'm giving this to Eeyore,' he explained, 'as a present. What are you going to give?'

'Couldn't I give it too?' said Piglet. 'From both of us?'

'No,' said Pooh. 'that would *not* be a good plan.'

'All right, then, I'll give him a balloon. I've got one left from my party. I'll go and get it now, shall I?'...

So off Piglet trotted; and in the other direction went Pooh, with his jar of honey.

It was a warm day, and he had a long way to go. He hadn't gone more than half-way when a sort of funny feeling began to creep over him. It began at the tip of his nose and trickled all through him and out at the soles of his feet. It was just as if somebody inside him was saying, 'Now then, Pooh, time for a little something.'

'Dear, dear,' said Pooh, 'I didn't know it was as late as that.' So he sat down and took the lid off his jar of honey...

'Now let me see,' he thought as he took his last lick of the inside of the jar, 'where was I going?'...

And then, suddenly, he remembered. He had eaten Eeyore's birthday present!

'*Bother!*' said Pooh. 'What *shall* I do? I *must* give him *something*.'

Then he thought: 'Well, it's a very nice pot, even if there's no honey in it, and if I washed it clean, and got somebody to write "*A Happy Birthday*" on it, Eeyore could keep things in it, which might be useful.'...

While all this was happening, Piglet had gone back to his own house to get Eeyore's balloon. He held it very tightly against himself, so that it shouldn't blow away, and he ran as fast as he could so as to get to Eeyore before Pooh did... And running along, and thinking how pleased Eeyore would be, he didn't look where he was going... and suddenly he put his foot in a rabbit hole, and fell down flat on his face.

BANG!!!???***!!!

Piglet lay there, wondering what had happened...

'I wonder what that bang was... And where's my balloon? And what's that small piece of damp rag doing?'

> *Piglet carried his burst balloon to Eeyore, but was mortified when Eeyore sadly enquired about the size and colour of the original – his favourite size and colour. Then Pooh arrived.*

'I've brought you a little present,' Pooh said excitedly... 'It's a useful pot... And it's for putting things in. There!'

When Eeyore saw the pot, he became quite excited.

'Why!' he said, 'I believe my Balloon will just go into that Pot!'

'Oh, no, Eeyore,' said Pooh. 'Balloons are much too big to go into Pots...'

'Not mine!' said Eeyore proudly. 'Look, Piglet!' And as Piglet looked sorrowfully round, Eeyore picked up the balloon with his teeth, and placed it carefully in the pot; picked it out and put it on the ground; and then picked it up again and put it carefully back...

'I'm very glad,' said Pooh happily, 'that I thought of giving you a Useful Pot to put things in.'

'I'm very glad,' said Piglet happily, 'that I thought of giving you Something to put in a Useful Pot.'

But Eeyore wasn't listening. He was taking the balloon out, and putting it back again, as happy as could be...

From *Winnie-the-Pooh*, 1926

## The Venerable Bede (c. 673–735)

# *King Oswald's generosity*

King Oswald, with the nation of the English which he governed, instructed by the teaching of... [Bishop Aidan], not only learned to hope for a heavenly kingdom unknown to his progenitors, but also obtained of the same of Almighty God, who made heaven and earth, larger earthly kingdoms than any of his ancestors. In short, he brought under his dominion all the nations and provinces of Britain, which are divided into four languages, viz. the Britons, the Picts, the Scots, and the English. When raised to that height of dominion, wonderful to relate, he always continued humble, affable, and generous to the poor and strangers.

In short, it is reported, that when he was once sitting at dinner, on the holy day of Easter, with the aforesaid bishop, and a silver dish of dainties before him, and they were just ready to bless the bread, the servant, whom he had appointed to relieve the poor, came in on a sudden, and told the king, that a great multitude of needy persons from all parts were sitting in the streets begging some alms of the king; he immediately ordered the meat set before him to be carried to the poor, and the dish to be cut in pieces and divided among them.

From *Ecclesiastical History of the English People*, 731

**Louisa May Alcott (1832–88)**

# *Christmas angels*

*'Christmas won't be Christmas without any presents,' Jo had grumbled, as she and her three sisters, Meg, Beth and Amy, waited for their mother to return from an early visit. It was Christmas morning. At last they heard the welcome sound of the street door banging:*

'Merry Christmas, Marmee! Many of them!...'

'Merry Christmas, little daughters!... But I want to say one word before we sit down. Not far away from here lies a poor woman with a little new-born baby. Six children are huddled into one bed to keep from freezing, for they have no fire. There is nothing to eat over there, and the oldest boy came to tell me that they were suffering hunger and cold. My girls, will you give them your breakfast as a Christmas present?'

They were all unusually hungry, having waited nearly an hour, and for a minute no one spoke – only a minute, for Jo exclaimed impetuously, 'I'm so glad you came before we began!'

'May I go and help carry the things to the poor little children?' asked Beth eagerly.

'*I* shall take the cream and the muffins,' added Amy, heroically giving up the articles she most liked.

Meg was already covering the buckwheats, and piling the bread into one big plate.

'I thought you'd do it,' said Mrs March, smiling as if satisfied. 'You shall all go and help me, and when we come back we will have bread and milk for breakfast, and make it up at dinnertime.'

They were soon ready, and the procession set out. Fortunately it was early, and they went through back streets, so few people saw them, and no one laughed at the queer party.

A poor, bare, miserable room it was, with broken windows, no fire, ragged bedclothes, a sick mother, wailing baby, and a group of pale, hungry children cuddled under one old quilt, trying to keep warm.

How the big eyes stared and the blue lips smiled as the girls went in!

'*Ach, mein Gott!* It is good angels come to us!' said the poor woman, crying for joy.

'Funny angels in hoods and mittens,' said Jo, and set them laughing.

In a few minutes it really did seem as if kind spirits had been at work there. Hannah, who had carried wood, made a fire, and stopped up the broken panes with old hats and her own cloak. Mrs March gave the mother tea and gruel, and comforted her with promises of help, while she dressed the little baby as tenderly as if it had been her own. The girls meantime spread the table, set the children round the fire, and fed them like so many hungry birds – laughing, talking, and trying to understand the broken English.

'*Das ist gut!*' '*Die Engel-kinder!*' cried the poor things as they ate and warmed their purple hands at the comfortable blaze.

The girls had never been called angel-children before, and thought it very agreeable... That was a very happy breakfast, though they didn't get any of it; and when they went away, leaving comfort behind, I think there were not in all the city four merrier people than the hungry little girls who gave away their breakfasts and contented themselves with bread and milk on Christmas morning.

From *Little Women*, 1868

## Charles Dickens (1812–70)

# 'The best of times and the worst of times'

*In A Tale of Two Cities Dickens tells of the terrors of the*
*French Revolution. Charles Darnay (a.k.a. Evremonde) and*
*Sidney Carton are both in love with the same woman. She*
*marries Darnay, the virtuous man, who is condemned to die,*
*but the ne'er-do-well Carton redeems himself by the supreme act*
*of going to the guillotine in his place:*

Along the Paris streets the death-carts rumble, hollow and harsh. Six tumbrils carry the day's wine to La Guillotine...

As the sombre wheels of the six carts go round, they seem to plough up a long crooked furrow among the populace in the streets. Ridges of faces are thrown to this side and that, and the ploughs go steadily forward. So used are the regular inhabitants of the houses to the spectacle, that in many windows there are no people, and in some the occupation of the hands is not so much as suspended, while the eyes survey the faces in the tumbrils...

The clocks are on the stroke of three, and the furrow ploughed among the populace is turning round, to come on into the place of execution, and end. The ridges thrown to this side and to that, now crumble in and close behind the last plough as it passes on, for all are following to the Guillotine. In front of it, seated in chairs, as in a garden of public diversion, are a number of women, busily knitting...

The tumbrils begin to discharge their loads. The ministers of Sainte Guillotine are robed and ready. Crash! – A head is held up, and the knitting women who scarcely lifted their eyes to look at it a moment ago when it could think and speak, count One.

The second tumbril empties and moves on; the third comes up. Crash! – And the knitting women, never faltering or pausing in their work, count Two.

The supposed Evremonde descends, and the seamstress is lifted out next after him. He has not relinquished her patient hand in getting out, but still holds it as he promised. He gently places her with her back to the crashing engine that constantly whirrs up and falls, and she looks into his face and thanks him.

'But for you, dear stranger, I should not be so composed, for I am naturally a poor little thing, faint of heart; nor should I have been able to raise my thoughts to Him who was put to death, that we might have hope and comfort here today. I think you were sent to me by Heaven.'

'Or you to me,' says Sidney Carton. 'Keep your eyes upon me, dear child, and mind no other object.'

'I mind nothing while I hold your hand. I shall mind nothing when I let it go, if they are rapid.'

'They will be rapid. Fear not!'...

She goes next before him – is gone; the knitting women count Twenty-two.

'I am the Resurrection and the Life, saith the Lord: he that believeth in me, though he were dead, yet shall he live: and he that liveth and believeth in me shall never die.'

The murmuring of many voices, the upturning of many faces, the pressing on of many footsteps in the outskirts of the crowd, so that it swells forward in a mass, like one heave of water, all flashes away. Twenty-three.

They said of him, about the city that night, that it was the peacefullest man's face ever beheld there... If he had given utterance to his [thoughts], they would have been these...

'I see the lives for which I lay down my life, peaceful, useful, prosperous and happy, in that England which I shall see no more... I see that I hold a sanctuary in their hearts, and in the hearts of their descendants, generations hence...

'It is a far, far better thing that I do, than I have ever done; it is a far, far better rest that I go to than I have ever known.'

From *A Tale of Two Cities*, 1859

### John Foxe (1516–87)

# 'True servant and martyr of God'

*Foxe's* History of the Acts and Monuments of the Church – *popularly known as* Foxe's Book of Martyrs – *is a vivid account of the Protestant martyrs from the fourteenth century to Foxe's own day. It had widespread influence as at one time it was almost the only book, other than the Bible, available to be read by ordinary people:*

William Tyndale, the faithful minister of Christ, was born about the borders of Wales, and brought up from a child in the University of Oxford, where he, by long continuance, increased as well in the knowledge of tongues, and other liberal arts, as especially in the knowledge of the Scriptures, whereunto his mind was singularly addicted... All they that knew him reputed him to be a man of most virtuous disposition, and of life unspotted...

Master Tyndale considered this only, or most chiefly, to be the cause of all mischief in the Church, that the Scriptures of God were hidden from the people's eyes...

For these and such other considerations this good man was stirred up of God to translate the Scripture into his mother tongue, for the profit of the simple people of his country; first setting in hand with the New Testament, which came forth in print about AD 1525. Cuthbert Tonstal, Bishop of London, with Sir Thomas More, being sore aggrieved, devised how to destroy that false erroneous translation, as they called it...

After that, Master Tyndale took in hand to translate the Old Testament, finishing the five books of Moses, with sundry most learned and godly prologues most worthy to be read and read again by all good Christians. These books being sent over in England, it cannot be spoken what a door of light they opened to the eyes of the whole English nation, which before were shut up in darkness...

The godly books of Tyndale, and especially the New Testament of his translation, after that they began to come into men's hands, and to spread abroad, wrought great and singular profit to the godly; but the ungodly (envying and disdaining that the people should be anything wiser than they and, fearing lest by the shining beams of truth, their works of darkness should be discerned) began to stir with no small ado...

So great were then the froward devices of the English clergy (who should have been the guides of light unto the people) to drive the people from the knowledge of the Scripture, which neither they would translate themselves, nor yet abide it to be translated by others...

The bishops and prelates never rested until they had brought the king to their consent; by reason whereof, a proclamation was devised and set forth under public authority, that the Testament of Tyndale's translation was inhibited – which was about 1537. And not content herewith, they proceeded further, how to entangle him in their nets, and to bereave him of his life; which how they brought it to pass, now it remaineth to be declared...

At last, after much reasoning, when no reason would serve, although he deserved no death, he was condemned by virtue of the emperor's decree, made in the assembly at Augsburg. Brought forth to the place of execution, he was tied to the stake, strangled by the hangman, and afterwards consumed with fire, at the town of Vilvorde, AD 1536; crying at the stake with a fervent zeal, and a loud voice, 'Lord! open the king of England's eyes.'

From *Foxe's Book of Martyrs*, 1554

**O. Henry (William Sydney Porter) (1862–1910)**

# *The gift of the magi*

One dollar and eighty-seven cents. That was all. And sixty cents of it was in pennies... There was clearly nothing to do but flop down on the shabby little couch and howl. So Della did it...

Della finished her cry and attended to her cheeks with a powder rag. She stood by the window and looked out dully at a grey cat walking a grey fence in a grey backyard. Tomorrow would be Christmas Day and she had only $1.87 with which to buy Jim a present. Many a happy hour she had spent planning for something nice for him. Something fine and rare and sterling...

Suddenly she whirled from the window and stood before the glass. Her eyes were shining brilliantly, but her face had lost its colour within twenty seconds. Rapidly she pulled down her hair and let it fall to its full length.

Now there were two possessions of the James Dillingham Youngs in which they both took a mighty pride. One was Jim's gold watch, that had been his father's and grandfather's. The other was Della's hair...

So now Della's beautiful hair fell about her rippling and shining like a cascade of brown waters. It reached below her knee and made itself almost a garment for her. And then she did it up again nervously and quickly. Once she faltered for a minute and stood still while a tear or two splashed on the worn red carpet.

On went her old brown jacket; on went her old brown hat. With a whirl of skirts and with the brilliant sparkle still in her eyes, she fluttered out the door and down the stairs to the street.

Where she stopped the sign read 'Mme Sofronie. Hair Goods of All Kinds.' One flight up Della ran, and collected herself, panting. Madame, large, too white, chilly, hardly looked the 'Sofronie.'

'Will you buy my hair?' asked Della.

'I buy hair,' said Madame. 'Take yer hat off and let's have a sight at the looks of it.'

Down rippled the brown cascade.

'Twenty dollars,' said Madame, lifting the mass with a practised hand.

'Give it to me quick,' said Della.

*Della hunted the stores until she found the perfect gift – a platinum fob chain, just right for Jim's watch. It cost $21 – leaving her with 87 cents. Once home she went to work with curling tongs, to repair 'the ravages made by generosity added to love'.*

At 7 o'clock the coffee was made and the frying-pan was on the back of the stove hot and ready to cook the chops.

Jim was never late. Della doubled the fob chain in her hand and sat on the corner of the table near the door that he always entered. Then she heard his step on the stair... She had a habit of saying little silent prayers about the simplest everyday things, and now she whispered: 'Please God, make him think I am still pretty.'

The door opened and Jim stepped in and closed it. He looked thin and very serious. Poor fellow, he was only twenty-two – and to be burdened with a family! He needed a new overcoat and he was without gloves... His eyes were fixed on Della, and there was an expression in them that she could not read, and it terrified her. It was not anger, nor surprise, nor disapproval, nor horror, nor any of the sentiments that she had been prepared for. He simply stared at her fixedly with that peculiar expression on his face...

'Jim darling,' she cried, 'don't look at me that way. I had my hair cut off and sold it because I couldn't have lived through Christmas without giving you a present...

'You've cut off your hair?' asked Jim laboriously... 'You say your hair is gone?'

Out of his trance Jim seemed quickly to wake... drew a package from his overcoat pocket and threw it upon the table.

'Don't make any mistake, Dell,' he said, 'about me. I don't think there's anything in the way of a haircut or a shave or a shampoo that could make me love my girl any less. But if you'll unwrap that package you may see why you had me going a while at first.'

White fingers and nimble tore at the string and paper. And then an ecstatic scream of joy; and then, alas! a quick feminine change to hysterical tears and wails...

For there lay The Combs – the set of combs, side and back, that Della had worshipped for long in a Broadway window. Beautiful combs, pure tortoise shell, with jewelled rims – just the shade to wear in the beautiful vanished hair...

At length she was able to look up with dim eyes and a smile and say: 'My hair grows so fast, Jim!'...

Jim had not yet seen his beautiful present. She held it out eagerly to him upon her open palm. The dull precious metal seemed to flash with a reflection of her bright and ardent spirit.

'Isn't it dandy, Jim? I hunted all over town to find it... Give me your watch. I want to see how it looks on it.'

Instead of obeying, Jim tumbled down on the couch and put his hands under the back of his head and smiled.

'Dell,' said he, 'let's put our Christmas presents away and keep 'em a while. They're too nice to use just at present. I sold the watch to get the money to buy your combs. And now suppose you put the chops on.'

The magi, as you know, were wise men – wonderfully wise men – who brought gifts to the Babe in the manger... But in a last word to the wise of these days let it be said that of all who give gifts these two were the wisest... Everywhere they are the wisest. They are the magi.

From *The Gift of the Magi*, c. 1904

## Alan Paton (1903–88)

# *The judge's gift*

*In* Ah, But Your Land is Beautiful *Alan Paton writes movingly
of the fear and the bitterness – as well as the courage and love –
that were part of South Africa's lifestyle in the 1950s:*

The Reverend Isaiah Buti, pastor of the Holy Church of Zion in
Bochabela, entered the room of the Acting Chief Justice, if not with awe,
then certainly with deference. And certainly with respect too, for not only
did Judge Olivier occupy one of the highest seats in the land, but he was
held in high esteem by all the black people of Blomfontein. Was he not
the man who had tried to prevent parliament from removing coloured
voters from the common roll?...

Welcome, Mr Buti. I got your letter, and now you are here. Sit down
and tell me all about it.

> *Encouraged by the Judge, Mr Buti explains his concerns that
> feeling against whites is growing and asks the judge to take part
> in a work of reconciliation. On the Thursday before Good
> Friday, a service of Washing of the Feet was to be held. He asks
> Judge Olivier if he would wash the feet of Martha Fortuin, once
> a servant in his household:*

– Martha?

– Yes, judge.

She has washed the feet of all my children. Why should I hesitate to
wash her feet?

Mr Buti's face was filled with joy. He stood up and opened wide his
arms...

It will be simple, judge. I shall call out the name of Martha Fortuin, and
she will come up and take a seat at the front of the altar. Than I shall call
out the name of Jan Christiaan Olivier – you will not mind, judge, if I do
not call you a judge?

No.

Then you come up to the altar, and I shall give you a towel to put round
yourself, and then a basin of water. I shall take off her shoes, and you will

wash her feet and dry them, and go back to your seat. Then I shall put on her shoes, and she will go back to her seat.

Does she know that I am to wash her feet?

She knows that her feet are to be washed, but she does not know who is going to wash them.

Will she be embarrassed?

I do not think so, judge. She is a holy woman. She knows the meaning of it. After all, the disciples' feet were washed by the Lord, and no one was embarrassed but Peter, and he was rebuked for it...

On the evening of the day before Good Friday, Judge Olivier set out privately for the Holy Church of Zion in Bochabela. He parked his car near the church, and set out to walk the short distance...

The judge was welcomed at the door by Mr Buti and was taken to a seat at the back of the church.

I am sorry to put you at the back, judge, but I do not want Martha to see you.

*At the appointed time Mr Buti called out:*

Martha Fortuin, I ask you to come forward.

So Martha Fortuin, who thirty years earlier had gone to work in the home of the newly married Advocate Olivier of Bloemfontein, and had gone with him to Cape Town and Pretoria when he became a judge, and had returned with him to Bloemfontein when he became a Justice of the Appellate Court, now left her seat to walk to the chair before the altar. She walked with head downcast, as becomes a modest and devout woman, conscious of the honour that had been done to her by the Reverend Isaiah Buti. Then she heard him call out the name of Jan Christiaan Olivier, and, though she was herself silent, she heard the gasp of the congregation as the great judge of Bloemfontein walked up to the altar to wash her feet.

Then Mr Buti gave the towel to the judge, and the judge, as the words say, girded himself with it, and took the dish of water and knelt at the feet of Martha Fortuin. He took her right foot in his hands and washed and dried it with the towel. Then he took her other foot in his hands and washed it and dried it with the towel. Then he took both her feet in his hands with gentleness, for they were no doubt tired with much serving, and kissed them both. Then Martha Fortuin, and many others in the Holy Church of Zion, fell a-weeping in that holy place.

From *Ah, But Your Land is Beautiful*, 1981

# SUFFERING

## Lament

*In 586* BC *the city of Jerusalem fell to the invading Babylonian army with terrible destruction. In the Old Testament book of Lamentations five poems by unknown eyewitnesses tell of the poet's (or poets') sense of national guilt and the intense suffering, recognized as God's just judgement.*

*I am one who has seen affliction
    under the rod of God's wrath;
he has driven and brought me
    into darkness without any light;
against me he turns his hand,
    again and again, all day long.*

*He has made my flesh and my skin waste away,
    and broken my bones;
he has besieged and enveloped me
    with bitterness and tribulation;
he has made me sit in darkness
    like the dead of long ago.*

*He has walled me about so that I cannot escape;
    he has put heavy chains on me;
though I call and cry for help,
    he shuts out my prayer;
he has blocked my way with hewn stones,
    he has made my paths crooked.*

*He is a bear lying in wait for me,
    a lion in hiding;
he led me off my way and tore me to pieces;*

*he has made me desolate;*
*he bent his bow and set me*
   *as a mark for his arrow...*

*He has made my teeth grind on gravel*
   *and made me cower in ashes;*
*my soul is bereft of peace;*
   *I have forgotten what happiness is;*
*so I say, 'Gone is my glory,*
   *and all that I had hoped for from the Lord.'*

*The thought of my affliction and my homelessness*
   *is wormwood and gall!*
*My soul continually thinks of it*
   *and is bowed down within me.*
*But this I call to mind,*
   *and therefore I have hope:*

*The steadfast love of the Lord never ceases,*
   *his mercies never come to an end;*
*they are new every morning;*
   *great is your faithfulness.*
*'The Lord is my portion,' says my soul,*
   *'therefore I will hope in him.'*

From Lamentations 3

# *Prepared to suffer*

*The book of Daniel tells the story of three young Jewish 'high-flyers', taken as captives to Babylon, who had achieved high office there under the king.*

King Nebuchadnezzar had a gold statue made, twenty-seven metres high and nearly three metres wide, and he had it set up in the plain of Dura in the province of Babylon. Then the king gave orders for all his officials to come together – the princes, governors, lieutenant-governors, commissioners, treasurers, judges, magistrates, and all the other officials of the provinces. They were to attend the dedication of the statue which

King Nebuchadnezzar had set up. When all these officials gathered for the dedication and stood in front of the statue, a herald announced in a loud voice, 'Peoples of all nations, races and languages! You will hear the sound of the trumpets, followed by the playing of oboes, lyres, zithers, and harps; and then all the other instruments will join in. As soon as the music starts, you are to bow down and worship the gold statue that King Nebuchadnezzar has set up. Anyone who does not bow down will immediately be thrown into a blazing furnace.' And so, as soon as they heard the sound of the instruments, the people of all the nations, races, and languages bowed down and worshipped the gold statue which King Nebuchadnezzar had set up.

It was then that some Babylonians took this opportunity to denounce the Jews. They said to King Nebuchadnezzar, 'May Your Majesty live for ever! Your Majesty has issued an order that as soon as the music starts, everyone is to bow down and worship the gold statue, and that anyone who does not bow down and worship it is to be thrown into a blazing furnace. There are some Jews whom you put in charge of the province of Babylon – Shadrach, Meshach and Abednego – who are disobeying Your Majesty's orders. They do not worship your god or bow down to the statue you set up.'

At that, the king flew into a rage and ordered the three men to be brought before him. He said to them, 'Shadrach, Meshach, and Abednego, is it true that you refuse to worship my god and to bow down to the gold statue I have set up? Now then, as soon as you hear the sound of the trumpets, oboes, lyres, zithers, harps, and all the other instruments, bow down and worship the statue. If you do not, you will immediately be thrown into a blazing furnace. Do you think there is any god who can save you?'

Shadrach, Meshach, and Abednego answered, 'Your Majesty, we will not try to defend ourselves. If it is true that we refuse to worship your god or bow down to the gold statue you set up, the God whom we serve is able to save us from the blazing furnace and from your power – and he will. But even if he doesn't, Your Majesty may be sure that we will not worship your god, and we will not bow down to the gold statue that you have set up.'

From Daniel 3

# *Suffering – and comfort – for the sake of others*

All praise to the God and Father of our Lord Jesus Christ. He is the source of every mercy and the God who comforts us. He comforts us in all our troubles so that we can comfort others. When others are troubled, we will be able to give them the same comfort God has given us. You can be sure that the more we suffer for Christ, the more God will shower us with his comfort through Christ. So when we are weighed down with troubles, it is for your benefit and salvation! For when God comforts us, it is so that we, in turn, can be an encouragement to you.

From 2 Corinthians 1

**Blaise Pascal (1623–62)**

# Distress and steadfastness

Who taught the evangelists the qualities of a perfectly heroic soul, so that they could depict one so perfectly in Jesus? Why do they make him weak in his agony? Do they not know how to depict a steadfast death? Yes, because the same St Luke describes the death of St Stephen more heroically than that of Jesus.

They make him capable of fear, before death had become inevitable and then absolutely steadfast.

But when they show him so distressed it is when he distresses himself; when men distress him he is steadfast.

From *Pensées*, 1669

John Newton (1725–1807)

# The benefits of affliction

The advantages of afflictions, when the Lord is pleased to employ them for the good of his people, are many and great. Permit me to mention a few of them; and the Lord grant that we may all find those blessed ends answered to ourselves, by the trials he is pleased to appoint us.

Afflictions quicken us to prayer. It is a pity it should be so; experience testifies that a long course of ease and prosperity, without painful changes, has an unhappy tendency to make us cold and formal in our secret worship; but troubles rouse our spirits, and constrain us to call upon the Lord in good earnest, when we feel a need of that help which we only can have from him...

They are useful, and in a degree necessary, to keep alive in us a conviction of the vanity and unsatisfying nature of the present world, and all its enjoyments; to remind us that this is not our rest, and to call our thoughts upwards, where our true treasure is, and where our conversation ought to be. When things go on much to our wish, our hearts are too prone to say, It is good to be here... Thus the Lord, by pain, sickness, and disappointments... weakens our attachment to this world, and makes the thought of quitting it more familiar and more desirable.

A child of God cannot but greatly desire a more enlarged and experimental acquaintance with his holy word; and this attainment is greatly promoted by our trials. The far greater part of the promises in Scripture are made and suited to a state of affliction; and though we may believe they are true, we cannot so well know their sweetness, power, and suitableness, unless we ourselves are in a state to which they refer... Thus afflictions likewise give occasion of our knowing and noticing more of the Lord's wisdom, power, and goodness, in supporting, and relieving, than we should otherwise have known.

I have not time to take another sheet, and must therefore contract my homily. Afflictions evidence to ourselves, and manifest to others, the reality of grace. And when we suffer as Christians, exercise some measure of that patience and submission, and receive some measure of these supports and supplies, which the Gospel requires and promises to believers, we are more confirmed that we have not taken up with mere notions; and others may be convinced that we do not follow cunningly devised fables... Methinks, if we might go to heaven without suffering, we should be unwilling to desire it. Why should we ever go by any other path than that which he has consecrated and endeared by his own example? especially as his people's sufferings are not penal; there is no wrath in them; the cup he puts in their hands is very different from that which he drank for their sakes, and is only medicinal to promote their chief good. Here I must stop; but the subject is fruitful, and might be pursued through a quire of paper.

Letter from Newton on the advantages of affliction

## Susan Howatch (b. 1940)

# *Creative suffering*

*The year was 1965 and Charles Ashworth, bishop of Starbridge (the 'I' of this story) visited the studio of Harriet March, who had sculpted the hands of his dean – and adversary – Neville ('Stephen') Aysgarth.*

'I always wanted to do those hands of his,' she said, 'but I could never see the right way to present them. Then about a year ago they began to haunt me. I dreamed about them, thought of them night and day – until finally I saw how they had to be done.'

'And after that did everything go smoothly?'

'Good God, no! Quite the reverse.' She sighed before adding: 'Creation has to be the greatest pleasure in the universe, but it can be pretty damned harrowing when the work's in process.'

I gestured towards the hands. 'You never thought of giving up?'

'Don't be ridiculous! When things go wrong I don't chuck in the towel,' she said, caressing the hands again with her forefinger. 'I just slave harder than ever to make everything come right... That's what it's all about. No matter how many disasters happen, no matter how many difficulties I encounter, I can't rest until I've brought order out of chaos and made everything come right...

'Of course I made a lot of mistakes... I turned down various blind alleys and had to rework everything to get back on course. But that's normal. You can't create without waste and mess and sheer undiluted slog – you can't create without pain. It's part of the process. It's in the nature of things.'

On the counter behind us the electric kettle was coming to the boil but she was oblivious of it. She was almost oblivious of me. At that moment she had eyes only for those ugly hands which were so beautiful...

Suddenly she swivelled to face me. 'You theologians talk a lot about creation,' she said, 'but as far as I can see none of you knows the first damn thing about it. God didn't create the world in seven days and then say: gee whizz, that's great! He created the first outlines of his project to end all projects and he said: "Yes, that's got a lot of potential but how the hell do I realise it without making a first-class balls-up?" And then the real hard work began.'

'And still continues. Theologians don't believe God withdrew from the world after the first creative blast and forgot about it.'

'Of course he couldn't forget! No creator can forget!... But no matter how much the mess and distortion make you want to despair, you can't abandon the work because you're *chained* to the bloody thing, it's absolutely woven into your soul and you know you can never rest until you've brought truth out of all the distortion and beauty out of all the mess – but it's agony, agony, *agony* – while simultaneously being the most wonderful and rewarding experience in the world – and *that's* the creative process which so few people understand. It involves an indestructible sort of fidelity, an insane sort of hope, an indescribable sort of... well, it's love, isn't it? You love the work and you suffer with it and always – *always* – you're slaving away against all the odds to make everything come right...'

'And when the work's finally finished,' I said, 'does every step of the creation make sense? All the pain and slog and waste and mess – how do you reconcile yourself to that? Is every disaster finally justified?'

'Every step I take – every bit of clay I ever touch – they're all there in the final work. If they hadn't happened, then this –' she gestured to the sculpture – 'wouldn't exist. So in the end every major disaster, every tiny error, every wrong turning, every fragment of discarded clay, all the blood, sweat and tears – *everything* has meaning. I give it meaning. I reuse, reshape, recast all that goes wrong so that in the end nothing is wasted and nothing is without significance and nothing ceases to be precious to me.'

'So you're saying that the creative process includes a very strong doctrine of redemption.'

Again she turned away abruptly. 'I don't trust those theological words.'

'But why? Surely –'

'I don't rate that God of yours very highly. Speaking as a creator, I'd say he makes too damn many mistakes.'

'But if, as you've just said, all things work together for good by a creative process of redemption... if God never wills the suffering and works always to redeem it – if he's driven on by faith, hope and love to make everything come right – if he's inside the work as well as outside, sharing the pain and suffering alongside his creation –'

'I'd still want to kick him in the teeth and scream at him for making such a mess.'

'Now you're talking as one of the created. But when you were talking as a creator a moment ago you said very firmly that mess was inevitable, an unavoidable part of the creative process. You said –'

'Oh shut up, Charles, for God's sake, before I kick *you* in the teeth for turning this into a bloody theological debate!'...

From *Absolute Truths*, 1994

Daniel Defoe (1660–1731)

# Memories of the Great Plague

*Defoe detailed events of the Great Plague of 1665 under the initials H.F., and quoted records and statistics as well as realistic stories which combine to give us a horrific – and apparently eyewitness – account of the events of that terrible year in London; but he was only a child of five at the time:*

I remember, and while I am writing this Story, I think I hear the very Sound of it, a certain Lady had an only Daughter, a young Maiden about 19 Years old, and who was possessed of a very Considerable Fortune; they were only Lodgers in the House where they were: the young Woman, her Mother, and the Maid, had been abroad on some Occasion, I do not remember what, for the House was not shut up; but about two Hours after they came home, the young Lady complain'd she was not well; in a quarter of an Hour more, she vomited, and had a violent Pain in her Head. Pray God, says her Mother in a terrible Fright, my Child has not the Distemper! The Pain in her Head increasing, her Mother ordered the bed to be warm'd, and resolved to put her to Bed; and prepared to give her things to sweat, which was the ordinary Remedy to be taken, when the first Apprehensions of the Distemper began.

While the Bed was airing, the Mother undressed the young Woman, and just as she was laid down in the Bed, she looking upon her Body with a Candle, immediately discovered the fatal Tokens on the Inside of her Thighs. Her Mother not being able to contain herself, threw down her Candle, and shriekt out in such a frightful Manner, that it was enough to place Horror upon the stoutest Heart in the World; nor was it one Skream, or one Cry, but the Fright having seiz'd her Spirits, she fainted first, then recovered, then ran all over the House, up the Stairs and down the Stairs, like one distracted, and indeed really was distracted, and continued screeching and crying out for several Hours, void of all Sense, or at least, Government of her Senses, and as I was told, never came thoroughly to herself again. As to the young Maiden, she was a dead Corpse from that Moment; for the Gangren which occasions the Spots had spread [over] her whole body, and she died in less than two Hours: but still the Mother continued crying out, not knowing any Thing more of her child, several Hours after she was dead. It is so long ago, that I am not certain, but I think the Mother never recover'd, but died in two or three Weeks after.

From *A Journal of the Plague Year*, 1722

## Thomas More (1478–1535)

# 'Weeping may endure for a night...'

*More wrote these comforting words during his imprisonment in the Tower of London, where he was beheaded for treason less than a year afterwards:*

There is a time of weeping and there is a time of laughing. But as you see, he setteth the weeping time before, for that is the time of this wretched world and the laughing time shall come after in heaven. There is also a time of sowing, and a time of reaping too. Now must we in this world sow, that we may in the other world reap: and in this short sowing time of this weeping world, must we water our seed with the showers of our tears, and then shall we have in heaven a merry laughing harvest for ever.

From *A Dialogue of Comfort Against Tribulation*, 1534

## Charles Lamb (1775–1834)

# 'My poor dear, dearest sister'

*The poet Samuel Coleridge and Charles Lamb were schoolboys together at Christ's Hospital (The Bluecoat School) and remained lifelong friends.*

*To Coleridge, 27 September 1796*

My Dearest Friend – White, or some of my friends, or the public papers, by this time may have informed you of the terrible calamities that have fallen on our family. I will only give you the outlines: – My poor dear, dearest sister, in a fit of insanity, has been the death of her own mother. I was at hand only time enough to snatch the knife out of her grasp. She is at present in a madhouse, from whence I fear she must be moved to an hospital. God has preserved to me my senses: I eat, and drink, and sleep, and have my judgement, I believe, very sound. My poor father was slightly wounded, and I am left to take care of him and my aunt. Mr Norris, of the Bluecoat School, has been very kind to us, and we have no other friend; but, thank God, I am very calm and composed, and able to do the best that remains to do. Write as religious a letter as possible, but no mention of what is gone and done with. With me 'the former things are passed away,' and I have something more to do than feel.

God Almighty have us all in his keeping!

C. Lamb

*To Coleridge, 3 October 1796*

My Dearest Friend – Your letter was an inestimable treasure to me. It will be a comfort to you, I know, to know that our prospects are somewhat brighter. My poor dear, dearest sister, the unhappy and unconscious instrument of the Almighty's judgements on our house, is restored to her senses, – to a dreadful sense and recollection of what has past, awful to her mind, and impressive (as it must be to the end of life), but tempered with religious resignation and the reasonings of a sound judgement, which, in this early stage, knows how to distinguish between a deed committed in a transient fit of frenzy and the terrible guilt of a mother's murder. I have seen her, I found her, this morning, calm and serene; far, very very far from an indecent forgetful serenity; she has a most affectionate and tender concern for what has happened. Indeed, from the beginning – frightful and hopeless as her disorder seemed – I had confidence enough in her strength of mind and religious principle, to look forward to a time when even she might recover tranquillity. God be praised, Coleridge! wonderful as it is to tell, I have never once been otherwise than collected and calm; even on the dreadful day, and in the midst of the terrible scene, I preserved a tranquillity which bystanders may have construed into indifference – a tranquillity not of despair. Is it folly or sin in me to say that it was a religious principle that most supported me?... I felt that I had something else to do than to regret. On that first evening my aunt was lying insensible – to all appearance like one dying; my father, with his poor forehead plaistered over from a wound he had received from a daughter, dearly loved by him, and who loved him no less dearly; my mother a dead and murdered corpse in the next room; yet was I wonderfully supported. I closed not my eyes that night, but lay without terrors and without despair. I have lost no sleep since...

On the very second day (I date from the day of horrors), as is usual in such cases, there were a matter of twenty people, I do think, supping in our room: they prevailed on me to eat with them (for to eat I never refused). They were all making merry in the room! Some had come from friendship, some from busy curiosity, and some from interest. I was going to partake with them, when my recollection came that my poor dead mother was lying in the next room – the very next room; – a mother who, through life, wished nothing but her children's welfare. Indignation, the rage of grief, something like remorse, rushed upon my mind. In an agony of emotion I found my way mechanically to the adjoining room, and fell on my knees by the side of her coffin, asking forgiveness of Heaven, and sometimes of her, for forgetting her so soon. Tranquillity returned, and it was the only violent emotion that mastered me. I think it did me good...

Charles Lamb

Letter to Coleridge, 1796

## Eleanor Spence (b. 1928)

# *Suffering that continues*

*In* The October Child *Eleanor Spence tells the story of a happy Australian family whose lives were completely disrupted by the birth of a fourth child, emotionally and mentally impaired. All were deeply affected but especially Douglas, the second son, sensitive and music-loving. The family uprooted from their home by the sea to live in Sydney, where Carl could attend special school. One day when Douglas was trusted to take the four-year-old Carl for a walk, the young child's violent tantrums became too much for him. He abandoned Carl, phoned his parents, then went to the flat of adult friends, where he found Kerry, a teacher at Carl's special school:*

'Start at the beginning,' Kerry suggested.

When he had finished she went to the telephone...

The phone was so close to him that he could hear his father's voice, and... he heard Kerry ask if he could stay the night, and was grateful. She seemed to be the kind of person who understood a lot of things without having them spelt out...

'They found Carl twenty minutes after your phone call,' Kerry told him, 'he was perfectly all right... he wasn't even crying. It was you your parents were worrying about.'

'Do you think that's true?' asked Douglas. 'About them worrying over me?'

'Why wouldn't it be true? Do you honestly think that Carl is more important to them than you are?'

Douglas frowned into his coffee mug.

'I don't know. Well, I'm pretty sure I'm important to Dad, though I don't see much of him. But Mum – she's always fussing over Carl such a lot... It was pretty stupid running off and leaving Carl the way I did,' he confessed. 'Adrienne's only eleven, and she wouldn't have done it.'

'But she wouldn't have had the responsibility of taking him for a walk, would she? Your mother says you're the only one she can trust with Carl.'

'Until tonight, that is,' said Douglas. 'It wasn't just because he bit me that I ran away – it was because he seemed to hate me so much. I used to think he *liked* me.'

'He doesn't love you, or hate you,' Kerry said. 'He doesn't, because he can't. He has no feelings about other people, because he has no feelings about himself – except the really basic ones, like pain and frustration. All the higher feelings have to be taught to him, like lessons. And even then, he may never be able to express them.'

'But he laughs and cries like other children,' Douglas objected. 'And he smiles and sings.'

'But he doesn't do any of those things for the right reasons,' Kerry said gently... 'Carl can't communicate at all.'

'Will he ever?' asked Douglas

'I don't know,' said Kerry. 'I'm painting a pretty gloomy picture so that none of you will hope for too much. All I can say is – if Carl does improve, it will be by a series of very small steps. And he won't even take those steps without the help of his family.'

'It sounds kind of grim,' said Douglas.

'I know, and I'm sorry. But there are a couple of important things to remember, and they could help just a fraction. The first thing is *never* to feel guilty or ashamed about Carl being what he is. It's nobody's fault... and the other aspect is... have you ever thought about how much Carl's existence has altered your life – for the better, this time?'...

'I suppose if it hadn't been for him, we'd never have left Chapel Rocks. And I wouldn't have gone to the Music College and met all my friends. Those are pretty important things. And maybe Adrienne and Ken could think of something too.'

'I'm afraid,' said Kerry, 'that's the best I can do for you right now. The only advice I can give you is to go home tomorrow, and just keep on trying, as far as Carl's concerned. Does that sound too awful?'

'It sounds the same as before,' admitted Douglas.

'Not quite,' said Kerry. 'Because you know a tiny bit more – about Carl *and* yourself.

From *The October Child*, 1976

## Alexander Whyte (1836–1921)

# *The blessings of adversity*

*Whyte's study of Joseph tells of the Old Testament hero who was the bane of his stepbrothers' lives. He was spoiled by his doting father, Jacob, and not only told tales on his brothers but recounted to them his dreams in which they and his parents were bowing down to him. When Joseph was sent by Jacob to check on his brothers and their flocks in Dothan, they seized the opportunity and threw him down a disused cistern in the ground while they planned his murder. Instead, they decided to sell him as a slave to traders passing by on the caravan route to Egypt:*

That dreadful pit in Dothan was the beginning of Joseph's salvation...
The good work that the pit in Dothan began in Joseph, those still more terrible days and nights on the way down to Egypt carried on. Lashed to the loaded side of a huge cane-waggon, and himself loaded with the baggage of Gilead for the Egyptian market, Joseph toiled on under the mid-day sun, thankful to be left alone of his churlish masters in the red-hot air. Put yourself in Joseph's place. The fondling of his father; a child on whom no wind was ever let blow, and no sun was ever let strike; with servants to wait on his every wish, and to dress and anoint him for every meal; with loving looks and fond words falling continually upon him from the day he was born; and now, lashed to the side of a slave caravan, and with the whistling whip of his Ishmaelite owner laid on his shoulder till he sank in the sand. But you must add this to the picture or you will not have the picture complete: 'The Lord was with Joseph, and Joseph found grace in the sight of the Lord.' Yes, the Lord was more with Joseph, more and better far, than ever he had been as long as Joseph was the spoilt child of his father, and the continual snare of his brothers. And there are young men in this city suffering hardships and persecutions in workshops and offices as sore to bear as was Joseph's load of labour and ill-usage of the Ishmaelites. And the Lord is with them also as he never was so long as they were spoilt sons at home, getting all things their own way...

Even if Potiphar paid thirty or even forty pieces of silver for his Hebrew slave, we now know what a good bargain he got that day. For that handful of silver the captain of Pharaoh's guard came into all the splendid talents that lay hid in Joseph's greatly gifted mind, and all the magnificent moral character the first foundations of which had been laid in the pit in Dothan, and had been built up in God every step of the long wilderness journey. All Joseph's deep repentance also, and all his bitter remorse; all his self-discovery and all his self-condemnation; with all his reticence and all his continence, – Potiphar took all that home from the slave-market that day in exchange for his handful of Egyptian silver. Joseph was now to be plunged into the most corrupt society... and had he not come into that pollution straight out of a sevenfold furnace of sanctifying sorrow, Joseph would no more have been heard of. The sensuality of Egypt would have soon swallowed him up. But... the Lord was with Joseph to protect him, to guide him, and to give him the victory. The Lord was with him to more imprisonment, and then to more promotion...

And, through it all, Joseph became a better and an even better man all his days.

From *Bible Characters: Adam to Achan*, 1896

# GRIEF AND LOSS

## My son!

*King David, now an old man, was threatened by an uprising led by his son, Absalom. The king fled Jerusalem with his followers who persuaded him not to take part in the battle that followed. He gave orders to his generals: 'Deal gently for my sake with the young man, even with Absalom.'*

*The king's men were victorious and Absalom, riding his mule under a great oak tree, was caught in the branches by his beautiful long hair. David's victorious general, Joab, killed him without compunction. But news must be taken to David.*

Then said Ahimaaz the son of Zadok, Let me now run, and bear the king tidings, how that the Lord hath avenged him of his enemies. And Joab said unto him, Thou shalt not bear tidings this day, but thou shalt bear tidings another day: but this day thou shalt bear no tidings, because the king's son is dead. Then said Joab to Cushi, Go tell the king what thou hast seen. And Cushi bowed himself unto Joab, and ran. Then said Ahimaaz the son of Zadok yet again to Joab, But howsoever, let me, I pray thee, also run after Cushi. And Joab said, Wherefore wilt thou run, my son, seeing thou hast no tidings ready? But howsoever, said he, let me run. And he said unto him, Run. Then Ahimaaz ran by the way of the plain, and overran Cushi. And David sat between the two gates: and the watchman went up to the roof over the gate unto the wall, and lifted up his eyes, and looked, and behold a man running alone. And the watchman cried, and told the king. And the king said, If he be alone, there is tidings in his mouth. And he came apace and drew near. And the watchman saw another man running: and the watchman called unto the porter, and said, Behold another man running alone. And the king said, Behold he also bringeth tidings. And the watchman said, Me thinketh the running of the foremost is like the running of Ahimaaz the son of Zadok. And the king said, He is a good man, and cometh with good tidings. And Ahimaaz called, and said unto the king, All is well. And he fell down to the earth upon his face before the king, and said, Blessed be the Lord thy God, which hath delivered up the men that lifted up their hand against my lord the king. And the king said, Is the young man Absalom safe? And Ahimaaz answered, When Joab sent the king's servant, and me thy servant, I saw a great tumult, but I knew not what it was. And the king said unto him, Turn aside, and stand here. And he turned aside, and stood still. And, behold, Cushi came; and Cushi said, Tidings, my lord the king: for the Lord hath avenged thee this day of all them that rose up against thee. And the king said unto Cushi, Is the young man Absalom safe? And Cushi answered, The enemies of my lord the king, and all that arise against thee to do thee hurt, be as that young man is.

And the king was much moved, and went up to the chamber over the gate, and wept: and as he went, thus he said, O my son Absalom, my son, my son Absalom! Would God I had died for thee, O Absalom, my son, my son!

From 2 Samuel 18

Laurence Sterne (1713–68)

# The green satin nightgown

*When Tristram Shandy's older brother is reported dead, Obadiah the coachman brings the news to the servants' hall:*

My young master in London is dead! said Obadiah.

A green sattin night-gown of my mother's which had been twice scoured, was the first idea which Obadiah's exclamation brought into Susannah's head. – Well might Locke write a chapter upon the imperfection of words. – Then, quoth Susannah, we must all go into mourning. – But note a second time: the word mourning, notwithstanding Susannah made use of it herself – failed also of doing its office; it excited not one single idea, tinged either with grey or black, – all was green. – The green sattin night-gown hung there still.

O! 'twill be the death of my poor mistress, cried Susannah. – My mother's whole wardrobe followed. – What a procession! her red damask, – her orange tawney, – her white and yellow lutestrings, – her brown taffeta, – her bone-laced caps, – her bed-gowns, and comfortable under-petticoats. – Not a rag was left behind. – 'No, she will never look up again,' said Susannah…

Here is sad news, Trim, cried Susannah, wiping her eyes as Trim stepp'd into the kitchen, – master Bobby is dead and buried – the funeral was an interpolation of Susannah's – we shall all have to go into mourning, said Susannah.

I hope not, said Trim. – You hope not! cried Susannah earnestly. – The mourning ran not in Trim's head whatever it did in Susannah's. – I hope – said Trim, explaining himself, I hope in God the news is not true. – I heard the letter read with my own ears, answered Obadiah… Oh! he's dead, said Susannah. – As sure, said the scullion, as I'm alive.

From the ten-volume edition of *Tristram Shandy*, 1781

### Charles Dickens (1812–70)

# 'She is dead'

*Dickens's own childhood and youth were harsh and* David Copperfield *is thought to be partly autobiographical.*

*David was born after his father died, and his happy life with his mother ended when she married again. His harsh stepfather sent him to boarding school and he last saw his mother with her new baby in the Christmas holidays. Now, two months later, it was his birthday:*

It was after breakfast, and we had been summoned in from the playground, when Mr Sharp entered and said:

'David Copperfield is to go into the parlour.'

I expected a hamper from Peggotty, and brightened at the order. Some of the boys about me put in their claim not to be forgotten in the distribution of the good things, as I got out of my seat with great alacrity.

'Don't hurry, David,' said Mr Sharp. 'There's time enough, my boy, don't hurry.'

I might have been surprised at the feeling tone in which he spoke, if I had given it a thought; but I gave it none until afterwards. I hurried away to the parlour; and there I found Mr Creakle, sitting at his breakfast with the cane and a newspaper before him, and Mrs Creakle with an opened letter in her hand. But no hamper.

'David Copperfield,' said Mrs Creakle, leading me to a sofa and sitting down beside me. 'I want to speak to you very particularly. I have something to tell you, my child.'

Mr Creakle, at whom of course I looked, shook his head without looking at me, and stopped up a sigh with a very large piece of buttered toast.

'You are too young to know how the world changes every day,' said Mrs Creakle, 'and how the people in it pass away. But we all have to learn it, David; some of us when we are young, some of us when we are old, some of us at all times of our lives.' I looked at her earnestly. 'When you came away from home at the end of the vacation,' said Mrs Creakle, after a pause, 'were they all well?' After another pause, 'Was your mama well?'

I trembled without distinctly knowing why, and still looked at her earnestly, making no attempt to answer. 'Because,' said she, 'I grieve to tell you that I hear this morning your mama is very ill.'

A mist rose between Mrs Creakle and me, and her figure seemed to move in it for an instant. Then I felt the burning tears run down my face, and it was steady again. 'She is very dangerously ill,' she added.

I knew all now. 'She is dead.'

There was no need to tell me so. I had already broken out into a desolate cry, and felt an orphan in the wide world.

She was very kind to me. She kept me there all day, and left me alone sometimes; and I cried, and wore myself to sleep, and awoke and cried again. When I could cry no more, I began to think... I thought of my father's grave in the churchyard, by our house, and of my mother lying there beneath the tree I knew so well. I stood upon a chair, when I was left alone, and looked into the glass to see how red my eyes were, and how sorrowful my face... I am sensible of having felt that a dignity attached to me among the rest of the boys, and that I was important in my affliction.

If ever child was stricken with sincere grief, I was. But I remembered that this importance was a kind of satisfaction to me, when I walked in the playground that afternoon, while the boys were in school. When I saw them glancing at me out of the windows, as they went up to their classes, I felt distinguished, and looked more melancholy, and walked slower. When school was over, and they came out and spoke to me, I felt it rather good in myself not to be proud to any of them, and to take exactly the same notice of them all, as before.

From *David Copperfield*, 1849–50

## C.S. Lewis (1898–1963)

# 'Meanwhile, where is God?'

*Lewis's marriage to the American academic, Joy Davidman, was brief but exceedingly happy. After her death he published his journal, entitled* A Grief Observed, *under the pseudonym of N.W. Clerk. It was only after his death that the author's real identity was revealed.*

No one ever told me that grief felt so like fear. I am not afraid, but the sensation is like being afraid. The same fluttering in the stomach, the same restlessness, the yawning. I keep on swallowing...

And no one ever told me about the laziness of grief. Except at my job – where the machine seems to run on much as usual – I loathe the slightest effort. Not only writing but even reading a letter is too much... They say an unhappy man wants distractions – something to take him out of himself. Only as a dog-tired man wants an extra blanket on a cold night; he'd rather lie there shivering than get up and find one...

Meanwhile, where is God? This is one of the most disquieting symptoms. When you are happy, so happy that you have no sense of needing him, so happy that you are tempted to feel his claims upon you as an interruption, if you remember yourself and turn to him with gratitude and praise, you will be – or so it feels – welcomed with open arms. But go to him when your need is desperate, when all other help is vain, and what do you find? A door slammed in your face, and a sound of bolting and double bolting on the inside. After that, silence. You may as well turn away. The longer you wait, the more emphatic the silence will become... Why is he so present a commander in our time of prosperity and so very absent a help in time of trouble?...

(Later)

'It was too perfect to last,' so I am tempted to say of our marriage. But it can be meant in two ways. It may be grimly pessimistic – as if God no sooner saw two of his creatures happy than he stopped it ('None of that here!') As if he were like the Hostess at the sherry-party who separates two guests the moment they show signs of having got into a real conversation. But it could also mean 'This had reached its proper perfection. This had become what it had in it to be. Therefore of course it would not be prolonged.' As if God said, 'Good; you have mastered that exercise. I am very pleased with it. And now you are ready to go on to the next.' When you have learned to do quadratics and enjoy doing them you will not be set them much longer. The teacher moves you on.

From *A Grief Observed*, 1961

### Francis Kilvert (1840–79)

# *Decking the graves*

*In his* Diary, *Francis Kilvert describes the old country custom of dressing graves with moss and flowers on Easter Eve, ready for Easter Day, which witnesses to new life and resurrection from the dead:*

*Saturday, Easter Eve, 16 April 1870*
When I started for Cefn y Blaen only two or three people were in the churchyard with flowers. But now the customary beautiful Easter Eve Idyll had fairly begun and people kept arriving from all parts with flowers to dress the graves. Children were coming from the town and from neighbouring villages with baskets of flowers and knives to cut holes in the turf. The roads were lively with people coming and going and the churchyard a busy scene with women and children and a few men moving about among the tombstones and kneeling down beside the green mounds flowering the graves...

More and more people kept coming into the churchyard as they finished their day's work. The sun went down in glory behind the dingle, but still the work of love went on through the twilight and into the dusk until the moon rose full and splendid. The figures continued to move about among the graves and to bend over the green mounds in the calm clear moonlight and warm air of the balmy evening.

At 8 o'clock there was a gathering of the Choir in the Church to practise the two anthems for tomorrow. The moonlight came streaming in broadly through the chancel windows. When the choir had gone and the lights were out and the church quiet again, as I walked down the Churchyard alone the decked graves had a strange effect in the moonlight and looked as if the people had laid down to sleep for the night out of doors, ready dressed to rise early on Easter morning.

From *Kilvert's Diary*, 1870

Susan Hill (b. 1942)

# Easter in the churchyard

*Ruth is twenty and her young husband, a forester, has been
tragically killed by a falling tree. Her grief is inexpressible as she
battles against the overwhelming loss. But when Easter comes,
she and Ben's brother Jo, join other villagers to dress the graves
of those they love:*

It was seven o'clock, there would be an hour more of the evening light,
which was paler now, as though the sun had faded in colour as it had lost
its warmth. The old headstones threw blurred shadows across the grass...

She went alone, around the side of the church, carrying her basket of
moss and golden flowers, she began, alone, to dress Ben's grave. It was
darker here, the sun had dropped down behind the tower. The moss felt
like seaweed, and the turf of the new-mounded grave was cold. She
thought, then, of that other body, carried away from the terrible cross at
dusk, and the great stone rolled in front of the tomb, imagined how it
must have been inside, echoing and fusty as a cave, with the limp figure
drained of all its blood and bound about in cloths, she felt, within
herself, the bewilderment and fear and despair of those men and women.

'Ben,' she said once, and rested her hand on a part of the turf she had
not yet dressed with moss. But she felt only calmness, still, and did not
try to imagine whatever might be underneath the soil now.

She could scarcely see the colour of the flowers, they were no longer
bright, as they had been when she picked them, and would be again
tomorrow, under the first sun. The cross she made was dense, each flower
packed tightly to the next one, so that the spiked petals of the dandelions
and the rounded buttercups overlapped, with the primroses pushed
between.

By the time Jo came over to her, it was almost dark, and the grave was
nearly finished. Ruth's back and legs ached. She handed the basket to Jo.

'You should do some – part of it ought to be yours.'

Some of the other people had brought lanterns and the churchyard was
lit here and there by their unsteady, silvery light, rings of it lay about the
grass and the graves like glow-worms... Jo said, pausing for a moment, and

resting back on his heels, 'Tomorrow...' and there was an excitement in his voice, 'Tomorrow, think how it will be!'

Yes, Ruth thought, and so it will be, for it is true, and the sun will shine and the grave-flowers will be like the raiment of the risen dead. But if he is risen, where do I find him, or see him? *How can I know?*

From *In the Springtime of the Year*, 1973

**William Shakespeare (1564–1616)**

# *The cause*

*Othello, the Moorish general, wrongly believes that his wife, Desdemona, has been unfaithful to him. He enters her bedchamber, where a light is burning, while she innocently sleeps:*

*It is the cause, it is the cause, my soul: –*
*Let me not name it to you, you chaste stars! –*
*It is the cause. Yet I'll not shed her blood;*
*Nor scar that whiter skin of hers than snow,*
*And smooth as monumental alabaster.*
*Yet she must die, else she'll betray more men.*
*Put out the light, and then put out the light:*
*If I quench thee, thou flaming minister,*
*I can again thy former light restore,*
*Should I repent me: but once put out thy light,*
*Thou cunning'st pattern of excelling nature,*
*I know not where is that Promethean heat*
*That can thy light relume. When I have pluck'd the rose,*
*I cannot give it vital growth again.*
*It must needs wither...*

*[He smothers her]*

*What noise is this? Not dead? Not yet quite dead?*
*I that am cruel am yet merciful;*
*I would not have thee linger in thy pain:*
*So, so... No more moving?*
*Still as the grave... I think she stirs again...*
*My wife! My wife! What wife? I have no wife.*
*O, insupportable! O heavy hour!*
*Methinks it should be now a huge eclipse*
*Of sun and moon, and that the affrighted globe*
*Should yawn at alteration.*

From *The Tragedy of Othello, the Moor of Venice*, 1622

**Penelope Lively (b. 1933)**

# *The weight of grief*

*Frances's husband, Steven, an international celebrity, has died very suddenly; Frances is stunned and overwhelmed with grief as she tries to survive the loss, and the impact of others' reactions:*

Loss clamped her every morning as she woke; it sat its grinding weight on her and rode her, like the old man of the sea. It roared in her ears when people talked to her so that frequently she did not hear what they said. It interrupted her when she spoke, so that she faltered in mid-sentence, lost track. A little less, now; remissions came and went. The days stalked by, taking her with them.

On the first day, on the morning of the first day, the day after Steven was found dead from a heart-attack in his car in the car park of the BBC Television Centre she had woken in a world that had no right to be as it was, from which Steven had gone and in which all should be numbed with her. Instead of which birds sang beyond the window and sunshine lay in hazy blobs on the bedspread. She had lain fuddled still from the sleeping pills… and had fretted, absurdly and irrelevantly, because she did not even know for the recording of what programme he had gone there. He was often on television. The known and loved face talked to her, bizarrely, from beyond the glass as though she were a roomful of strangers.

The sunshine lay on the bed and beyond the closed door was the day, into which she had to go. And the next day, and the next.

And this one, eight months two weeks one day on, in which she drove now into the gathering traffic of outer London and eventually into the driveway of the house…

She unlocked the door and picked up the post from the doormat. Letters still came for Steven; there was one now, a circular from a publisher. She walked into the kitchen and filled the kettle. The house stretched emptily around her in the same silence that once, in the days of young children, she would have greedily savoured. Solitude is enjoyed only by those who are not alone; the lonely feel differently about it.

Frances had ceased, nowadays, to weep. There was a time when she was always crying. Tears came out of her in an unstoppable flow as though she bled from inexhaustible arteries. She could not see what she was doing, shuttered off by her tears, moving through a world that swam and shimmered, dripping into the kitchen sink, on to the wheel of the car, over the papers on the desk. Now, except for the occasional lapse, she was dry-eyed.

From *Perfect Happiness*, 1983

### Thomas Gray (1716–71)

# *A letter of sympathy*

*William Mason (1725–97), English clergyman and poet, was a friend of the poet Gray. Mason published this letter because, he said, 'it then breathed, and still seems to breathe, the very voice of friends…'*

I break in upon you at a moment, when we least of all are permitted to disturb our friends, only to say, that you are daily and hourly present to my thoughts. If the worst be not yet past, you will neglect and pardon me; but if the last struggle be over, if the poor object of your long anxieties be no longer sensible of your kindness, or to her own sufferings, allow me (at least in idea, for what could I do, were I present, more than this?) to sit by you in silence, and pity from my heart not her, who is at rest, but you, who lost her. May He, who made us, the master of our pleasures and of our pains, preserve and support you! Adieu.

Letter of sympathy from Gray to Mason

# HUMAN LOVE

## Love song

As the lily among thorns, so is my love among the daughters. As the apple tree among the trees of the wood, so is my beloved among the sons. I sat down under his shadow with great delight, and his fruit was sweet to my taste. He brought me to the banqueting house, and his banner over me was love. Stay me with flagons, comfort me with apples: for I am sick of love. His left hand is under my head and his right hand doth embrace me. I charge you, O ye daughters of Jerusalem, by the roes, and by the hinds of the field, that ye stir not up nor awake my love, till he please.

The voice of my beloved! behold, he cometh leaping upon the mountains, skipping upon the hills. My beloved is like a roe or a young hart: behold, he standeth behind our wall, he looketh forth at the windows, shewing himself through the lattice. My beloved spake and said unto me, Rise up, my love, my fair one, and come away. For, lo, the winter is past, the rain is over and gone; The flowers appear on the earth; the time of the singing of birds is come, and the voice of the turtle[dove] is heard in our land; The fig tree putteth forth her green figs, and the vines with the tender grape give a good smell. Arise, my love, my fair one, and come away...

My beloved is mine, and I am his: he feedeth among the lilies. Until the day break, and the shadows flee away, turn, my beloved, and be thou like a roe or a young hart upon the mountains of Bether.

From Song of Songs 2

### Dante Alighieri (1265–1321)

# *The beatific vision*

*In* Vita Nuova *(the 'new life' that began with his encounter with Love), Dante prefaces thirty-one poems about love by introductions and explanations in which he describes first seeing Beatrice and the beginning of his love for her.*

### II

Nine times already since my birth the heaven of light had circled back to almost the same point when the now glorious lady of my mind first appeared to my eyes. She was called Beatrice... She appeared to me almost in the beginning of her ninth year, and I first saw her near the end of my ninth year. She appeared dressed in the most noble of colours, a subdued and decorous crimson, girded and adorned in a style suitable to her years. At that moment, and what I say is true, the vital spirit, the one that dwells in the most secret chamber of the heart, began to tremble so violently that even the least pulses of my body were strangely affected... let me say that from that time on Love governed my soul.

### III

After so many days had passed that precisely nine years had been completed since the appearance I have just described of this very gracious lady, it happened that on the last day of this nine-year period the blessed lady appeared to me dressed in pure white standing between two ladies of high bearing both older than herself. While walking down a street, she turned her eyes to where I was standing faint-hearted and, with that indescribable graciousness that today is rewarded in the eternal life, she greeted me so miraculously that I felt I was experiencing the very summit of bliss. It was precisely the ninth hour of that day (three o'clock in the afternoon), when her sweet greeting reached me. And since that was the first time her words had entered my ears, I was so overcome with ecstasy that I departed from everyone as if intoxicated. I returned to my room and began thinking of this most gracious lady.

### IV

After that vision my natural spirit began to slacken in its working for I had become wholly absorbed in the thought of this most gracious lady. It was but a short time before I became so weak and so frail that many of my friends were concerned about my appearance; others, full of envy, were striving to learn about me that which above all I wished to keep secret. Then I... would answer by saying that it was Love that had governed me. I said that it was Love because on my face so many of his signs were clearly marked that they were impossible to conceal. And when people would ask, 'For whom has Love so undone you?' I, smiling, would look at them and say nothing.

> *In section XXVIII Dante tells how 'the God of Justice called this most gracious one to glory under the banner of the Blessed Virgin Mary, whose name was always spoken with the greatest reverence by the blessed Beatrice'.*

## XLII

There appeared to me a miraculous vision in which I saw things that made me resolve to say no more about this blessed one until I would be capable of writing about her in a more worthy fashion. And to achieve this I am striving as hard as I can, and this she truly knows. Accordingly, if it be the wish of Him through whom all things flourish that my life continue for a few more years, I hope to write of her that which has never been written of any other woman. And then may it please that One who is the Lord of Graciousness that my soul ascend to behold the glory of its lady, that is, of that blessed Beatrice, who in glory gazes upon the countenance of the One *who is through all ages blessed.*

From *Vita Nuova*, c. 1292

**George Eliot (Mary Ann Evans) (1819–80)**

# The love of a child

*The little child, whose mother had died in the snow and who had found her way into Silas's cottage, seemed to him to have replaced the gold he had hoarded and so cruelly lost. He brought little Eppie up himself, in spite of others' misgivings, and found the people of Raveloe warmed towards him:*

No child was afraid of approaching Silas when Eppie was near him: there was no repulsion around him now, either for young or old; for the little child had come to link him once more with the whole world. There was love between him and the child that blent them into one, and there was love between the child and the world – from men and women with parental looks and tones, to the red lady-birds and the round pebbles.

Silas began now to think of Raveloe life entirely in relation to Eppie: she must have everything that was good in Raveloe; and he listened docilely, that he might come to understand better what this life was, from which, for fifteen years, he had stood aloof, as from a strange thing, with which he could have no communion: as some man who has a precious plant to which he would give a nurturing home in a new soil, thinks of the rain and the sunshine, and all influences, in relation to his nursling... The disposition to hoard had been utterly crushed at the very first by the loss of his long-stored gold: the coins he earned afterwards seemed as irrelevant as stones brought to complete a house suddenly buried by an earthquake; the sense of bereavement was too heavy upon him for the old thrill of satisfaction to arise again at the touch of the newly earned coin. And now something had come to replace his hoard which gave a growing purpose to the earnings, drawing his hope and joy continually onward beyond the money.

In old days there were angels who came and took men by the hand and led them away from the city of destruction. We see no white-winged angels now. But yet men are led away from threatening destruction; a hand is put into theirs, which leads them forth gently towards a calm and bright land, so that they look no more backward; and the hand may be a little child's.

From *Silas Marner*, 1861

Aldous Huxley (1894–1963)

# The world their love

*Brian had been brought up by a deeply religious and overpowering mother; here he remembers the time that the vicar's wife called on them and introduced him to her daughter:*

'And this is Joan.'

The girl held out her hand, and as he took it, her slender body swayed away from his alien presence in a movement of shyness that was yet adorably graceful, like the yielding of a young tree before the wind. That movement was the most beautiful and at the same time the most touching thing he had ever seen.

'We've been hearing you're keen on birds,' said Mrs Thursley, with an oppressive politeness and intensifying that all too bright, professionally Christian smile of hers. 'So's Joan. A regular ornithologist.'

Blushing, the girl muttered a protest...

Looking at her flushed, averted face, Brian was filled with compassionate tenderness. His heart began to beat very hard. With a mixture of fear and exultation he realised that something extraordinary, something irrevocable had happened.

And then, he went on to think, there was that time, some four or five months later, when they were staying together at her uncle's house in East Sussex. Away from her parents, she was as though transformed – not into another person; into her own fundamental self, into the happy, expansive girl that it was impossible for her to be at home... but there, in that spacious house at Iden, among its easy-going inhabitants, she was liberated into a transfiguring happiness. Brian fell in love with her all over again.

He thought of the day when they had gone walking in Winchelsea marshes. The hawthorn was in bloom; dotted here and there on the wide, flat expanse of grass, the sheep and their lambs were like white constellations; overhead, the sky was alive with white clouds gliding in the wind. Unspeakably beautiful! And suddenly it seemed to him that they were walking through the image of their love. The world was their love, and their love was the world; and the world was significant, charged with depth beyond depth of mysterious meaning. The proof of God's goodness floated in those clouds, crept in those grazing sheep, shone from every bush of incandescent blossom – and, in himself and Joan, walked hand in hand across the grass and was manifest in their happiness. His love, it seemed to him, in that apocalyptic moment, was more than merely *his*; it was in some mysterious way the equivalent of this wind and sunshine, these white gleams against the green and blue of spring. His feeling for Joan was somehow implicit in the world, had a divine and universal significance. He loved her infinitely, and for that reason was able to love everything in the world as much as he loved her.

From *Eyeless in Gaza*, 1936

## George Bernard Shaw (1856–1950)

# *Sex and the theatre*

*In the preface to his* Three Plays for Puritans, *Shaw savagely attacks the triviality and false romantic notions that dominated the plays of the time. Meanwhile he was being criticised for his own plays which dealt with such genuine – but publicly shocking – issues as prostitution and racketeer landlords.*

When the managers tried to put their principle of trying to please everybody into practice, Necessity, ever ironical towards Folly, had driven them to seek a universal pleasure to appeal to. And since many have no ear for music or eye for colour, the search for the universality inevitably flung the managers back on the instinct of sex as the avenue to all hearts. Of course the appeal was a vapid failure...

I found that the whole business of stage sensuousness... finally disgusted me, not because I was Pharisaical, or intolerantly refined, but because I was bored; and boredom is a condition which makes men as susceptible to disgust and irritation as headache makes them to noise and glare...

The English novelist, like the tramp who can think of nothing but his hunger, seems to be unable to escape from the obsession of sex... no editor, publisher or manager, will now accept a story or produce a play without 'love interest' in it. Take, for a recent example, Mr H.G. Wells's *War of the Worlds*, a tale of the invasion of the earth by the inhabitants of the planet Mars: a capital story, not to be laid down until finished. Love interest is impossible on its scientific plane: nothing could be more impertinent or irritating. Yet Mr Wells has had to pretend that the hero is in love with a young lady manufactured for the purpose, and to imply that it is on her account alone that he feels concerned about the apparently inevitable destruction of the human race by the Martians...

I have, I think, always been a Puritan in my attitude to Art. I am as fond of fine music and handsome buildings as Milton was, or Cromwell, or Bunyan; but if I found that they were becoming the instruments of a systematic idolatry of sensuousness, I would hold it good statesmanship to blow every cathedral in the world to pieces... without the least heed to the screams of the art critics and cultured voluptuaries. And when I see that the nineteenth century has crowned the idolatry of Art with the deification of Love... I feel that Art was safer in the hands of the most fanatical of Cromwell's major generals than it will be if ever it gets into mine. The pleasures of the senses I can sympathise with and share; but the substitution of sensuous ecstasy for activity and intellectual honesty is the very devil.

From the preface to *Three Plays for Puritans*, 1901

# The pangs of love

*In* Swann's Way, *volume 1 of Proust's great, continuous novel,* Remembrance of Things Past, *he tells the story of Swann's growing love for Odette and his obsessive jealousy. A letter confirms his suspicion that Odette has indeed been deceiving him:*

He was not jealous, at first, of the whole of Odette's life, but of those moments only in which an incident, which he had perhaps misinterpreted, had led him to suppose that Odette might have played him false. His jealousy, like an octopus which throws out a first, then a second, and finally a third tentacle, fastened itself irremovably first to that moment, five o'clock in the afternoon, then to another, then to another again. But Swann was incapable of inventing his sufferings. They were only the memory, the perpetuation of a suffering that had come to him from without.

From without, however, everything brought him fresh suffering. He decided to separate Odette from Forcheville, by taking her away for a few days to the south. But he imagined that she was coveted by every male person in the hotel, and that she coveted them in return. And so he, who in old days, when he travelled, used always to seek out new people and crowded places, might now be seen fleeing savagely from human society as if it had cruelly injured him. And how could he not have turned misanthrope, when in every man he saw a potential lover for Odette? Thus his jealousy did even more than the happy, passionate desire which he had originally felt for Odette had done to alter Swann's character, completely changing, in the eyes of the world, even the outward signs by which that character had been intelligible...

He did not have (as I had, afterwards, at Combray in my childhood) happy days in which to forget the sufferings that would return with the night. For his days, Swann must pass them without Odette; and as he told himself, now and then, to allow so pretty a woman to go out by herself in Paris was just as rash as to leave a case of jewels in the middle of the street. In this mood he would scowl furiously at the passers-by, as though they were so many pickpockets. But their faces – a collective and formless mass

– escaped the grasp of his imagination, and so failed to feed the flame of his jealousy. The effort exhausted Swann's brain, until, passing his hand over his eyes, he cried out: 'Heaven help me!' as people, after lashing themselves into an intellectual frenzy in their endeavours to master the problem of the reality of the external world, or that of the immortality of the soul, afford relief to their weary brains by an unreasoning act of faith. But the thought of his absent mistress was incessantly, indissolubly blended with all the simplest actions of Swann's daily life – when he took his meals, opened his letter, went for a walk or to bed – by the fact of his regret at having to perform those actions without her.

From *Swann's Way*, 1922, translated by C.K. Scott-Moncrieff from *Du côté de chez Swann*, 1913; volume 1 of *Remembrance of Things Past*

## Jane Austen (1775–1817)

# *The course of true love*

*In* Persuasion, *Jane Austen's last published novel, Anne Elliot, daughter of a snobbish but impoverished baronet, rejects her suitor, Frederick Wentworth, at the persuasion of the family friend, Lady Russell, who fears he is 'a nobody'. Some years later the two young people meet again, their love undeclared but as strong as ever. Misunderstandings obstruct the path of love before the two are reunited.*

*Captain Wentworth writes to Anne, sitting at a desk in the room where Anne and her friends are talking:*

'I can no longer listen in silence. I must speak to you by such means as are within my reach. You pierce my soul. I am half agony, half hope. Tell me that I am not too late, that such precious feelings are gone for ever. I offer myself to you again with a heart even more your own than when you almost broke it, eight years and a half ago. Dare not say that man forgets sooner than woman, that his love has an earlier death. I have loved none but you. Unjust I may have been, weak and resentful I have been, but never inconstant. You alone have brought me to Bath. For you alone, I think and plan. Have you not seen this? Can you fail to have understood my wishes? I had not waited even these ten days, could I have read your feelings, as I think you have penetrated mine. I can hardly write. I am every instant hearing something which overpowers me. You sink your voice, but I can distinguish the tones of that voice when they would be lost on others. Too good, too excellent creature! You do us justice indeed. You do believe that there is true attachment and constancy among men. Believe it to be most fervent, most undeviating, in
F. W.

'I must go, uncertain of my fate; but I shall return hither or follow your party, as soon as possible. A word, a look, will be enough to decide whether I enter your father's house this evening or never.'

Such a letter was not to be soon recovered from. Half an hour's solitude and reflection might have tranquillized her; but the ten minutes only which now passed before she was interrupted, with all the restraints of her situation, could do nothing towards tranquillity. Every moment rather brought fresh agitation. It was an overpowering happiness. And before she was beyond the first stage of full sensation, Charles, Mary, and Henrietta, all came in.

*Later, Charles insists on seeing Anne home:*

They were in Union Street, when a quicker step behind, a something of familiar sound, gave her two moments' preparation for the sight of Captain Wentworth. He joined them; but, as if irresolute whether to join or pass on, said nothing, only looked. Anne could command herself enough to receive that look, and not repulsively. The cheeks which had been pale now glowed, and the movements which had hesitated were decided. He walked by her side.

From *Persuasion*, 1818

Fyodor Dostoevsky (1821–81)

# *Love that redeems*

*Raskolnikov had committed a murder, for what he deemed to be utilitarian and rational reasons. But a whole gamut of unexpected emotions followed the cold-blooded deed. He confessed to Sonya, a virtuous girl who had been driven to prostitution to support her family, ruined by her father's drinking. When Raskolnikov was condemned to exile, Sonya, who loved him with utter loyalty, went with him:*

The day was again bright and warm. Early in the morning, at about six o'clock, he went off to his work on the river-bank, where gypsum was calcined in a kiln set up in a shed, and afterwards crushed. Three convicts altogether had been sent there. One of them, with the guard, had gone to the fortress for a tool, the other began splitting wood and putting it in the kiln. Raskolnikov went out of the shed on to the bank, sat down on a pile of logs and looked at the wide, solitary river. From the high bank a broad landscape was revealed. From the other bank, far away, was faintly borne the sound of singing. There, in the immensity of the steppe, flooded with sunlight, the black tents of the nomads were barely visible dots. Freedom was there, there other people lived, so utterly unlike those on this side of the river... Raskolnikov sat on and his unwavering gaze remained fixed on the farther bank; his mind had wandered into day-dreams; he thought of nothing, but an anguished longing disturbed and tormented him.

Suddenly Sonya appeared at his side. She had come up almost soundlessly and sat down beside him. It was early; the chill of the morning still lingered. She wore her shabby old pelisse and the green shawl. Her face still bore traces of her illness; it was thinner and paler and hollow-cheeked. She gave him a joyful welcoming smile, but she held out her hand as timidly as ever.

She always stretched out her hand to him timidly, sometimes even half withdrawing it, as if she feared he would repulse her. He always grasped it reluctantly, always greeted her with a kind of irritation, sometimes remained obstinately silent all through her visit. There had been occasions when she had quailed before him and gone away deeply hurt. But this time their hands remained joined; he gave her a rapid glance, but said nothing and turned his eyes to the ground. They were alone; there was nobody to see them. The guard had turned away.

How it happened he himself did not know, but suddenly he seemed to be seized and cast at her feet. He clasped her knees and wept. For a moment she was terribly frightened, and her face grew white. She sprang up and looked down at him, trembling. But at once, in that instant, she understood. Infinite happiness shone in her eyes; she had understood, and she no longer doubted that he loved her, loved her for ever, and that now at last the moment had come...

They tried to speak, but they could not; tears stood in their eyes. They were both pale and thin, but in their white sick faces there glowed the dawn of a new future, a perfect resurrection into a new life. Love had raised them from the dead, and the heart of each held endless springs of life for the heart of the other...

That same evening, after the barrack was locked, Raskolnikov lay on his plank-bed and thought... He was thinking of her. He remembered how ceaselessly he had tormented her and harrowed her heart; he remembered her pale, thin little face; but those memories now hardly troubled him: he knew with what infinite love he would now expiate all her sufferings...

There was a New Testament under his pillow. Mechanically he took it out. It was hers, the very one from which she had read to him the raising of Lazarus. At the beginning of his religious life he had been afraid that she would pester him with religion, talk about the gospels and press books on him. But to his great astonishment she did not once speak of it, and never even offered him a New Testament. He himself had asked her for it not long before his illness and she had brought it to him without a word. He had not yet opened it.

He did not open it even now, but an idea flashed through his mind: 'Could not her beliefs become my beliefs now? Her feelings, her aspirations, at least...'

From *Crime and Punishment*, 1866

PART THREE

# *KNOWING GOD*

# THE CROSS AND THE RESURRECTION

## New life through death

Christ... his own self bare our sins in his own body on the tree, that we, being dead to sins, should live unto righteousness.

From 1 Peter 2

## He died... he rose again

For I delivered unto you first of all that which I also received, how that Christ died for our sins according to the scriptures; and that he was buried, and that he rose again the third day, according to the scriptures... If Christ be not risen, then is our preaching vain, and your faith is also vain.

From 1 Corinthians 15

C.S. Lewis (1898–1963)

# The death of Aslan

*Lewis's* Narnia *books for children have been recognised by many as an allegory of the Christian faith. Aslan the Lion gives his life for others, to atone for their wrongdoing and overcome the powers of evil. Then he rises to new life.*

A howl and a gibber of dismay went up from the creatures when they first saw the great Lion pacing towards them, and for a moment even the Witch seemed to be struck with fear. Then she recovered herself and gave a wild fierce laugh.

'The fool!' she cried. 'The fool has come. Bind him fast.'

Lucy and Susan held their breaths waiting for Aslan's roar and his spring upon his enemies. But it never came…

'Bind him, I say!' repeated the White Witch. The Hags made a dart at him and shrieked with triumph when they found that he made no resistance at all. Then others – evil dwarfs and apes – rushed in to help them, and between them they rolled the huge Lion over on his back and tied all his four paws together, shouting and cheering as though they had done something brave, though, had the Lion chosen, one of those paws could have been the death of them all. But he made no noise, even when the enemies, straining and tugging, pulled the cords so tight that they cut into his flesh. Then they began to drag him towards the Stone Table.

'Stop!' said the Witch. 'Let him first be shaved.'…

Snip-snip-snip went the shears and masses of curling gold began to fall to the ground…

'Muzzle him!' said the Witch. And even now, as they worked about his face, putting on the muzzle, one bite would have cost two or three of them their hands. And this seemed to enrage all that rabble… For a few minutes the two girls could not even see him – so thickly was he surrounded by the whole crowd of creatures kicking him, spitting on him, jeering at him.

At last the rabble had had enough of this. They began to drag the bound and muzzled Lion to the Stone Table, some pulling and some pushing. He was so huge that even when they got him there it took all their efforts to hoist him onto the surface of it.

When once Aslan had been tied (and tied so that he was really a mass of cords) on the flat stone, a hush fell on the crowd. Four hags, holding four torches, stood at the corners of the Table. The Witch bared her arms... then she began to whet her knife. It looked to the children, when the gleam of the torchlight fell upon it, as if the knife were made of stone, not of steel, and it was of a strange and evil shape.

At last she drew near. She stood by Aslan's head. Her face was working and twitching with passion, but his looked up at the sky, still quiet, neither angry nor afraid, but a little sad. Then, just before she gave the blow, she stooped down, and said in a quivering voice, 'And now, who has won?'

From *The Lion, the Witch and the Wardrobe*, 1950

**John Bunyan (1628–88)**

# Burdens loosed

*In a second term of imprisonment, for preaching openly without a licence, Bunyan wrote the first part of* Pilgrim's Progress. *In his dream, Bunyan sees Christian, burdened with his sins, leave wife and family in his home town – The City of Destruction – to set out on a journey to the Celestial City:*

Now I saw in my dream, that the highway up which Christian was to go, was fenced on either side with a Wall, and that Wall is called Salvation. Up this way therefore did burdened Christian run, but not without great difficulty, because of the load on his back.

He ran thus till he came at a place somewhat ascending; and upon that place stood a Cross, and little below in the bottom, a sepulchre. So I saw in my dream, that just as Christian came up with the Cross, his burden loosed from off his shoulders, and fell from off his back; and began to tumble, and so continued to do till it came to the mouth of the sepulchre, where it fell in, and I saw it no more.

Then was Christian glad and lightsome, and said with a merry heart, 'He hath given me rest, by his sorrow, and life, by his death.' Then he stood still a while, to look and wonder; for it was very surprising to him that the sight of the Cross should thus ease him of his burden. He looked therefore, and looked again, even till the springs that were in his head sent the waters down his cheeks. Now as he stood looking and weeping, behold three Shining Ones came to him, and saluted him, with 'Peace be to thee.' So the first said to him, 'Thy sins be forgiven.' The second stripped him of his rags, and clothed him with change of raiment. The third also set a mark on his forehead, and gave him a roll with a seal upon it, which he bid him look on as he ran, and that he should give it in at the Celestial Gate: so they went their way. Then Christian gave three leaps for joy, and went on singing,

*Thus far did I come, laden with my sin,*
*Nor could aught ease the grief that I was in,*
*Till I came hither. What a place is this!*
*Must here be the beginning of my bliss?*

*Must here the burden fall from off my back?*
*Must here the strings that bound it to me crack?*
*Blessed Cross! Blessed Sepulchre! Blessed rather be*
*The man that there was put to death for me.*

From *Pilgrim's Progress*, part 1, 1678

Dorothy L. Sayers (1893–1957)

# The shock of the cross

*When Dorothy L. Sayers' play cycle for radio – The Man Born to Be King – was first broadcast (from December 1941 to October 1942), it was condemned by many churchgoers. They considered the modern idiom and realistic treatment to be blasphemous. In her introduction to the plays, Sayers vindicates her treatment of the sacred subjects:*

It is necessary for the playwright to work with a divided mind. He must be able at will to strip off his knowledge of what is actually taking place, and present, through his characters, the events and people as they appeared to themselves at the time. This would seem obvious and elementary; but its results are in fact the very thing that gives offence to unimaginative piety...

Sacred personages, living in a far-off land and time, using dignified rhythms of speech... They mocked and railed on him and smote him, they scourged and crucified him. Well, they were people very remote from ourselves... We should not like to think otherwise.

Unhappily, if we think about it at all, we must think otherwise. God was executed by people painfully like us, in a society very similar to our own – in the over-ripeness of the most splendid and sophisticated empire the world has ever seen. In a nation famous for its religious genius and under a government renowned for its efficiency, he was executed by a corrupt church, a timid politician, and a fickle proletariat led by professional agitators. His executioners made vulgar jokes about him, called him filthy names, taunted him, smacked him in the face, flogged him with the cat, and hanged him on the common gibbet – a bloody, dusty, sweaty and sordid business.

If you show people that, they are shocked. So they should be. If that does not shock them, nothing can. If the mere representation of it has an air of irreverence, what is to be said about the deed? It is curious that people who are filled with horrified indignation whenever a cat kills a sparrow can hear that story of the killing of God told Sunday after Sunday and not experience any shock at all...

Tear off the disguise of the Jacobean idiom, go back to the homely and vigorous Greek of Mark or John, translate it into its current English counterpart, and there every man may see his own face. *We* played the parts in that tragedy, nineteen and a half centuries since, and are perhaps playing them today, in the same good faith and in the same ironic ignorance. But today we cannot see the irony, for we the audience are now the actors and do not know the end of the play. But it may assist us to know what we are doing if the original drama is shown to us again, with ourselves in the original parts.

From the introduction to *The Man Born to Be King*, 1943

## Thomas à Kempis (1379–1471)

# *On the royal road of the holy cross*

'Renounce yourself, take up your cross and follow Jesus.' There are many to whom that seems a hard saying; but how much harder will it be to hear that word of final judgement: *Go far from me, you that are accursed, into eternal fire.* Those who now gladly hear the word of the cross and keep what it commands will not be afraid then when they hear the doom of everlasting loss...

Why, then, are you afraid to take up your cross? It is your road to the kingdom of Christ. In the cross lies our salvation, our life; in the cross we have a defence against our foes. In the cross we have a pouring-in of heavenly sweetness, a strengthening of our minds and spiritual joy. In the cross is the peak of virtue, the perfection of holiness. There is no salvation for our souls, no hope of life everlasting, but in the cross. Take up your cross, then, and follow Jesus; and you will go into life that has no end. He has gone ahead of you, bearing his own cross; on that cross he has died for you, that you may bear your own cross and on that cross yearn to die. If you have died together with him, together with him you will have life; if you have shared his suffering, you will also share his glory.

You see, the cross is at the root of everything; everything is based upon our dying there. There is no other road to true inward peace, but the road of the cross, of dying daily to self. Walk where you will, seek whatever you have a mind to; you will find no higher road above, no safer road below, than the road of the holy cross...

The cross, then, is at all times ready for you; never a place on earth but you will find it awaiting you. Dash off here or there, you can't get away from it; because, wherever you go, you take yourself along with you, and at every moment you will find yourself. Look above yourself or below, outside yourself or within; everywhere you will find the cross. And everywhere you must keep patient, if you would have inward peace and gain an everlasting crown.

Set out, then, as a good and faithful servant of Christ, to bear like a man the cross of your Lord, that cross to which he was nailed for love of you. Be prepared to endure much thwarting and many a difficulty in this life of sadness; because that's how things are going to be for you... there's no cure, no getting round the fact of trouble and sorrow; you just have to put up with them. If you long to be the Lord's friend, you must drink his cup and like it. As for consolations, let God see about that...

If there had been anything better for men, more profitable for their salvation, than suffering, you may be sure that Christ, by his teaching and by his own example, would have pointed it out. But no; addressing the disciples who were following him, and all those who wish to follow him, he clearly urges them to carry the cross, when he says: *If any man has a mind to come my way, let him renounce self, and take up his cross, and follow me.* So then, when we have made an end of reading and studying, this is the conclusion we should reach at last: *that we cannot enter the kingdom of heaven without many trials.*

From *The Imitation of Christ*, 1418

## William Penn (1644–1718)

# *No cross, no crown*

*William Penn was imprisoned in the Tower of London for eight months on a charge of blasphemy and it was here that he wrote the earliest version of* No Cross, No Crown.

Come, Reader, hearken to me awhile; I seek thy salvation; that's my plot; thou wilt forgive me. A Refiner is come near thee, his grace hath appeared to thee; receive its leaven, and it will change thee; his medicine, and it will cure thee; he is as infallible as free; without money and with certainty. A touch of his garment did it of old; it will do it still; his virtue is the same, it cannot be exhausted. He turns vile things into things precious; for he maketh saints out of sinners, and almost gods of men. What rests to us then, that we must do, to be thus witnesses of his power and love? This is the Crown; but where is the Cross?

Christ's Cross is Christ's way to Christ's Crown. This is the subject of the following discourse, first writ during my confinement in the Tower of London, in the year 1668, now reprinted (1682) with enlargements that thou, Reader, mayest be won to Christ; and if won already, brought nearer to him. 'Tis the path God in his everlasting kindness guided my feet into, in the flower of my youth, when about two and twenty years of age; then he took me by the hand and led me out of the pleasures, vanities and hopes of the world. I have tasted of Christ's judgements, and of his mercies, and of the world's frowns, and reproaches. I rejoice in my experience and dedicate it to thy service in Christ.

To my country, and to the world of Christians I leave it. May God, if he please, make it effectual to them all and turn their hearts from that envy, hatred, and bitterness they have one against another about worldly things (sacrificing humanity and charity to ambition and covetousness, for which they fill the earth with trouble and oppression) that receiving the spirit of Christ into their hearts, the fruits of which are love, peace, joy, temperance and patience, brotherly kindness and charity, they may in body, soul, and spirit, make a triple league against the world, the flesh, and the devil, the only common enemies of mankind; and having conquered them through a life of self-denial and the power of the cross of Jesus, they may at last attain to the eternal rest and kingdom of God.

*So desireth, so prayeth,*
*Friendly Reader,*
*Thy fervent Christian friend*

William Penn

From the preface to *No Cross, No Crown,* 1682

John Grisham (b. 1955)

# The road to restoration

*Nate O'Reilly, lawyer and alcoholic, emerges from a spell in a rehabilitation clinic, to be sent by his firm to find Rachel, the illegitimate daughter of a multi-millionaire American. She is missionary to a remote tribe of Indians in the Brazilian forests. On his return journey he develops dengue fever; in a hospital in Corumba Rachel appears to come to encourage and comfort him. Later, Nate looks for her in the city. He sees lights from a small chapel and goes in hoping to find Rachel among the scattered worshippers:*

He could wait. He had the time; she might appear. He shuffled along the back row and sat alone. He studied the crucifixion, the nails through His hands, the sword in His side, the agony in His face. Did they really kill Him in such a dreadful manner?...

Three more stragglers came from the street. A young man with a guitar appeared from a side door and went to the pulpit. It was exactly nine-thirty. He strummed a few chords and began singing, his face glowing with words of faith and praise... Maybe the music would draw Rachel...

When the song was finished, the young man read some scripture and began teaching... Nate was mesmerised by the soft, slurring sounds, and the unhurried cadence. Though he understood not a word, he tried to repeat the sentences. Then his thoughts drifted.

His body had purged the fevers and chemicals. He was well fed, alert, rested. He was his old self again, and that suddenly depressed him. The present was back, hand in hand with the future. The burdens he'd left with Rachel had found him again, found him then and there in the chapel. He needed her to sit with him, hold his hand and help him pray.

He hated his weaknesses. He named them one by one, and was saddened by the list. The demons were waiting at home – the good friends and the bad friends, the haunts and habits, the pressures he couldn't stand anymore...

The young man was praying, his eyes clenched tightly, his arms waving gently upward. Nate closed his eyes too, and called God's name. God was waiting.

With both hands, he clenched the back of the pew in front of him. He repeated the list, mumbling softly every weakness and flaw and affliction and evil that plagued him. He confessed them all. In one long glorious acknowledgement of failure, he laid himself bare before God. He held nothing back. He unloaded enough burdens to crush any three men, and when he finally finished Nate had tears in his eyes. 'I'm sorry,' he whispered to God. 'Please help me.'

As quickly as the fever had left his body, he felt the baggage leave his soul. With one gentle brush of the hand, his slate had been wiped clean...

He heard the guitar again. He opened his eyes and wiped his cheeks. Instead of seeing the young man in the pulpit, Nate saw the face of Christ, in agony and pain, dying on the cross. Dying for him.

From *The Testament*, 1999

### Malcolm Muggeridge (1903–90)

# *The crucifixion*

I suppose every age has its own particular fantasy. Ours is science. A seventeenth-century man like Pascal, though himself a mathematician and scientist of genius, found it quite ridiculous that anyone should suppose that rational processes could lead to any ultimate conclusions about life, but easily accepted the authority of the Scriptures. With us it is the other way round.

What, then, does the Crucifixion signify in an age like ours? I see it in the first place as a sublime mockery of all earthly authority and power. The crown of thorns, the purple robe, the ironical title 'King of the Jews', were intended to mock or parody Christ's pretensions to be the Messiah; in fact, they rather hold up to ridicule and contempt all crowns, all robes, all kings that ever were. It was a sick joke that back-fired. No one it seems to me, who has fully grasped the Crucifixion can ever again take seriously any expression or instrument of worldly power, however venerable, glittering or seemingly formidable.

When Christ was tempted in the wilderness he declined the Devil's offer to give him sway over the kingdoms of the earth (a refusal that must be intensely irritating to those who believe that it is possible through Christian good-will to set up a kingdom of heaven on earth); the Crucifixion demonstrated why – because the Devil's offer was bogus. There are no kingdoms for him to bestow; only pseudo or notional ones presided over by mountebanks masquerading as emperors and kings and governments...

In this sense, Christ's death on the cross may be seen as the exact converse of the next most famous death as far as our civilisation is concerned – that of Socrates. Socrates obediently drank hemlock and died to support and enhance the State: Christ died on the cross in derisive defiance of all States, whether Roman, Judaic, or any other.

From Socrates' death emanate all plans for the collective betterment of mankind, whether embodied in a nation, a regime, a leader, an ideology, a social system, or, for that matter a Church; from the cross, the notion of individual salvation, of individual souls journeying through life like Bunyan's Pilgrim, all equal in their capacity as children of God and in that Christ died for them equally, and all buoyed up by the expectation of deliverance through death from the demands and imperfections of their fleshly existence.

From an article in *The Observer*, 26 March 1967

Leo Tolstoy (1828–1910)

# Easter at church

*Resurrection is Tolstoy's last great novel. Nekhlyudov, a wealthy Russian prince, falls in love with Katusha, his aunt's servant girl, and seduces her. Years later she comes before the court when he is serving as a juror, as a prostitute and convicted murderer. The theme of new beginnings is pictured in the Easter service which Nekhlyudov attended years before at his aunt's church:*

This midnight service remained for ever after one of the happiest and most vivid memories of Nekhlyudov's life.

The service had already begun when he rode into the churchyard out of the black night, relieved only here and there by patches of white snow, his horse splashing through the water and pricking its ears at the sight of the little lights around the church.

Some peasants, recognizing Marya Ivanovna's nephew, led him to a dry place to dismount, tied his horse up and conducted him into the church, which was full of people.

On the right stood the men: old men in home-spun caftans, bast shoes and clean white leg-bands; the younger ones in new cloth tunics with bright-coloured belts round their waists, and top-boots. On the left were the women, with red silk kerchiefs on their heads, sleeveless velveteen jackets, bright red blouses and gay-coloured skirts of blue, green and red, and boots with steel heel-plates. The more staid, older women with white kerchiefs, grey jackets and old-fashioned linen petticoats, and leather or new bast shoes on their feet, stood behind; between them and the others were the children, their hair greased, and dressed in their best clothes. The men were crossing themselves and bowing, shaking back their hair when they brought their heads up; the women, especially the old women, riveting their faded eyes upon one of the many ikons, each with lighted candles burning before it, made the sign of the cross, firmly pressing their bent fingers to the kerchief on their foreheads, to each shoulder and their stomachs, moving their lips all the while, and bowed or fell to their knees. The children imitated their elders and prayed earnestly when anyone was looking at them...

Nekhlyudov passed up to the front. In the middle of the church stood the local gentry: a landed proprietor with his wife and son, the latter wearing a blouse, the district police-officer, the telegraph operator, a tradesman in top-boots, the village elder with a medal on his chest; and to the right of the reading desk, behind the wife of the landowner, stood Matriona Pavlovna in a shot-silk lilac gown and fringed white shawl, and Katusha in a white dress with a tucked bodice and blue sash, and a little red bow in her black hair.

Everything was festive, solemn, happy and beautiful: the clergy in their silver cloth vestments with gold crosses; the deacon and subdeacon in their gala silver and gold surplices; the choir singers in their best clothes, with their hair well oiled; the gay dancing melodies of the Easter hymns; the continual blessing of the people by the clergy with their triple flower-bedecked candles; and the ever-repeated salutation: 'Christ is risen! Christ is risen!' It was all lovely, but best of all was Katusha in her white dress and blue sash, with the little red bow on her dark head, and her sparkling rapturous eyes.

From *Resurrection*, 1899

## Piers Paul Read (b. 1941)

# *Whose skeleton?*

*On the Third Day is an intellectual thriller which has at its
centre the importance of Christ's resurrection. A skeleton
discovered by an Israeli archaeologist is identified as that of
Christ. Believers and unbelievers alike are stirred by the find, the
suspicious death that follows and the possible political fall-out.*

*Henry – the agnostic brother of the young monk, Andrew –
has been involved in an affair with Anna, daughter of the
archaeologist who discovered the skeleton:*

When Anna had first told him that her father had discovered the skeleton
of Christ, he had been neither particularly surprised nor particularly
interested. Now, he realized, the truth or falsity of her claim could not
only affect the psychological state of those who had faith... it could also
have considerable political ramifications all over the world – in Eastern
Europe, in Africa, in Latin America.

Isolated for so long among like-minded agnostics, whose values were of
a secular kind, it came as a shock to Henry to realize quite how many
people throughout the world still believed in the Resurrection of Christ.
Seldom since adolescence had he himself stopped to consider questions of
this kind. There had been moments, mostly on holiday, when, staring at
the stars, he had been awed by the mystery of infinity, and had wondered
about the origin of the universe; but almost at once, when he had
returned to London, he had been distracted once again by the practical
concerns of his daily life.

Now, however, he had the uneasy feeling that there might, after all, be
more to life than he had supposed; that perhaps the imperatives of
instinct did not lead to fulfilment; and that perhaps the faculty of reason,
unique though it was to the human species, was insufficient to explain the
mystery which lay in the kernel of the human condition...

He went out onto the small balcony at the back of his flat... and while
he picked the chives and parsley for an omelette for supper, he continued
to think about the skeleton, and grew increasingly agitated by the thought
that, if reason could not explain the human condition, it was
unreasonable to be sure that there was no God. Nor could it be

impossible, if there was a God, that he should have been born a Jew, have died on a cross, and, after dying, have risen from the dead.

If such a story was not certainly false, then it must be possibly true. Thus, incontrovertible evidence – even evidence which pushed the balance of probability one way or the other – would be of critical importance, not merely to those political developments in different parts of the world which were influenced by people's religious convictions, but also to the individual speculations of a man such as Henry about the value of his actions or the meaning of his life.

He cooked his omelette and ate it in the kitchen, his mood swinging between excitement and gloom. He still felt a repugnance for religion, and thought it absurd to suggest that a God powerful enough to bring the whole universe into existence should choose to become a sweating, defecating, human being. Yet he had to acknowledge that, if there was a God, then what appeared absurd to us might seem sensible to him. He would be privy to knowledge beyond the range of human understanding which made it necessary for God to become man to enable man to become a god.

From *On the Third Day*, 1990

John Irving (b. 1942)

# *Believing in Easter*

*Owen Meany – friend from boyhood of the narrator – is a one-off. He is extremely small and has an extraordinary voice (indicated in the text by capital letters); he is also very clever and, most important, has a deep sense of the presence of God and of the part he is destined to play in fulfilling God's purposes. John Wheelwright begins his story, set in the United States:*

I am doomed to remember a boy with a wrecked voice – not because of his voice, or because he was the smallest person I ever knew, or even because he was the instrument of my mother's death, but because he is the reason I believe in God. I am a Christian because of Owen Meany... I have a church-rummage faith – the kind that needs patching up every week-end. What faith I have I owe to Owen Meany, a boy I grew up with. It is Owen who made me a believer.

*Toronto: 12 April 1987*
A rainy Palm Sunday. It is not a warm spring rain – not a 'seasonal' rain, as my grandmother liked to say. It is a raw cold rain, a suitable day for the Passion of our Lord Jesus Christ. At Grace Church on-the-Hill, the children and the acolytes stood huddled in the narthex; holding their palm-fronds, they resembled tourists who'd landed in the tropics on an unseasonably cold day. The organist chose Brahms for the processional – 'O Welt ich muss dich lassen' 'O world I must leave you'.

Owen hated Palm Sunday: the treachery of Judas, the cowardice of Peter, the weakness of Pilate.

'IT'S BAD ENOUGH THAT THEY CRUCIFIED HIM,' Owen said, 'BUT THEY MADE FUN OF HIM, TOO!'

Canon Mackie read heavily from Matthew: how they mocked Jesus, how they spit on him, how he cried, 'My God, my God, why hast thou forsaken me?'

I find that Holy Week is draining; no matter how many times I have lived through his crucifixion, my anxiety about his resurrection is undiminished – I am terrified that, this year, it won't happen; that, that year, it didn't. Anyone can be sentimental about the Nativity; any fool can feel like a Christian at Christmas. But Easter is the main event; if you don't believe in the resurrection, you're not a believer.

'IF YOU DON'T BELIEVE IN EASTER,' Owen Meany said, 'DON'T KID YOURSELF – DON'T CALL YOURSELF A CHRISTIAN.'...

'EASTER MEANS WHAT IT SAYS,' said Owen Meany.

At Christ Church on Easter Sunday, Rector Wiggin always said: 'Alleluia. Christ is risen.'

And we, the People – we said: 'The Lord is risen indeed. Alleluia.'

From *A Prayer for Owen Meany*, 1989

# REPENTANCE, FORGIVENESS AND RECONCILIATION

## *The prodigal son*

Then drew near unto him [Jesus] all the publicans and sinners for to hear him. And the Pharisees and scribes murmured, saying, This man receiveth sinners and eateth with them.

And he spake this parable unto them saying...

A certain man had two sons. And the younger of them said to his father, Father, give me the portion of goods that falleth to me. And he divided unto them his living. And not many days after the younger son gathered all together, and took his journey into a far country, and there wasted his substance with riotous living. And when he had spent all, there arose a mighty famine in that land, and he began to be in want. And he went and joined himself to a citizen of that country; and he sent him into his fields to feed swine. And he would fain have filled his belly with the husks that the swine did eat: and no man gave unto him. And when he came to himself, he said, How many hired servants of my father's have bread enough and to spare, and I perish with hunger! I will arise and go to my father and will say unto him, Father, I have sinned against heaven, and before thee, and am no more worthy to be called thy son: make me as one of thy hired servants. And he arose, and came to his father. But when he was yet a great way off, his father saw him, and had compassion, and ran, and fell on his neck and kissed him. And the son said unto him, Father, I have sinned against heaven and in thy sight and am no more worthy to be called thy son. But the father said to his servants, Bring forth the best robe and put it on him, and put a ring on his hand, and shoes on his feet: and bring hither the fatted calf and kill it; and let us eat and be merry: for this my son was dead, and is alive again; he was lost, and is found. And they began to be merry. Now his elder son was in the field, and as he came and drew nigh to the house, he heard musick and dancing. And he called one of the servants, and asked what these things meant. And he said unto him, Thy brother is come, and thy father hath killed the fatted calf, because he hath received him safe and sound. And he was angry, and would not go in: therefore came his father out, and intreated him. And he answering said to his father: Lo, these many years do I serve thee, neither transgressed I at any time thy commandment: and yet thou never gavest me a kid, that I might make merry with my friends: But as soon as this thy son was come, which hath devoured thy living with harlots, thou hast killed for him the fatted calf. And he said unto him, Son, thou art ever with me, and all that I have is thine. It was meet that we should make merry, and be glad, for this thy brother was dead, and is alive again; and was lost, and is found.

From Luke 15

**Aldous Huxley (1894–1963)**

# *Change of mind*

Repentance is *metanoia*, or 'change of mind'; and without it there cannot be even a beginning of the spiritual life – for the life of the spirit is incompatible with the life of the 'old man', whose acts, whose thoughts, whose very existence are the obstructing evils which have to be repented. This necessary change of mind is normally accompanied by sorrow and self-loathing. But these emotions are not to be persisted in and must never be allowed to become a settled habit of remorse. In Middle English 'remorse' is rendered, with a literalness which to modern readers is at once startling and stimulating, as 'again-bite'. In this cannibalistic encounter, who bites whom? Observation and self-analysis provide the answer: the creditable aspects of the self bite the discreditable and are themselves bitten, receiving wounds that fester with incurable shame and despair. But in Fenelon's words, 'It is mere self-love to be inconsolable at seeing one's own imperfections.' Self-reproach is painful; but the very pain is a reassuring proof that the self is still intact; so long as attention is fixed on the delinquent ego, it cannot be fixed upon God and the ego (which lives upon attention and dies only when that sustenance is withheld) cannot be dissolved in the divine Light.

From *The Perennial Philosophy*, 1948

### G.K. Chesterton (1874–1936)

# *Hook, line and sinker*

*Father Brown was ensconced in a hotel office during a splendid dinner held by the exclusive club of the Twelve True Fishermen. In spite of the tightest security measures, their priceless, pearl-encrusted, fish-shaped knives and forks had been stolen during the meal. Father Brown not only solved the mystery of how it was done, but he identified the thief. He waited for him in the hotel cloakroom:*

He was an elegant man in very plain evening-dress… he tossed down a scrap of paper with a number and called out with amiable authority: 'I want my hat and coat, please; I find I have to go away at once.'

Father Brown took the paper without a word, and obediently went to look for the coat; it was not the first menial work he had done in his life. He brought it and laid it on the counter; meanwhile, the strange gentleman who had been feeling in his waistcoat pocket, said, laughing: 'I haven't got any silver; you can keep this.' And he threw down half a sovereign and caught up his coat.

Father Brown's figure remained quite dark and still; but in that instant he had lost his head. His head was always most valuable when he had lost it. In such moments he put two and two together and made four million. Often the Catholic church (which is wedded to common sense) did not approve of it. Often he did not approve of it himself. But it was a real inspiration – important at rare crises – when whosoever shall lose his head the same shall save it.

'I think, sir,' he said civilly, 'that you have some silver in your pocket.'

The tall gentleman stared. 'Hang it,' he cried, 'If I give you gold, why should you complain?'

'Because silver is sometimes more valuable than gold,' said the priest mildly: 'that is, in large quantities.'

The stranger looked at him curiously… He put one hand on the counter, vaulted over as easily as an acrobat, and towered over the priest, putting one tremendous hand upon his collar.

'Stand still,' he said in a hacking whisper. 'I don't want to threaten you, but –'

'I do want to threaten you,' said Father Brown, in a voice like a rolling drum. 'I want to threaten you with the worm that dieth not, and the fire that is not quenched.'

'You're a rum sort of cloak-room clerk,' said the other.

'I am a priest, Monsieur Flambeau,' said Brown, 'and I am ready to hear your confession.'

*Later, the wealthy and decadent club members questioned Father Brown about the identity of the thief:*

'I don't know his real name,' said the priest placidly; 'but I know something of his fighting weight, and a great deal about his spiritual difficulties. I formed the physical estimate when he tried to throttle me, and the moral estimate when he repented.'

'Oh, I say – repented!' cried young Chester, with a sort of crow of laughter.

Father Brown got to his feet, putting his hands behind him. 'Odd, isn't it,' he said, 'that a thief and a vagabond should repent, when so many who are rich and secure remain hard and frivolous, and without fruit for God or man? But there, if you will excuse me, you trespass a little upon my province. If you doubt the penitence as a practical fact, there are your knives and forks. You are the Twelve True Fishers, and there are all your silver fish. But He has made me a fisher of men.'

'Did you catch this man?' asked the colonel, frowning.

Father Brown looked him full in his frowning face. 'Yes,' he said, 'I caught him, with an unseen hook and an invisible line which is long enough to let him wander to the ends of the world, and still to bring him back with a twitch upon the thread.'

From *The Innocence of Father Brown*, 1911

### Charles Dickens (1812–70)

# *All is forgiven*

*Pip, orphaned, was brought up by his hard-hearted, married sister whose husband Joe, the blacksmith, gave the young boy love and protection. When Pip went to London to better himself, thanks to an unknown benefactor, he felt superior to his childhood friends and treated Joe shabbily. But when Pip lay desperately ill, in debt and alone in his London rooms, Joe came to nurse him:*

After I had turned the worst point of my illness, I began to notice that while all its other features changed, this one consistent feature did not change. Whoever came about me, still settled down into Joe. I opened my eyes in the night, and I saw in the great chair at the bedside, Joe. I opened my eyes in the day, and, sitting on the window-seat, smoking his pipe in the shaded open window, still I saw Joe. I asked for cooling drink, and the dear hand that gave it me was Joe's. I sank back on my pillow after drinking, and the face that looked so hopefully and tenderly upon me was the face of Joe.

At last, one day, I took courage, and said, '*Is* it Joe?'

And the dear old home-voice answered, 'Which it air, old chap.'

'Oh Joe, you break my heart! Look angry at me, Joe! Strike me, Joe! Tell me of my ingratitude. Don't be so good to me!'

For Joe had actually laid his head down on the pillow at my side and put his arm round my neck, in his joy that I knew him.

'Which dear old Pip, old chap,' said Joe, 'you and me was ever friends. And when you're well enough to go out for a ride – what larks!'

After which, Joe withdrew to the window, and stood with his back towards me, wiping his eyes. And as my extreme weakness prevented me from getting up and going to him, I lay there, penitently whispering, 'O God bless him! God bless this gentle Christian man!'

From *Great Expectations*, 1860–61

## John Bunyan (1628–88)

# 'Wonderful glory'

*John Bunyan tells the story of his conversion and the transformation that took place:*

At another time, though just before I was pretty well and savoury in my spirit, yet suddenly there fell upon me a great cloud of darkness, which did so hide from me the things of God and Christ, that I was as if I had never seen or known them in my life; I was also so overrun in my soul, with a senseless, heartless frame of spirit, that I could not feel my soul to move or stir after grace and life by Christ...

After I had been in this condition some three or four days, as I was sitting by the fire, I suddenly felt this word to sound in my heart, that I must go to Jesus; at this my former darkness and atheism fled away, and the blessed things of heaven were set within my view. While I was on this sudden thus overtaken with surprise, Wife, said I, is there ever such a scripture, I must go to Jesus? She said she could not tell, therefore I sat musing still to see if I could remember such a place; I had not sat above two or three minutes but that came bolting in upon me, 'And to an innumerable company of angels,' and withal, Hebrews the twelfth, about the mount Sion, was set before mine eyes (ver. 22–4).

Then with joy I told my wife, O now I know, I know! But that night was a good night to me, I never had but few better; I longed for the company of some of God's people that I might have imparted unto them what God had showed me. Christ was a precious Christ to my soul that night; I could scarce lie in my bed for joy, and peace, and triumph, through Christ; this great glory did not continue upon me until morning, yet that twelfth of the author to the Hebrews (ver. 22–4) was a blessed scripture to me for many days together after this.

The words are these, 'Ye are come unto mount Sion, and unto the city of the living God, the heavenly Jerusalem, and to an innumerable company of angels... to God the Judge of all... and to Jesus, the mediator of the new covenant, and to the blood of sprinkling, that speaketh better things than that of Abel.' Through this blessed sentence the Lord led me over and over, first to this word, and then to that, and showed me wonderful glory in every one of them. These words also have oft since this time been great refreshment to my spirit. Blessed be God for having mercy on me.

*From* Grace Abounding to the Chief of Sinners; or, a Brief Revelation of the Exceeding Mercy of God in Christ, to His Poor Servant, John Bunyan, *1666*

## Les Murray (b. 1918)

# *False repentance*

Black Australians are sometimes puzzled, and often made cynical, by the proxy vehemence of some of their white supporters. They hate their own a lot more than they love us, I've heard said. When a colleague of mine sent me a poem recently about teachers signing the Sorry Book at a high school – I wince at the dragooning of conscience which would have enforced that enterprise! – I shocked him by saying I'd sign too if he could convince me that the Jews, of all times down to the present, were guilty of killing Jesus. If you've never personally killed or even hurt an Aborigine and never approved of any such thing, then to apologise for treatment they've suffered means that you embrace the principle of collective, inherited guilt, the very notion laid on the Jews to such terrible effect. 'But surely you're living in a stolen country!' he exclaimed. Not stolen by me, I said; I was born here and have lived my life here; under Aboriginal law I have as much right to the country as they. The British government stole our continent two hundred years ago, and stranded a quarter of a million of their most troublesome and unfortunate folk here by force. No present day British government bears any guilt for this, however. No British person now alive did it. English people above a certain, not always very high, class line sometimes despise Australians for having convict ancestors, and I've told them they'll need someday to forgive us, because such dislike comes from an uneasy conscience. They'll have to forgive the Irish likewise, in a much more major way. Most people have some victim-group they need to forgive, because the victim has power over us and distorts our soul: we hate him for lowering our self-esteem. Abasing oneself with loud public apology is likely to make that resentment worse, not better. Perhaps the fury which some activists displace on to their fellow Australians comes from getting this wrong. Perhaps they and the supposed and real racists they scream at are unbearably close to each other. Whatever race is, both torment themselves about it.

From *The Quality of Sprawl: Thoughts About Australia*, 1999

### Herman Melville (1819–91)

# *Out of the belly of hell*

*Ishmael, preparing for his first whaling expedition, attended a Whaleman's Chapel, when a storm was raging. The minister, once a harpooner himself, ascended to the high pulpit by seaman's rope ladder:*

The preacher slowly turned over the leaves of the Bible, and at last, folding his hand down upon the proper page, said: 'Beloved shipmates, clinch the last verse of the first chapter of Jonah – "And God had prepared a great fish to swallow up Jonah."'

'Shipmates, this book, containing only four chapters – four yarns – is one of the smallest strands in the mighty cable of the Scriptures. Yet what depths of the soul does Jonah's deep sea-line sound! what a pregnant lesson to us is this prophet! what a noble thing is that canticle in the fish's belly! How billow-like and boisterously grand! We feel the floods surging over us; we sound with him to the kelpy bottom of the waters; sea-weed and all the slime of the sea is about us! But *what* is this lesson that the book of Jonah teaches? Shipmates, it is a two-stranded lesson; a lesson to us all as sinful men and a lesson to me as a pilot of the living God. As sinful men, it is a lesson to us all, because it is a story of the sin, hard-heartedness, suddenly awakened fears, the swift punishment, repentance, prayers, and finally the deliverance and joy of Jonah. As with all sinners among men, the sin of this son of Amittai was in his wilful disobedience of the command of God – never mind now what that command was, or how conveyed – which he found a hard command. But all the things that God would have us do are hard for us to do... If we obey God we must disobey ourselves; and it is in this disobeying ourselves wherein the hardness of obeying God consists.'

*In colourful language and seaman's imagery, Father Mapple retells the story of Jonah – his refusal to obey God's mission but his attempted escape on a ship to Tarshish; the fierce storm, the sailors' anguish and Jonah's admission of guilt and instructions to the crew to throw him overboard:*

'And now behold Jonah taken up as an anchor and dropped into the sea; when instantly an oily calmness floats out from the east, and the sea is still, as Jonah carries down the gale with him, leaving smooth water behind. He goes down in the heart of such a masterless commotion that he scarce heeds the moment when he drops seething into the yawning jaws awaiting him; and the whale shoots-to all his ivory teeth, like so many white bolts, upon his prison. Then Jonah prayed unto the Lord out of the fish's belly. But observe his prayer, and learn a weighty lesson. For sinful as he is, Jonah does not weep and wail for direct deliverance. He feels that his dreadful punishment is just. He leaves all his deliverance to God, contenting himself with this, that spite of all his pains and pangs, he will still look towards His holy temple... Shipmates, I do not place Jonah before you to be copied for his sin but I do place him before you as a model for repentance. Sin not; but if you do, take heed to repent of it like Jonah.'

While he was speaking these words, the howling of the shrieking, slanting storm without seemed to add new power to the preacher, who, when describing Jonah's sea-storm, seemed tossed by a storm himself. His deep chest heaved as with a ground-swell; his tossed arms seemed the warring elements at work; and the thunders that rolled away from off his swarthy brow, and the light leaping from his eye, made all his simple hearers look on him with a quick fear that was strange to them.

From *Moby Dick*, 1851

**Paul Scott (1920–78)**

# Mr Chaudhuri and Miss Crane

*After many years in India Miss Edwina Crane had become superintendent of the Mayapore district's Protestant mission schools. In 1942, on one of her regular visits to the Dibrapur school, where Mr Chaudhuri was in charge, there was trouble stirring. But Miss Crane was determined to return to Mayapore although phone lines had been cut and Congress rebels reported to be on the roads.*

Mr Chaudhuri was silent for a while. Presently he sighed and said, 'I don't follow your reasoning, Miss Crane. It is no doubt an example of British phlegm. You are mad. And I am mad to let you go and to go with you…'

She turned her head and again they looked at each other straight. She had stopped smiling, not because she was annoyed with him for calling her mad or had already stopped seeing the funny side, but because she felt there was between them an unexpected mutual confidence…

And for Miss Crane there was something else besides, a feeling she had often had before, a feeling in the bones of her shoulders and in the base of her skull that she was about to go over the hump thirty-five years of effort and willingness had never really got her over; the hump… which, however hard you tried, still lay in the path of thoughts you sent flowing out to a man or woman whose skin was a different colour from your own…

[She] wished that there were words she could use that would convey to him the regard she held him in at that moment, a regard deeper, harder than that she had felt for the ragged singing children years ago; deeper, harder, because her regard for the children had sprung partly from her pity for them – and for Mr Chaudhuri she had no pity; only respect and the kind of affection that came from the confidence one human being could feel in another, however little had been felt before.

'Then,' Mr Chaudhuri said, 'let us proceed.' His lips looked very dry. He was afraid, and so was she, but now perhaps they both saw the comic side, and she did not have to say anything special to him just because his skin was brown or because she had never understood him. After all, he had never fully understood her either.

*The car proceeded until they encountered rioters strung across the road. One man waved his arms and commanded them to stop. In spite of Mr Chaudhuri's instructions to drive straight on through them, Miss Crane found she could not obey. She stopped the car:*

'Don't speak,' Mr Chaudhuri said. 'Now leave it to me, don't speak.' He put a hand on her wrist. 'Trust me,' he said. 'I know you never have, but trust me now. Do whatever I say. *Whatever* I say.'

She nodded. 'I trust you. I'll do what you say.'

*Mr Chaudhuri tried to convince the rioters that Miss Crane was a friend of India, warning them:*

'Great evil will come to you and your seed if you so much as lay a finger on her.'

'Then we will lay one on you, brother,' the leader said, and dragged open the door, whose lock Miss Crane had failed, month after month, to have repaired...

'Go!' shrieked Mr Chaudhuri from outside the car, kicking the door shut, his arms held by four men, 'or do you only take orders from white men? Do you only keep promises you make to your own kind?'

*Obediently, Miss Crane drove forward, but looking back she saw the rioters attacking Mr Chaudhuri repeatedly with sticks. She confronted the rioters, brandishing the starting handle of the car but they only laughed at her and one hit her across the face and pushed her over into the ditch. When she regained consciousness, her overturned car was burning and the rioters disappearing into the distance.*

Limping, she walked to where Mr Chaudhuri still lay. Reaching him she knelt and said, 'Mr Chaudhuri,' but could not touch him because of his bloody face and open eyes and the awful thing that had happened to the side of his head. 'No,' she said, 'no, it isn't true. Oh God. Oh God, forgive me. Oh God, forgive us all,' and then covered her face and wept, which she had not done for years, and continued weeping for some time.

She dried her eyes by wiping them on the sleeve of her blouse, once, twice, three times. She felt the first heavy drops of rain. Her raincape had been in the back of the car. She said, in anguish, 'But there's nothing to cover him with, nothing, nothing,' and stood up, crouched, got hold of his feet and dragged him to the side of the road.

'I can't help it,' she said, as if to him, when he lay bloody and limp and inhuman in the place she had dragged him to. 'There's nothing I can do, nothing, nothing,' and turned away and began to walk with long unsteady strides through the rain, past the blazing car, towards Mayapore. As she walked she kept saying, 'Nothing I can do. Nothing. Nothing.'

A hundred yards past the car she stopped. 'But there is,' she said, and turned and walked back until she reached Mr Chaudhuri's body. She sat down in the mud at the side of the road, close to him, reached out and took his hand.

'It's taken me a long time,' she said, meaning not only Mr Chaudhuri, 'I'm sorry it was too late.'

From *The Jewel in the Crown*, 1966

# PRAYER AND THE PRESENCE OF GOD

## *True prayer*

[Jesus continued]: 'When you pray, don't be like those show-offs who love to stand up and pray in the meeting-places and on the street corners. They do this just to look good. I can assure you that they already have their reward.

'When you pray, go into a room alone and close the door. Pray to your Father in private. He knows what is done in private, and he will reward you.

'When you pray, don't talk on and on as people do who don't know God. They think God likes to hear long prayers. Don't be like them. Your Father knows what you need before you ask.

'You should pray like this:

*'Our Father in heaven,*
*help us to honour*
  *your name.*
*Come and set up*
  *your kingdom,*
*so that everyone on earth*
  *will obey you,*
*as you are obeyed*
  *in heaven.*
*Give us our food for today.*
*Forgive us for doing wrong,*
  *as we forgive others.*
*Keep us from being tempted*
  *and protect us from evil.*

'If you forgive others for the wrongs they do to you, your Father in heaven will forgive you. But if you don't forgive others, your Father will not forgive your sins.'

From Matthew 6

# The unexpected presence of God

*Jacob, Isaac's and Rebekah's son, had run away from home, afraid that his twin brother Esau might kill him; he had pretended to be Esau and tricked his half-blind father into giving him the eldest son's blessing. Championed only by his mother, he set out for his mother's home and family:*

Jacob left the town of Beersheba and set out for Haran. At sunset he stopped for the night and went to sleep, resting his head on a large rock. In a dream he saw a ladder that reached from earth to heaven, and God's angels were going up and down on it.

The Lord was standing beside the ladder and said:

I am the Lord God who was worshipped by Abraham and Isaac. I will give to you and your family the land on which you are now sleeping. Your descendants will spread over the earth in all directions and become as numerous as the specks of dust. Your family will be a blessing to all people. Wherever you go, I will watch over you, then later I will bring you back to this land. I won't leave you – I will do all I have promised.

Jacob woke up suddenly and thought, 'The Lord is in this place, and I didn't even know it. Then Jacob became frightened and said, 'This is a fearsome place! It must be the house of God and the ladder to heaven.'

When Jacob got up early the next morning, he took the rock that he had used for a pillow and stood it up for a place of worship. Then he poured olive oil over the rock to dedicate it to God, and he named the place Bethel.

From Genesis 28

William Law (1686–1761)

# *The practice of prayer*

I take it for granted that every Christian who is in good health is up early in the morning. It is much more reasonable to suppose a person is up early because he is a Christian, than because he is a labourer, or tradesman, or businessman or whatever. We naturally think it bad for a man to be in bed when he should be at his work. We could not imagine what to think of a person who is a slave to sleep so that he neglects his business affairs.

It teaches us then how bad we must appear in God's sight, if we are in bed, shut up in sleep and darkness, when we should be up and alert, praising God! How bad to be such slaves to sleep as to neglect our devotions because of it...

The first thing that you are to do when you are on your knees is to shut your eyes, and with a short silence let your soul place itself in the presence of God; that is, you are to use this, or some other better method, to separate yourself from all ordinary thoughts, and as much as you can make your heart aware of the divine presence.

Then if this recollection of spirit is necessary (and who can say it isn't?), then how paltry must be the devotions of those who are always in a hurry... Theirs is truly a matter of saying prayers rather than of praying.

If possible, you should always pray in a little room or part of a room and reserve that place for devotion. Do not allow yourself to do anything ordinary in it, never being there except in times of devotion. This kind of consecration of it as a place holy to God, will have an effect upon your mind. It will dispose you towards such attitudes which will greatly assist your devotion...

When you begin your petitions, use many varied expressions of the attributes of God which may make you most aware of the greatness and power of the divine nature... For these descriptions of the divine attributes, which show us in some degree the majesty and greatness of God, are an excellent way to raise our hearts in to lively acts of worship and adoration...

Although prayer does not consist in fine words or studied expressions, yet words speak to the soul and they have a certain power to lift up thoughts in the soul. Those words which speak of God in the highest way, which most fully express his power and presence, which raise thoughts in the soul most suitable to the greatness and providence of God, are the most useful and edifying in our prayers.

From *A Serious Call to a Devout and Holy Life*, 1729

**John Donne (1572–1631)**

## *Distractions at prayer*

When we consider with a religious seriousness the manifold weaknesses of the strongest devotions in time of prayer, it is a sad consideration. I throw myself down in my chamber, and I call in, and invite God, and his angels thither, and when they are there, I neglect God and his angels, for the noise of a fly, for the rattling of a coach, for the whining of a door; I talk on, in the same posture of praying; eyes lifted up; knees bowed down; as though I prayed to God; and, if God, or his angels should ask me, when I thought last of God in that prayer, I cannot tell: sometimes I find that I had forgot what I was about, but when I began to forget it, I cannot tell. A memory of yesterday's pleasures, a fear of tomorrow's dangers, a straw under my knee, a noise in mine ear, a light in mine eye, an any thing, a nothing, a fancy, a chimera in my brain, troubles me in my prayer. So certainly is there nothing, nothing in spiritual things, perfect in this world.

Preached at the funeral of Sir William Cockayne,
Knight, Alderman of London, 12 December 1626

Leo Tolstoy (1828–1910)

# Grisha at prayer

*'The idiot Grisha', as he was known, sometimes visited the Tolstoy estate, on his barefoot travels. Some thought him a saint, the outcast son of rich parents, others an idle peasant. When the children heard that Grisha wore heavy chains under his clothes, they determined to see them, and crowded into the store-room overlooking the servant's room where Grisha was to stay the night.*

We all felt a little uneasy in the thick darkness, so we pressed close to one another and said nothing. Before long Grisha arrived with his soft tread, carrying in one hand his staff and in the other a tallow candle set in a brass candlestick. We scarcely ventured to breathe.

'Our Lord Jesus Christ! Holy Mother of God! Father, Son and Holy Ghost!' he kept repeating...

Still praying, he placed his staff in a corner and looked at the bed; after which he began to undress. Unfastening his old black girdle, he slowly divested himself of his torn nankeen *kaftan*, and deposited it carefully on the back of a chair. His face had now lost its usual disquietude and idiocy. On the contrary, it had in it something restful, thoughtful, and even grand, while all his movements were deliberate and intelligent.

Next, he lay down quietly in his shirt on the bed, made the sign of the cross towards every side of him, and adjusted his chains beneath his shirt – an operation which, as we could see from his face, occasioned him considerable pain. Then he sat up again, looked gravely at his ragged shirt, and rising and taking the candle, lifted the latter towards the shrine where the images of the saints stood. That done, he made the sign of the cross again, and turned the candle upside down, when it went out with a hissing noise.

Through the window (which overlooked the wood) the moon (nearly full) was shining in such a way that one side of the tall white figure of the idiot stood out in the pale, silvery moonlight, while the other side was lost in the dark shadow which covered the floor, walls and ceiling. In the courtyard the watchman was tapping at intervals upon his brass alarm plate. For a while Grisha stood silently before the images and, with his large hands pressed to his breast and his head bent forward, gave occasional sighs. Then with difficulty he knelt down and began to pray...

Though disconnected, his prayers were very touching. He prayed for all his benefactors (so he called everyone who had received him hospitably) with, among them, Mama and ourselves. Next he prayed for himself, and besought God to forgive him his sins, at the same time repeating, 'God forgive also my enemies!' Then, moaning with the effort, he rose from his knees – only to fall to the floor again and to repeat his phrases afresh. At last he regained his feet, despite the weight of the chains, which rattled loudly whenever they struck the floor... Instead of the laughter and amusement which I had expected on entering the store-room, I felt my heart beating and overcome.

Grisha continued for some time in this state of religious ecstasy as he improvised prayers and repeated again and yet again, 'Lord, have mercy upon me!' Each time that he said, 'Pardon me, Lord, and teach me to do what thou wouldst have done,' he pronounced the words with added earnestness and emphasis... In the moonlight I could see a tear glistening on the white patch of his blind eye.

'Yes, thy will be done!' he exclaimed suddenly, with an expression which I cannot describe, as, prostrating himself with his forehead on the floor, he fell to sobbing like a child.

Much sand has run out since then, many recollections of the past have faded from my memory or become blurred in indistinct visions, and poor Grisha himself has long since reached the end of his pilgrimage; but the impression which he produced upon me, and the feelings which he aroused in my breast, will never leave my mind. O truly Christian Grisha, your faith was so strong that you could feel the actual presence of God; your love so great that the words fell of themselves from your lips...

Nevertheless, the sense of awe with which I had listened to Grisha could not last for ever. I had now satisfied my curiosity, and, being cramped with sitting in one position so long, desired to join in the tittering and fun going on in the dark store-room behind me... Grisha lifted his head, looked quietly about him, and, muttering a prayer, rose and made the sign of the cross towards each of the four corners of the room.

From *Childhood, Boyhood and Youth*, 1852, 1854, 1857

## Teresa of Avila (1515–82)

# A garden of prayer

In order to make great advance in prayer... we must remember that the business of prayer does not consist in *thinking much* but in *loving much*. Do therefore whatever may excite you most to love.

Perhaps we do not know what love is. I do not wonder at this, for it consists not in having greater delights, but in having greater resolutions and desires to please God in everything and in endeavouring not to offend him. It lies in beseeching him that he would promote the honour and glory of his Son and extend the bounds of the church universal...

A beginner in prayer must look upon himself as making a garden. There our Lord may take his delight, but in a soil that is unfruitful and full of weeds. His Majesty roots up the weeds to replace them with good plants. Let us take for granted that this is already done when a soul is determined to give itself to prayer and has begun the practice of it.

As good gardeners, we have by the help of God to see that the plants grow. We should water them carefully so that they will not die but rather produce blossoms. These will send forth much fragrance which is so refreshing to our Lord that he may come often for his delight into this garden and take pleasure himself in the midst of these virtues.

*Teresa describes four kinds of prayer, compared to four different ways of watering the garden.*

# The prayer of quietness

What the soul must do during these seasons of quiet amounts to no more that proceeding gently and noiselessly in prayer. What I mean by noise is running about with the intellect, looking for many words and meanings so as to give thanks for this gift, and piling up one's sins and faults in order to see that the gift is unmerited. Everything is in motion and rush. The intellect is thinking hard and the memory is hurrying about in the past...

Therefore, in such times of quietude, let the soul remain in its repose. Put aside learning. The time will come when learning will be useful for the Lord. It should be esteemed so that it is not abandoned for any treasure, but it should be used only to serve his Majesty. This alone is helpful.

Believe me, in the presence of infinite Wisdom, a little study of humility and one act of humility is worth all the knowledge of the world. For here there is no demand for reasoning, but simply for knowing what we are and that we are humbly in God's presence.

From *The Way of Perfection*, 1565–66

Alexander Solzhenitsyn (b. 1918)

# The right kind of prayer

One Day in the Life of Ivan Denisovich (*first published in 1962 in the literary magazine* Novy Mir), *describes a day in a Siberian labour camp under Stalin. Prisoners faced a brutal regime, bitter cold, hard labour and shortage of food, as well as the senseless rules and red tape that made the prisoners' lives unbelievably hard. As the day ended Shukhov climbs into his bunk across the way from Alyosha, a Baptist Christian:*

Head on the pillow, studded with shavings of wood: feet in jacket sleeve; coat on top of blanket and – Glory be to Thee, O Lord. Another day over. Thank you I'm not spending tonight in the cells. Here it's still bearable.

He lay head to the window, but Alyosha, who slept next to him on the same level, across a low wooden railing, lay the opposite way, to catch the light. He was reading his Bible again.

Alyosha heard Shukhov's whispered prayer, and turning to him:

'There you are, Ivan Denisovich, your soul is begging to pray. Why, then, don't you give it its freedom?'

Shukhov stole a look at him. Alyosha's eyes glowed like two candles.

'Well, Alyosha,' he said with a sigh, 'it's this way. Prayers are like those appeals of ours. Either they don't get through or they're returned with "rejected" scrawled across 'em.'

Outside the staff-hut were four sealed boxes – they were cleared by a security officer once a month. Many were the appeals that were dropped into them. The writers waited, counting the weeks: there'll be a reply in two months, in one month...

But the reply doesn't come. Or if it does it's only 'rejected'.

'But Ivan Denisovich, it's because you pray too rarely, and badly at that. Without really trying. That's why your prayers stay unanswered. One must never stop praying. If you have real faith you tell a mountain to move and it will move...'

Shukhov grinned and rolled another cigarette...

'Don't talk bunkum, Alyosha. I've never seen a mountain move. Well, to tell the truth, I've never seen a mountain. But you, now, you prayed in the Caucasus with all that Baptist club of yours – did you make a single mountain move?'...

'Oh, we didn't pray for that, Ivan Denisovich,' Alyosha said earnestly. Bible in hand, he drew nearer to Shukhov till they lay face to face. 'Of all earthly and mortal things Our Lord commanded us to pray only for our daily bread.'...

'Our ration, you mean?' asked Shukhov.

But Alyosha didn't give up. Arguing more with his eyes than his tongue, he plucked at Shukhov's sleeve, stroked his arm, and said:

'Ivan Denisovich, you shouldn't pray to get parcels or for extra skilly, not for that. Things that man puts a high price on are vile in the eyes of Our Lord. We must pray about things of the spirit – that the Lord Jesus should remove the scum of anger from our hearts.'

From *One Day in the Life of Ivan Denisovich*, 1962

## Maya Angelou (Marguerite Johnson) (b. 1928)

# *A morning prayer*

*Maya Angelou describes her early life, when she and her brother were brought up by their grandmother, who kept a store in the American South:*

Each year I watched the field across from the Store turn caterpillar green, then gradually frosty white. I knew exactly how long it would be before the big wagons would pull into the front yard and load on the cotton pickers at daybreak to carry them to the remains of slavery's plantations.

During the picking season my grandmother would get out of bed at four o'clock (she never used an alarm clock) and creak down to her knees and chant in a sleep-filled voice, 'Our Father, thank you for letting me see this New Day. Thank you that you didn't allow the bed I lay on last night to be my cooling board, nor my blanket my winding-sheet. Guide my feet this day along the straight and narrow, and help me to put a bridle on my tongue. Bless this house, and everybody in it. Thank you, in the name of your Son, Jesus Christ, Amen.'

Before she had quite arisen, she called our names and issued orders, and pushed her large feet into homemade slippers and across the bare lye-washed wooden floor to light the coal-oil lamp.

From *I Know Why the Caged Bird Sings*, 1969

## Teresa of Avila (1515–82)

# *God's presence of love*

Our Lord was pleased that I should have at times a vision of this kind: I saw an angel close by me, on my left side, in bodily form. This I am not accustomed to see, unless very rarely. Though I have visions of angels frequently, yet I see them only by intellectual vision, such as I have spoken of before. It was our Lord's will that in this vision I should see the angel in this wise. He was not large, but small of stature, and most beautiful – his face burning as if he were one of the higher angels, who seem to be all of fire: they must be those whom we call Cherubim. Their names they never tell me: but I see very well that there is in heaven so great a difference between one angel and another, and between these and the others, that I cannot explain it.

I saw in his hand a long spear of gold, and at the iron's point there seemed to be a little fire. He appeared to me to be thrusting it at times into my heart, and to pierce my very entrails; when he drew it out, he seemed to draw them out also, and to leave me all on fire with a great love of God. The pain was so great, that it made me moan; and yet so surpassing was the sweetness of this excessive pain, that I could not wish to be rid of it. The soul is satisfied now with nothing less than God. The pain is not bodily, but spiritual; though the body has its share in it, even a large one. It is a caressing of love so sweet which now takes place between the soul and God, that I pray God of his goodness to make him experience it who may think that I am lying.

From *Life of Saint Teresa of Avila*, 1565

**Margery Kempe (c. 1373–c. 1440)**

# Merry in heaven

*Margery Kempe was much given to visions and had the gift of tears – later to be a great annoyance to her fellow travellers on pilgrimage. In her autobiography, she refers to herself as 'this creature':*

One night, as this creature lay in bed with her husband, she heard a melodious sound so sweet and delectable that she thought she had been in paradise. And immediately she jumped out of bed and said, 'Alas that ever I sinned! It is full merry in heaven.' This melody was so sweet that it surpassed all the melody that might be heard in this world, without any comparison, and it caused this creature when she afterwards heard any mirth or melody to shed very plentiful and abundant tears of high devotion, with great sobbings and sighings for the bliss of heaven, not fearing the shames and contempt of this wretched world. And ever after her being drawn to God in this way, she kept in mind the joy and the melody that there was in heaven, so much so that she could not very well restrain herself from speaking of it. For when she was in company with any people she would often say, 'It is full merry in heaven!'

And those who knew of her behaviour previously and now heard her talk so much of the bliss of heaven said to her, 'Why do you talk so of the joy that is in heaven? You don't know it, and you haven't been there any more than we have.' And they were angry with her because she would not hear or talk of worldly things as they did, and as she did previously.

From *The Book of Margery Kempe*, 1420s

## Samuel Johnson (1709–84)

# 'The Lord is everywhere'

*James Boswell, friend and biographer of Dr Johnson, frequently visited London and told Johnson of his plan to worship in St Paul's Cathedral every Easter. Johnson wrote back:*

*March 1774*

... You must remember that your image of worshipping once a year in a certain place, in imitation of the Jews, is but a comparison; and *simile non est idem*; if the annual resort to Jerusalem was a duty to the Jews, it was a duty because it was commanded; and you have no such command, therefore no such duty. It may be dangerous to receive too readily, and indulge too fondly, opinions from which, perhaps, no pious mind is wholly disengaged, of local sanctity and local devotion. You know what strange effects they have produced over a great part of the Christian world. I am now writing, and you when you read this are reading, under the Eye of Omnipotence.

To what degree fancy is to be admitted into religious offices, it would require much deliberation to determine. I am far from intending totally to exclude it. Fancy is a faculty bestowed by our Creator, and it is reasonable that all his gifts should be used to his glory, that all our faculties should co-operate according to the will of him that gave them, according to the order which his wisdom has established... Fancy is always to act in subordination to Reason. We may take Fancy for a companion, but must follow Reason as our guide. We may allow Fancy to suggest certain ideas in certain places; but Reason must always be heard, when she tells us that those ideas and those places have no natural or necessary relation. When we enter a church we habitually recall to mind the duty of adoration, but we must not omit adoration for want of a temple; because we know, and ought to remember, that the universal Lord is everywhere present; and that, therefore, to come to Iona, or to Jerusalem, though it may be useful, cannot be necessary.

Thus I have answered your letter, and have not answered it negligently. I love you too well to be careless when you are serious...

Sam. Johnson

Letter from Johnson to Boswell, 1774

# DIVINE LOVE

## A parent's love

The Lord says,

'When Israel was a child, I loved him
    and called him out of Egypt as my son.
But the more I called to him,
    the more he turned away from me.
My people sacrificed to Baal;
    they burnt incense to idols.
Yet I was the one who taught Israel to walk.
I took my people up in my arms,
    but they did not acknowledge that I took care of them.
I drew them to me with affection and love.
    I picked them up and held them to my cheek;
    I bent down to them and fed them.

'They refuse to return to me, and so they must return to Egypt, and Assyria will rule them. War will sweep through their cities and break down the city gates... they insist on turning away from me...

'How can I give you up, Israel?
    How can I abandon you?
Could I ever destroy you as I did Admah,
    or treat you as I did Zeboiim?
My heart will not let me do it!
    My love for you is too strong.
I will not punish you in my anger;
    I will not destroy Israel again.
For I am God and not man.
    I, the Holy One, am with you.
I will not come to you in anger.'

From Hosea 11

# *God* is *love*

Beloved, let us love one another: for love is of God; and every one that loveth is born of God, and knoweth God. He that loveth not knoweth not God; for God is love. In this was manifested the love of God toward us, because that God sent his only begotten Son into the world, that we might live through him. Herein is love, not that we loved God, but that he loved us, and sent his Son to be the propitiation for our sins. Beloved, if God so loved us, we ought also to love one another.

From 1 John 4

## Julian of Norwich (c. 1342–after 1413)

# *The love of God*

He showed me more, a little thing, the size of a hazel-nut, on the palm of my hand, round like a ball. I looked at it thoughtfully and wondered, 'What is this?' And the answer came, 'It is all that is made.' I marvelled that it continued to exist and did not disintegrate; it was so small. And again my mind supplied the answer, 'It exists, both now and for ever, because God loves it.' In short, everything owes its existence to the love of God.

The love that God most high has for our soul is so great that it surpasses understanding.

No created being can comprehend how much, and how sweetly, and how tenderly our maker loves us.

As truly as God is our father, so just as truly is he our mother.

In our father God Almighty, we have our being; in our merciful mother we are remade and restored. Our fragmented lives are knit together and made perfect man. And by giving and yielding ourselves, through grace, to the Holy Spirit, we are made whole.

From *Revelations of Divine Love*, c. 1393

### William Langland (c. 1332–c. 1400)

# *Search for charity*

*The poet – Long Will – almost loses his reason after his first dream. Then he falls asleep again and meets a strange creature called Anima; from him the poet seeks answers to his questions.*

'What is charity?' I asked him then.

'A child-like thing,' he replied, 'for "unless you become as little children, you shall not enter into the kingdom of heaven". It is a frank and generous good-will, without folly or childishness.'

'But where can you find such an open-hearted friend?' I asked. 'I have lived all over the land, and men call me Long Will, but, search where I would, I have never yet found perfect charity... I have been told by the theologians that Christ is everywhere; yet I have never seen him in person – only his reflection in myself, as in a mirror... and from what I hear, I should think the same is true of charity. At any rate, I am sure of this, that he is not to be found in the tournaments of knights, or in the dealings of businessmen.'

'Charity never bargains,' said Anima, 'nor does he challenge his opponents or assert his rights. He is as proud of a penny as of a gold sovereign, and as pleased with a grey home spun coat, as with a tunic of Tartary silk or a finest scarlet. Charity rejoices with those who rejoice, returns good for evil and trusts and loves all whom our Lord created. He never curses and he bears no malice, and takes no delight in slander or making fun of others. For he trusts whatever men say and accepts it cheerfully, bearing patiently all manner of injuries. Nor does he covet any earthly goods, but seeks only the bliss of the kingdom of Heaven.'...

'O God! If only I knew him!' I cried. 'he is the one I seek above all others!'

'Unless Piers the Ploughman helps you,' he said, 'you will never see him truly, face to face... You will never recognize Charity by appearances, or by learning, or by words and actions – but only by knowing the heart. And no one on earth, not even a priest, can know that, but only Piers the Ploughman – *Peter, that is, Christ.*

From *Piers the Ploughman,* begun in 1362

### Simone Weil (1909–43)

# *Loving the right way?*

... I could not prevent myself from imagining him living, imagining his house as a possible place for me to listen to his delightful conversation. Thus the consciousness of the fact of his death made a frightful desert. Cold with metallic coldness. What did it matter to me that there were other people to love? The love that I directed towards him, together with the outlines shaping in my mind of exchanges of ideas which could take place with no one else, were without an object. Now I no longer imagine him alive and his death has ceased to be intolerable for me. The memory of him is sweet to me. But there are others that I did not know then and whose death would affect me in the same way.

D... is not dead, but the friendship that I bore him is dead, and a like sorrow goes with it. He is no more than a shadow.

But I cannot imagine the same transformation for X..., Y..., or Z..., who, nevertheless, so short a time ago did not exist in my consciousness.

Just as parents find it impossible to realise that three years ago their child was non-existent, I find it impossible to realise that I have not always known the beings I love.

I think I must love wrongly: otherwise things would not seem like this to me. My love would not be attached to a few beings. It would be extended to everything that is worthy of love.

'Be ye perfect even as your Father who is in heaven...' Love in the same way as the sun gives light. Love has to be brought back to ourselves in order that it may be shed on all things. God alone loves all things and he, only, loves himself.

To love in God is far more difficult than we think.

From *Gravity and Grace*, 1947

**Isak Dinesen (Karen Blixen) (1885–1962)**

# *The grace of giving*

*In* Babette's Feast, *Babette, a brilliant French cook and refugee from revolutionary France, is taken in by two poor Norwegian ladies. They belong to a strict puritanical sect, founded by their dead father, the dean. They know nothing of Babette's history, only that she makes wonderful meals for them from the sparse ingredients their ascetic life-style permits. After twelve years Babette wins a lottery and asks permission to provide a meal for the two ladies and their friends, for the anniversary of the dean's birthday. She cooks a gourmet meal, as served in the famous French restaurant where she cooked, but it is recognised only by General Loewenhielm, who had dined there years before.*

The talk round the table had turned to the smaller miracles of kindliness and helpfulness daily performed by [the Dean's] daughters. The old Brother who had first struck up the hymn quoted the Dean's saying: 'The only things which we may take with us from our life on earth are those which we have given away.'…

Then the General felt that the time had come to make a speech. He rose and stood up very straight…

'Mercy and truth, my friends, have met together,' said the General. 'Righteousness and bliss shall kiss one another…

'We have all of us been told that grace is to be found in the universe. But in our human foolishness and short-sightedness we imagine divine grace to be finite. For this reason we tremble…' Never till now had the General stated that he trembled; he was genuinely surprised and even shocked to hear his own voice proclaim the fact. 'We tremble before making our choice in life, and after having made it again tremble in fear of having chosen wrong. But the moment comes when our eyes are opened, and we see and realize that grace is infinite. Grace, my friends, demands nothing from us but that we shall await it with confidence and acknowledge it in gratitude. Grace, brothers, makes no conditions and singles out none of us in particular; grace takes us all to its bosom and proclaims general amnesty. See! that which we have chosen is given us, and that which we have refused is, also and at the same time, granted us. Ay, that which we have rejected is poured upon us abundantly. For mercy and truth have met together, and righteousness and bliss have kissed one another!'

The Brothers and Sisters had not altogether understood the General's speech, but his collected and inspired face and the sound of well-known and cherished words had seized and moved all hearts...

Of what happened later in the evening nothing definite can be stated. None of the guests later on had any clear remembrance of it. They only knew that the room had been filled with a heavenly light, as if a number of small halos had blended into one glorious radiance... Time itself had merged into eternity. Long after midnight the windows of the house shone like gold, and golden light flowed out into the winter air...

The old Dean's flock were humble people. When later in life they thought of this evening it never occurred to any of them that they might have been exalted by their own merit. They realized that the infinite grace of which General Loewenhielm had spoken had been allotted to them, and they did not even wonder at the fact, for it had been but the fulfilment of an ever-present hope. The vain illusions of this earth had dissolved before their eyes like smoke, and they had seen the universe as it really is. They had been given one hour of the millennium.

From 'Babette's Feast', *Anecdotes of Destiny*, 1958

**The Cloud of Unknowing (fourteenth century)**

# Longing love

*Although the identity of the author is unknown, internal evidence suggests that he was a priest, a contemplative and spiritual director, who had retired from a monastery and become a hermit:*

So, therefore, never give up your resolve, but beat away at this cloud of unknowing between you and God with that sharp dart of longing love. Dislike intensely all thoughts other than those of God himself. Let nothing put you off. It is the only way that you can destroy the very ground and root of sin. No amount of fasting, keeping watch, early rising, sleeping on bare boards, or self-flagellation, is of any use...

What else? Were you to weep sorrowful buckets over your sin, or Christ's suffering, or if you were to ponder limitlessly the joys of heaven, what good would it do? Surely a great deal of benefit would come to you and you would receive much grace. But in comparison with this blind stirring of love within you, there is little all those things can do for you. Love alone is the best part and it is the part Mary chose. Without it all else is useless. Not only does it succeed in destroying sin's roots, its very essence, but it produces virtue. If this love is truly present in you, then you will also know perfect and true goodness, without any mixed motives. A man may have as many virtues as he pleases but without this love they will all be tainted, imperfect.

For virtue is no more than an ordered, deliberate love clearly directed towards God for his own sake. And God is himself the pure cause of all virtue. In fact, should anyone be motivated to seek virtue for mixed reasons, even if the chief one were God, then that renders the virtue imperfect. This can be seen from the examples of the two virtues of love and humility. Anyone possessing these has everything: he needs no more.

From *The Cloud of Unknowing: A New Paraphrase*, edited by Halcyon Backhouse, 1985

Graham Greene (1904–91)

# *Justice and love*

*The little 'whisky priest' – proscribed like all priests under the communist regime of a South American state – has finally been caught. He has broken his priest's vows yet cannot find it in his heart to repent. The lieutenant who captured him, guards him through the night before they return to the police station.*

'You're a man of education,' the lieutenant said. He lay across the entrance of the hut with his head on his rolled cape and his revolver by his side. It was night, but neither man could sleep. The priest, when he shifted, groaned a little with stiffness and cramp; the lieutenant was in a hurry to get home, and they had ridden till midnight. They were down off the hills and in the marshy plain. Soon the whole State would be subdivided by swamp. The rains had really begun.

'I'm not that. My father was a storekeeper.'

'I mean, you've been abroad. You can talk like a Yankee. You've had schooling.'

'Yes.'

'I've had to think things out for myself. But there are some things you don't have to learn in a school. That there are rich and poor.' He said in a low voice, 'I've shot three hostages because of you. Poor men. It made me hate you.'

'Yes,' the priest admitted, and tried to stand to ease the cramp in his right thigh. The lieutenant sat up quickly, gun in hand: 'What are you doing?'

'Nothing. Just cramp. That's all.' He lay down again with a groan.

The lieutenant said, 'Those men I shot. They were my own people. I wanted to give them the whole world.'

'Well, who knows? Perhaps that's what you did.'

The lieutenant spat suddenly, viciously, as if something unclean had got upon his tongue. He said, 'You always have answers that mean nothing.'

'I was never any good at books,' the priest said. 'I haven't any memory. But there was one thing always puzzled me about men like yourself. You hate the rich and love the poor. Isn't that right?'

'Yes.'...

'We've always said the poor are blessed and the rich are going to find it hard to get to heaven. Why should we make it hard for the poor man too? Oh, I know we are told to give to the poor, to see they are not hungry – hunger can make a man do evil just as much as money can. But why should we give the poor power? It's better to let him die in dirt and wake in heaven – so long as we don't push his face in the dirt.'

'I hate your reasons,' the lieutenant said, 'I don't want reasons... I want to let my heart speak.'

'At the end of a gun.'

'Yes. At the end of a gun.'

'Oh well, perhaps when you're my age you'll know that the heart's an untrustworthy beast. The mind is too, but it doesn't talk about love. Love. And a girl puts her head under water or a child's strangled, and the heart all the time says love, love.'

They lay quiet for a while in the hut. The priest thought the lieutenant was asleep until he spoke again. 'You never talk straight. You say one thing to me – but to another man, or a woman, you say, "God is love." But you think that stuff won't go down with me, so you say different things. Things you think I'll agree with.'

'Oh,' the priest said, 'that's another thing altogether – God *is* love. I don't say the heart doesn't feel a taste of it, but what a taste. The smallest glass of love mixed with a pint of ditch-water. We wouldn't recognise *that* love. It might even look like hate. It would be enough to scare us – God's love. It set fire to a bush in the desert, didn't it, and smashed open graves and set the dead walking in the dark. Oh, a man like me would run a mile to get away if he felt that love around.'

'You don't trust him much, do you? He doesn't seem a grateful kind of God. If a man served me as well as you've served him, well, I'd recommend him for promotion, see he got a good pension... if he was in pain, with cancer, I'd put a bullet through his head.'

'Listen,' the priest said earnestly, leaning forward in the dark, pressing on a cramped foot, 'I'm not as dishonest as you think I am. Why do you think I tell people out of the pulpit that they're in danger of damnation if death catches them unawares? I'm not telling them fairy stories I don't believe myself. I don't know a thing about the mercy of God: I don't know how awful the human heart looks to him. But I do know this – that if there's ever been a single man in this state damned, then I'll be damned too. I wouldn't want it to be any different. I just want justice, that's all.'

From *The Power and the Glory*, 1940

# LAST THINGS

## Jesus is coming back

*In the days of the early Church, Christians believed that Jesus'*
*promise to return to earth would be fulfilled very soon – in their*
*own lifetime:*

In the last days cynical mockers will undoubtedly come – men whose only guide in life is what they want for themselves – and they will say, 'Where is his promised coming? Since our fathers fell asleep, everything remains exactly as it was since the beginning of creation!'...

But you should never lose sight of this fact, dear friends, that with the Lord a day may be a thousand years, and a thousand years only a day. It is not that he is dilatory about keeping his own promise as some men seem to think; the fact is that he is very patient with you. He has no wish that any man should be destroyed; he wishes that all men should find the way to repentance. Yet the day of the Lord will come as unexpectedly as a thief. In that day the heavens will vanish in a tearing blast, the very elements will disintegrate in heat and the earth and all its works will disappear.

In view of the fact that all these things are to be dissolved, what sort of people ought you to be? Surely men of good and holy character, who live expecting and working for the coming of the day of God. This day will mean that the heavens will disintegrate in fire and the burning elements will melt, but our hopes are set on new heavens and a new earth which he has promised us, in which justice will make its home.

From 2 Peter 3

# The future is bright

*When John was exiled for his faith, on the Island of Patmos
(perhaps quarrying stone), he had a vision of Jesus Christ which
gave him, and the persecuted Christians to whom he wrote,
courage to endure suffering. It confirmed to them that God is
still in control and that they would eventually be vindicated and
enjoy for ever the presence of their Lord.*

Then the angel showed me the river of the water of life, bright as crystal,
flowing from the throne of God and of the Lamb through the middle of
the street of the city. On either side of the river, is the tree of life with its
twelve kinds of fruit, producing its fruit each month; and the leaves of the
tree are for the healing of the nations. Nothing accursed will be found
there any more. But the throne of God and of the Lamb will be in it, and
his servants will worship him; they will see his face, and his name will be
on their foreheads. And there will be no more night; they need no light of
lamp or sun, for the Lord God will be their light, and they will reign for
ever and ever...

'See, I am coming soon; my reward is with me, to repay according to
everyone's work. I am the Alpha and the Omega, the first and the last, the
beginning and the end...

'It is I, Jesus, who sent my angel to you with this testimony for the
churches. I am the root and the descendant of David, the bright morning
star.'

The Spirit and the bride say, 'Come.'

And let everyone who hears say, 'Come.'

And let everyone who is thirsty come.

Let anyone who wishes take the water of life as a gift.'...

The one who testifies to these things says, 'Surely I am coming soon.'

Amen. Come, Lord Jesus!

From Revelation 22

John Donne (1572–1631)

# *Heaven*

Heaven is Glory, and heaven is Joy; we cannot tell which most; we cannot separate them; and this comfort is joy in the Holy Ghost. This makes all Job's states alike; as rich in the first chapter of his book, where all is suddenly lost, as in the last, where all is abundantly restored. This consolation from the Holy Ghost makes my midnight noon, mine executioner a physician, a stake and pile of faggots a bonfire of triumph. This consolation makes a satire and slander and libel against me a panegyric and an eulogy in my praise. It makes a *tolle* an *ave*... It makes my death-bed a marriage-bed and my passing-bell an epithalamium.

From 'Sermon XXXVI' preached at St Paul's
Cathedral, London, Whitsunday, 1625

# *The Day of Judgement*

*It is a fearful thing to fall into the hands of the living God*, if I do but fall into his hands in a fever in my bed, or in a tempest at sea, or in a discontent at home. But, to fall into the hands of the living God so as that, that living God enters into judgement with me, and passes a final and irrevocable judgement upon me, this is a consternation of all my spirits, an extermination of all my succours... I consider that I may be surprised by that day, the day of Judgement... And, as the Judgement itself, so the Judge himself says of himself, *I will come upon thee as a thief*. He says he will, and he does it. For it is not *Ecce veniam*, but *Ecce venio, Behold I do come upon thee as a thief*; there, the *future*, which might imply a dilatoriness, is reduced to an infallible *present*; it is so sure that he *will* do it that he is said to *have* done it already. I consider, *he will come as a thief*, and then, *as a thief in the night*. And I do not only not know *when* that night shall be (for himself, as he is the Son of man, knows not that), but I do not only not know *what* night, that is, *which* night, but not *what* night, that is, what kind of night he means. It is said so often, so often repeated, that *he will come as a thief in the night*, as that he may mean all kind of *nights*.

In my night of *Ignorance* he may come; and he may come in my night of *Wantonness*; in my night of inordinate and sinful *melancholy*, and *suspicion* of his *mercy*, he may come…

*Behold, he cometh with clouds, and every eye shall see him*; and, *plangent omnes, All the kindreds of the earth shall wail and lament*, and weep and howl *because of him*. I consider that I shall look upon him then, and see all my *Sins, Substance*, and *Circumstance* of sin, *Weight* and measure of sin, *heinousness*, and *continuance* of sin, all my sins imprinted in his wounds; and how shall I be affected then, confounded then to see him so mangled with my sins? But then I consider again, that I shall look upon him again, and not see all my sins in his wounds; My *forgotten* sins, mine *unconsidered, unconfessed, unrepented* sins, I shall not see there; and how shall I be affected then, when I shall stand in *Judgement*, under the guiltiness of some sins, not buried in the wounds, not drowned in the blood of my Saviour? *Many*, and *many*, and *very many, infinite* and *infinitely infinite*, are the *terrors* of that day.

From 'A Sermon of Commemoration of the
Lady Danvers, Late Wife of Sir John Danvers', 1627

## C.S. Lewis (1898–1963)

# *Heaven and hell*

It is objected that the ultimate loss of a single soul means the defeat of omnipotence. And so it does. In creating beings with free will, omnipotence from the outset submits to the possibility of such defeat. What you call defeat, I call miracle: for to make things which are not Itself, and thus to become, in a sense, capable of being resisted by its own handiwork, is the most astonishing and unimaginable feat we attribute to the Deity. I willingly believe that the damned are, in one sense, successful, rebels to the end; that the doors of hell are locked on the *inside*. I do not mean that the ghosts may not *wish* to come out of hell, in the vague sense in which an envious man 'wishes' to be happy: but they certainly do not will even the first preliminary stages of that self-abandonment through which alone the soul can reach any good. They enjoy for ever the horrible freedom they have demanded, and are therefore self-enslaved: just as the blessed, forever submitting to obedience, become more and more free.

In the long run the answer to all those who object to the doctrine of hell, is itself a question: 'What are you asking God to do?' to wipe out their past sins and, at all costs, to give them a fresh start, smoothing every difficulty and offering every miraculous help? But he has done so, on Calvary. To forgive them? They will not be forgiven. To leave them alone? Alas, I am afraid that is what he does...

In all discussions of Hell we should keep steadily before our eyes the possible damnation, not of our enemies nor our friends (since both these disturb the reason) but of ourselves. This chapter is not about your wife or son, nor about Nero or Judas Iscariot; it is about you and me.

From *The Problem of Pain*, 1940

## John Bunyan (1628-88)

# *The gates of heaven and hell*

Now I saw in my dream that these two men [Christian and Hopeful] went in at the Gate; and lo, as they entered they were transfigured, and they had raiment put on that shone like gold. There were also that met them with harps and crowns, and gave them to them, the harps to praise withal, and the crowns in token of honour. Then I heard in my dream, that all the bells in the City rang again for joy; and that it was said unto them, *'Enter ye into the joy of your Lord.'* I also heard the men themselves, that they sang with a loud voice, saying, *'Blessing, honour, glory and power, be to him that sitteth upon the throne, and to the Lamb for ever and ever.'*

Now just as the Gates were opened to let in the men, I looked in after them; and behold, the City shone like the sun, the streets also were paved with gold...

Now while I was gazing upon these things, I turned my head to look back and Ignorance was coming... so he, as the other I saw, did ascend the hill to come up to the Gate, only he came alone, neither did any man meet him with the least encouragement. When he was come up to the Gate, he... began to knock, supposing that entrance should have been quickly administered to him. But he was asked by the men who looked over the top of the Gate, 'Whence came you, and what would you have?' He answered, 'I have ate and drank in the presence of the King, and he has taught in our streets.' Then they asked for his certificate, that they might go in and show it to the King. So he fumbled in his bosom for one and found none. Then said they, 'Have you none?' But the man answered never a word. So they told the King, but he would not come down to see him; but commanded the two Shining Ones that conducted Christian and Hopeful to the City to go out and take Ignorance and bind him hand and foot, and have him away. Then they took him up, and carried him through the air to the door that I saw in the side of the hill, and put him in there. Then I saw that there was a way to Hell, even from the Gates of Heaven.

From *Pilgrim's Progress*, part 1, 1678

### The Brothers Grimm: Jacob Ludwig Carl Grimm (1785–1863) and Wilhelm Carl Grimm (1786–1859)

# At the pearly gates

Once upon a time a poor pious peasant died, and arrived before the gate of heaven. At the same time a very rich, rich lord came there who also wanted to get into heaven. Then Saint Peter came with the key, and opened the door, and let the great man in, but apparently did not see the peasant, and shut the door again. And now the peasant outside heard how the great man was received in heaven with all kinds of rejoicing, and how they were making music, and singing within. At length all became quiet again, and Saint Peter came and opened the gate of heaven, and let the peasant in. The peasant, however, expected that they would make music and sing when he went in also, but all remained quite quiet; he was received with great affection, it is true, and the angels came to meet him, but no one sang. Then the peasant asked Saint Peter how it was that they did not sing for him as they had done when the rich man went in, and said that it seemed to him that there in heaven things were done with just as much partiality as on earth. Then said Saint Peter: 'By no means, you are just as dear to us as anyone else, and will enjoy every heavenly delight that the rich man enjoys, but poor fellows like you come to heaven every day, but a rich man like that does not come more than once in a hundred years!'

'The Peasant in Heaven', *Grimm's Fairy Tales*, 1812, 1815, 1822

### Richard Baxter (1615–91)

# 'The saints' everlasting rest'

*The best known of Richard Baxter's books is* The Saints'
Everlasting Rest, *reaching twelve editions in his lifetime, in
spite of its length (some eight hundred thousand words). In
1754 John Wesley abridged it and it has exercised great
influence on centuries of Christian readers in many countries.
The 'Rest' of which Baxter tells us, 'chiefly intends' the 'Rest of
Eternal Glory':*

There is contained in this Rest, a cessation from motion or action; not of
all action, but of that which hath the nature of a means, and implies the
absence of the end. When we have obtained the haven, we have done
sailing; when the workman hath his wages, it is implied he hath done his
work; when we are at our journey's end, we have done with the way. All
motion ends at the centre, and all means cease when we have the way...

There shall be no more prayer, because no more necessity, but the
full enjoyment of what we prayed for... Neither shall we need to fast,
and weep, and watch any more, being out of the reach of sin and
temptations...

The Rest containeth a perfect freedom from all the evils that
accompanied us through our course, and which necessarily follow our
absence from the chief good... As God will not know the wicked so as to
own them; so neither will heaven know iniquity to receive it: for there
entereth nothing that defileth or is unclean; all that remains without. And
doubtless there is not such a thing as grief and sorrow known there. Nor
is there such a thing as a pale face, a languid body, feeble joints, unable
infancy, decrepit age, peccant humours, dolorous sickness, griping fears,
consuming cares nor whatsoever deserves the name of evil. Indeed a gale
of groans and sighs, a stream of tears accompanied us to the very gates,
and there bid us farewell, for ever. We did weep and lament when the
world did rejoice; but our sorrow is turned to joy, and our joy shall no man
take from us. God were not the chief and perfect good if full fruition of
him did not free us from all evil.

From *The Saints' Everlasting Rest*, 1650

# PART FOUR

# GOOD AND EVIL

# ANGELS AND DEVILS

## Angels

In the sixth month the angel Gabriel was sent by God to Nazareth, a town in Galilee, with a message for a girl betrothed to a man named Joseph, a descendant of David; the girl's name was Mary. The angel went in and said to her, 'Greetings, most favoured one! The Lord is with you.' But she was deeply troubled by what he said and wondered what this greeting could mean. Then the angel said to her, 'Do not be afraid, Mary, for God has been gracious to you; you will conceive and give birth to a son, and you are to give him the name Jesus. He will be great, and will be called Son of the Most High...'

'How can this be?' said Mary. 'I am still a virgin.' The angel answered, 'The Holy Spirit will come upon you, and the power of the Most High will overshadow you; for that reason the holy child to be born will be called Son of God...'

'I am the Lord's servant,' said Mary; 'may it be as you have said.' Then the angel left her.

From Luke 1

## The Devil

Be on your guard and stay awake. Your enemy, the devil, is like a roaring lion, prowling around to find someone to attack. But you must resist the devil and stay strong in your faith. You know that all over the world the Lord's followers are suffering just as you are. But God shows undeserved kindness to everyone... You will suffer for a while, but God will make you complete, steady, strong, and firm. God will be in control for ever!

From 1 Peter 5

## Beryl Bainbridge (b. 1934)

# *Devil or Angel?*

*Beryl Bainbridge tells the story of Scott's ill-fated expedition to the South Pole through the eyes – and consecutive accounts – of five members of the team. Dr Wilson – a self-confessed Christian and an artist – tells of a startling vision he saw and later recounted to fellow officer 'Birdie' Bowers:*

Something happened to me on the morning of July 16th – the ninth anniversary of my wedding-day – which disturbs me. It was dawn, and I was standing on the crow's-nest... when suddenly my head was filled with pictures of my time at medical school... my experiences as a Sunday School teacher at the Caius Mission in Battersea...

I was seeing the mission-room in my mind's eye, those rows of shaven heads illuminated in a slant of sunlight writhing with dust, when, by some trick of the early light in the sky above me, the sea broke into a thousand glittering fragments, and in that heavenly dazzle I clearly saw a creature, half man, half bird, soaring above the waves.

The moment before I had been as warm as toast, and now I was so cold I shuddered, and in that shuddering blinked, and the creature was gone, though not before I had gazed down into those lidless eyes fixed on mine, observed where its powerful shoulders jutted into wings, followed the silver spray kicked up by its cruel talons as it skimmed the bright water. There was no doubt in my mind that the apparition was a harbinger of death, and yet, in the blaze of that terrible second a sensation akin to joy, something pitched between sexual arousal and fear bubbled up inside me. Still my body shook, and through chattering teeth I heard myself stuttering over and over, 'So cold... so cold... so cold.'

From *The Birthday Boys*, 1991

## John Bunyan (1628–88)

# *Battle with Apollyon*

But now in this Valley of Humiliation poor Christian was hard put to it, for he had gone but a little way before he espied a foul fiend coming over the field to meet him; his name is Apollyon. Then did Christian begin to be afraid, and to cast in his mind whether to go back, or to stand his ground. But he considered again that he had no armour for his back, and therefore... he resolved to venture, and stand his ground.

So he went on, and Apollyon met him; now the monster was hideous to behold, he was clothed with scales like a fish (and they are his pride); he had wings like a dragon, feet like a bear, and out of his belly came fire and smoke, and his mouth was as the mouth of a lion. When he was come up to Christian he beheld him with a disdainful countenance and thus began to question with him.

'Whence come you, and whither are you bound?'

'I come from the City of Destruction, which is the place of all evil, and am going to the City of Sion.'

'By this I perceive thou art one of my subjects, for all that country is mine; and I am the prince and god of it...'

'But I have let myself to another, even to the King of Princes, and how can I with fairness go back to thee?... and besides (O thou destroying Apollyon), to speak truth, I like his service, his wages, his servants, his government, his company, and country better than thine: and therefore leave off to persuade me further, I am his servant, and I will follow him.'...

Then Apollyon straddled quite over the whole breadth of the way, and said, 'I am void of fear in this matter, prepare thyself to die, for I swear by my infernal den that thou shalt go no further, here will I spill thy soul:' and with that he threw a flaming dart at his breast; but Christian had a shield in his hand, with which he caught it, and so prevented the danger of that. Then did Christian draw, for he saw 'twas time to bestir him; and Apollyon as fast made at him, throwing darts as thick as hail... This sore combat lasted for above half a day, even till Christian was almost quite spent. For you must know, that Christian, by reason of his wounds, must needs grow weaker and weaker.

Then Apollyon, espying his opportunity, began to gather up close to Christian, and wrestling with him, gave him a dreadful fall; and with that

Christian's sword flew out of his hand. Then said Apollyon, 'I am sure of thee now,' and with that he had almost pressed him to death, so that Christian began to despair of life. But as God would have it, while Apollyon was fetching of his last blow thereby to make a full end of this good man, Christian nimbly reached out his hand for his sword , and caught it, saying *'Rejoice not against me, O mine enemy! When I fall I shall arise,'* and with that gave him a deadly thrust, which made him give back as one that had received his mortal wound: Christian perceiving that, made at him again, saying, *'Nay, in all these things we are more than conquerors through him that loved us.'* And with that Apollyon spread forth his dragon's wings, and sped him away, that Christian saw him no more.

From *Pilgrim's Progress*, part 1, 1678

C.S. Lewis (1898–1963)

# A devil's view of God

*In* The Screwtape Letters *Lewis created the imagined letters to Wormwood – a novice devil – from his experienced uncle Screwtape. The older devil advises his nephew on the best ways to induce his 'patient' – now a Christian – to give up his faith or fail to practise it:*

My dear Wormwood,

So! Your man is in love... I have looked up this girl's dossier and am horrified at what I find. Not only a Christian but such a Christian – a vile, sneaking, simpering, demure, monosyllabic, mouse-like, watery, insignificant, virginal, bread-and-butter miss. The little brute. She makes me vomit... Looks as if butter wouldn't melt in her mouth and yet has a satirical wit... Filthy insipid little prude – and yet ready to fall into this booby's arms like any other breeding animal. Why doesn't the Enemy blast her for it, if He's so moonstruck by virginity – instead of looking on there, grinning?

He's a hedonist at heart. All those fasts and vigils and stakes and crosses are only a façade. Or only like foam on the sea shore. Out at sea, out in His sea, there is pleasure, and more pleasure. He makes no secret of it; at his right hand are 'pleasures for evermore'. Ugh! I don't think He has the least inkling of that high and austere mystery to which we rise in the Miserific Vision. He's vulgar, Wormwood. He has a bourgeois mind. He has filled his world full of pleasures. There are things for humans to do all day long without his minding in the least – sleeping, washing, eating, drinking, making love, playing, praying, working. Everything has to be *twisted* before it's any use to us. We fight under cruel disadvantages. Nothing is naturally on our side...

Then, of course, he gets to know this woman's family and whole circle. Could you not see that the very house she lives in is one that he ought never to have entered? The whole place reeks of that deadly odour... It bears a sickening resemblance to the description one human writer made of Heaven; 'the regions where there is only life and therefore all that is not music is silence'.

Music and silence – how I detest them both! How thankful we should be that ever since our Father entered Hell... no square inch of infernal space and no moment of infernal time has been surrendered to either of those abominable forces, but all has been occupied by Noise – Noise... which alone defends us from silly qualms, despairing scruples and impossible desires. We will make the whole universe a noise... The melodies and silences of Heaven will be shouted down in the end.

From *The Screwtape Letters*, 1942

**Joseph Conrad (1857–1924)**

# *Warding off devils*

*In* Heart of Darkness Marlow, *a seafarer, recounts his journey
to take over as skipper of a river steam-boat, after the mysterious
death of its previous captain. He sailed hundreds of miles
upriver in a dark continent; finally the Swedish captain pointed
out the Company station and Marlow was set down:*

'A rocky cliff appeared, mounds of turned-up earth by the shore, houses
on a hill, others with iron roofs, amongst a waste of excavations... A
continuous noise of the rapids above hovered over this scene of inhabited
devastation. A lot of people, mostly black and naked, moved about like
ants. A jetty projected into the river. A blinding sunlight drowned all this
at times in a recrudescence of glare...

'I... found a path leading up the hill. It turned aside for the boulders,
and also for an undersized railway-truck lying there on its back with its
wheels in the air. One was off. The thing looked as dead as the carcass of
some animal. I came across more pieces of decaying machinery, a stack of
rusty nails. To the left a clump of trees made a shady spot, where dark
things seemed to stir feebly. I blinked, the path was steep. A horn tooted
to the right, and I saw the black people run. A heavy and dull detonation
shook the ground, a puff of smoke came out of the cliff, and that was all.
No change appeared on the face of the rock. They were building a railway.
The cliff was not in the way of anything; but this objectless blasting was
all the work going on.

'A slight clinking behind me made me turn my head. Six black men
advanced in a file, toiling up the path. They walked erect and slow,
balancing small baskets full of earth on their heads, and the clink kept
time with their footsteps. Black rags were wound round their loins, and
the short ends behind waggled to and fro like tails. I could see every rib,
the joints of their limbs were like knots in a rope; each had an iron collar
on his neck, all were connected together with a chain whose bights swung
between them, rhythmically clinking... All their meagre breasts panted
together, the violently dilated nostrils quivered, the eyes stared stonily
uphill. They passed me within six inches, without a glance, with...
complete, deathlike indifference... Behind this raw matter, one of the

reclaimed, the product of the new forces at work, strolled despondently, carrying a rifle by its middle. He had a uniform jacket with one button off, and seeing a white man on the path, hoisted his weapon to his shoulder with alacrity. This was simple prudence, white men being so alike at a distance that he could not tell who I might be...

'Instead of going up, I turned and descended to the left. My idea was to let that chain-gang get out of sight before I climbed the hill. You know I am not particularly tender; I've had to strike and to fend off. I've had to resist and to attack sometimes – that's only one way of resisting – without counting the exact cost, according to the demands of such sort of life as I had blundered into. I've seen the devil of violence, and the devil of greed, and the devil of hot desire; but, by all the stars! These were strong, lusty, red-eyed devils, that swayed and drove men – men, I tell you. But as I stood on the hillside, I foresaw that in the blinding sunshine of that land I would become acquainted with a flabby, pretending, weak-eyed devil of a rapacious and pitiless folly. How insidious he could be, too, I was only to find out several months later and a thousand miles farther. For a moment I stood appalled, as though by a warning. Finally I descended the hill, obliquely, towards the trees I had seen.'

From *Heart of Darkness*, 1902

## C.S. Lewis (1898–1963)

# *Lewis meets an angel*

Perelandra *was the second of Lewis's trilogy of space novels for adults.*

*The narrator has been summoned to the country cottage of his friend Ransom. His journey to the cottage is tense and fraught. As he enters the house, he stumbles in the darkness:*

I was just preparing to... hunt systematically round the room for a candle when I heard Ransom's name pronounced; and almost, but not quite, simultaneously I saw the thing I had feared so long to see... The sound was quite astonishingly unlike a voice. It was perfectly articulate: it was even, I suppose, rather beautiful. But it was, if you understand me, inorganic... Blood and lungs and the warm, moist cavity of the mouth are somehow indicated in every Voice. Here they were not. The two syllables sounded more as if they were played on an instrument than as if they were spoken: and yet they did not sound mechanical either... more as if rock or crystal or light had spoken of itself. And it went through me from chest to groin like the thrill that goes through you when you think you have lost your hold while climbing a cliff.

That was what I heard. What I saw was simply a very faint rod or pillar of light. I don't think it made a circle of light either on the floor or the ceiling, but I am not sure of this... But it had two other characteristics which are less easy to grasp. One was its colour. Since I saw the thing I must obviously have seen it white or coloured; but no efforts of my memory can conjure up the faintest image of what the colour was. I try blue, and gold, and violet, and red, but none of them will fit... The other was its angle. It was not at right angles to the floor... What one actually felt at the moment was that the column of light was vertical but the floor was not horizontal – the whole room seemed to have heeled over as if it were on board ship...

I had no doubt at all that I was seeing an eldil... and now that the thing had happened I was no longer in a condition of abject panic. My sensations were, it is true, in some ways very unpleasant... On the other hand, all those doubts which I had felt before I entered the cottage as to whether these creatures were friend or foe... had for the moment vanished. My fear was now of another kind. I felt sure that the creature was what we call 'good', but I wasn't sure whether I liked 'goodness' as much as I had supposed. This is a very terrible experience.

From *Perelandra* (later renamed *Voyage to Venus*), 1943

# GOODNESS AND STRIVINGS FOR GOODNESS

## Struggle and success

*The apostle Paul wrote about his own striving to be good.*

I know that good does not live in me – that is, in my human nature. For even though the desire to do good is in me, I am not able to do it. I don't do the good I want to do; instead, I do the evil that I do not want to do...

So I find that this law is at work: when I want to do what is good, what is evil is the only choice I have. My inner being delights in the law of God. But I see a different law at work in my body – a law that fights against the law which my mind approves of. It makes me a prisoner to the law of sin which is at work in my body. What an unhappy man I am! Who will rescue me from this body that is taking me to death? Thanks be to God, who does this through our Lord Jesus Christ!

From Romans 7

## The goodness God requires

'With what shall I come before the Lord, and bow myself before God on high? Shall I come before him with burnt-offerings, with calves a year old? Will the Lord be pleased with thousands of rams, with tens of thousands of rivers of oil? Shall I give my firstborn for my transgression, the fruit of my body for the sin of my soul?'

He has told you, O mortal, what is good; and what does the Lord require of you but to do justice, and to love kindness, and to walk humbly with your God?

From Micah 6

## Charles Lamb (1775–1834)

# Charity regretted

My good old aunt, who never parted from me at the end of a holiday without stuffing a sweetmeat, or some nice thing, into my pocket, had dismissed me one evening with a smoking plum-cake, fresh from the oven. In my way to school (it was over London Bridge) a grey-headed old beggar saluted me (I have no doubt at this time of day that he was a counterfeit). I had no pence to console him with, so in the vanity of self-denial, and the very coxcombry of charity, school-boy-like, I made him a present of – the whole cake! I walked on a little, buoyed up, as one is on such occasions, with a sweet soothing of self-satisfaction; but before I had got to the end of the bridge, my better feelings returned, and I burst into tears, thinking how ungrateful I had been to my good aunt, to go and give her good gift away to a stranger, that I had never seen before, and who might be a bad man, for aught I knew; and then I thought of the pleasure my aunt would be taking in thinking that I – I myself, and not another – would eat her nice cake – and what should I say to her the next time I saw her – how naughty I was to part with her pretty present – and the odour of that spicy cake came back upon my recollection, and the pleasure and the curiosity I had taken in seeing her make it, and her joy when she sent it to the oven, and how disappointed she would feel that I never had a bit of it in my mouth at last – and I blamed my impertinent spirit of alms-giving, and out-of-place hypocrisy of goodness, and above all I wished never to see the face again of that insidious, good-for-nothing, old grey impostor.

'Dissertation on Roast Pig', *Essays of Elia*, 1823, 1833

Samuel Butler (1835–1902)

# Black pudding

At... times, Christina would, to do her justice, have doubts whether she was in all respects as spiritually minded as she ought to be. She must press on, press on, till every enemy to her salvation was surmounted and Satan himself lay bruised under her feet. It occurred to her on one of these occasions that she might steal a march over some of her contemporaries if she were to leave off eating black puddings, of which whenever they had killed a pig she had hitherto partaken freely; and if she were also careful that no fowls were served at her table which had had their necks wrung, but only such as had had their throats cut and been allowed to bleed. St Paul and the Church of Jerusalem had insisted upon it as necessary that even Gentile converts should abstain from things strangled and from blood, and they had joined this prohibition with that of a vice about the abominable nature of which there could be no question; it would be well therefore to abstain in future and see whether any noteworthy spiritual result ensued. She did abstain, and was certain that from the day of her resolve she had felt stronger, purer in heart, and in all respects more spiritually minded than she had ever felt hitherto.

From *The Way of All Flesh*, 1903 (published posthumously)

**Mark Twain (Samuel Langhorne Clemens) (1835–1910)**

# *Right or wrong?*

*Huckleberry Finn had run away from his drunken father and
taken to the Mississippi river by raft, with Jim, an escaping
black slave, in a bid for freedom.*

*Torn between his duty to report a runaway slave and his
loyalty to Jim, Huck decided to lie to protect him. But he faced
a crisis of conscience:*

'Good-bye, sir,' says I, 'I won't let no runaway niggers get by me if I can
help it.'

They went off and I got aboard the raft, feeling bad and low, because I
knowed very well I had done wrong, and I see it warn't no use for me to
try to learn to do right; a body that don't get *started* right when he's little,
ain't got no show – when the pinch comes there ain't nothing
to back him up and keep him to his work, and so he gets beat. Then I
thought a minute and says to myself, hold on, – s'pose you'd a done right
and give Jim up; would you felt better than what you do now? No, says I,
I'd feel bad – I'd feel just the same way I do now. Well, then, says I, what's
the use you learning to do right, when it's troublesome to do right and
ain't no trouble to do wrong, and the wages is just the same? I was stuck.
I couldn't answer that. So I reckoned I wouldn't bother no more about it,
but after this always do whichever come handiest at the time.

From *The Adventures of Huckleberry Finn*, 1884

Oscar Wilde (1854–1900)

# *The selfish giant*

*When the Giant, who never allowed children into his beautiful garden, was away for seven years, the children played there happily. But on his return, the Giant banished the children and built a high wall around the grounds. Spring came to the outside world but spring, summer and autumn never visited his winter-locked garden:*

One morning the Giant was lying awake in bed when he heard some lovely music... it was so long since he had heard a bird sing in his garden that it seemed to him to be the most beautiful music in the world. Then the Hail stopped dancing over his head, and the North Wind ceased roaring, and a delicious perfume came to him through the open casement. 'I believe the Spring has come at last,' said the Giant; and he jumped out of bed and looked out.

What did he see?

He saw a most wonderful sight. Through a little hole in the wall the children had crept in, and they were sitting in the branches of the trees. In every tree that he could see there was a little child. And the trees were so glad to have the children back again that they had covered themselves with blossoms... It was a lovely scene, only in one corner it was still winter. It was the farthest corner of the garden, and in it was standing a little boy. He was so small that he could not reach up to the branches of the tree, and he was wandering all round it, crying bitterly...

And the Giant's heart melted as he looked out. 'How selfish I have been!' he said; 'now I know why the Spring would not come here. I will put that poor little boy on the top of the tree, and then I will knock down the wall, and my garden shall be the children's playground for ever and ever.' He was really very sorry for what he had done.

So he crept downstairs and opened the front door quite softly, and went out into the garden. But when the children saw him they were so frightened that they all ran away, and the garden became winter again. Only the little boy did not run, for his eyes were so full of tears that he did not see the Giant coming. And the Giant stole up behind him and took him gently in his hand, and put him up into the tree. And the tree broke at once into blossom, and the birds came and sang on it, and the little boy stretched out his two arms and flung them round the Giant's neck, and kissed him. And the other children, when they saw that the Giant was not wicked any longer, came running back, and with them came the Spring. 'It is your garden now, little children,' said the Giant, and he took a great axe and knocked down the wall...

All day long they played, and in the evening they came to the Giant to bid him good-bye.

'But where is your little companion?' he said, 'the boy I put into the tree.' The Giant loved him the best because he had kissed him.

'We don't know,' answered the children, 'he has gone away.'...

Every afternoon, when school was over, the children came and played with the Giant. But the little boy whom the Giant loved was never seen again...

Years went by, and the Giant grew very old and feeble...

One winter morning he looked out of the window as he was dressing... Suddenly he rubbed his eyes in wonder, and looked and looked. It certainly was a marvellous sight. In the farthest corner of the garden was a tree quite covered with lovely white blossoms. Its branches were all golden, and silver fruit hung down from them, and underneath it stood the little boy he had loved.

Downstairs ran the Giant in great joy, and out into the garden. He hastened across the grass, and came near to the child. And when he came quite close his face grew red with anger, and he said, 'Who hath dared to wound thee?' For on the palms of the child's hands were the prints of two nails, and the prints of two nails were on the little feet.

'Who hath dared to wound thee?' cried the Giant; 'tell me, that I may take my big sword and slay him.'

'Nay!' answered the child; 'but these are the wounds of Love.'

'Who art thou?' said the Giant, and a strange awe fell on him, and he knelt before the little child.

And the child smiled on the Giant, and said to him, 'You let me play once in your garden, to-day you shall come with me to my garden, which is paradise.'

And when the children ran in that afternoon, they found the Giant lying dead under the tree, all covered with white blossoms.

'The Selfish Giant', *The Happy Prince and Other Stories*, 1888

## Melvyn Bragg (b. 1939)

# *Negative good?*

*Melvyn Bragg's* Credo *charts the coming of Christianity to Britain in a fictional historical epic. Bega – an Irish princess – had been given a small piece of the true cross. Cuthbert convinced her that she must therefore renounce the man she loved and set up a small community that would come under the authority of Hilda at Whitby. She found the ideal spot then visited Reggiani, a local pagan priestess, for provisions:*

'You do not remember me?' Reggiani asked, as she handed over the milk.

Bega stared at her, reluctant to be reminded of her weakness. She took in Reggiani properly for the first time.

She saw a woman she guessed to be a few years older than her, about the same height, though plumper. Everything about Reggiani appeared soft and yielding. Even under the coarse full-length dress the undulating softness of easy curves could be seen or suspected. Her thick fair hair was spread over her shoulders and, like Bega's, reached down to her waist but, unlike the attempt on Bega's part to regiment the hair, this seemed cultivated to a seductive, entangling wilderness, seductiveness being the most marked characteristic about Reggiani; in the parted red lips, the fine-coloured cheeks, in the slow saunter, but above all in the eyes, hazel brown and always, Bega was to find, seeming half-closed...

'On the island, on Erebert's island,' Bega acknowledged, somehow rather angrily. 'When I was ill.'

'You were very badly,' replied Reggiani.

Bega felt uncomfortable at what she thought was a rather mocking stare. 'You helped me.'

Reggiani waved a lazy hand towards a large and heavily stocked herb garden. 'That was what helped you.'

'That and God,' said Bega.

'God.' Reggiani smiled and her eyes brimmed with fun. 'Ah yes. You are one of the God-ones, aren't you? The Christians.'

'You are not.'

'He is much too difficult for me,' Reggiani replied, shrugging to avoid any argument. 'I have much simpler gods. But mostly, when people are badly, I have herbs.'

'The herbs are the gifts of God.'

'Ah yes. Your God makes everything, doesn't he?'

'He does.'...

'And that is why you starve?'

'That is why we fast. That is why we pray.'...

'But no,' she shook her head, 'it's all too much *against*. Look at the monks and nuns I met... Against any intercourse.' She laughed, clearly enjoying what she thought of as a ridiculous rule. 'They say that God wants them to have no intimacy. The monks must avoid women, the nuns must avoid men. What is the purpose of that?'

'To serve God with all our strength. To be pure for him alone. To be his perfect vessel on earth. I too am chaste,' said Bega hotly.

'Oh,' said Reggiani, 'Are you now?'

From *Credo*, 1996

### Jeremy Taylor (1613–67)

# *True goodness*

Lastly there is a sort of God's dear servants, who walk in perfectness...
and they have a degree of charity and divine knowledge, more than we can
discourse of, and more certain than the demonstrations of geometry, and
indeficient as the light of heaven... But I shall say no more of this at this
time, for this is to be felt, not talked of; and they that never touched it
with their finger may, secretly perhaps, laugh at it in their heart and be
never the wiser. All that I shall now say of it is that a good man is united
to God as a flame touches flame.

From a sermon preached in Dublin between 1651 and 1653

**Anthony Trollope (1815–82)**

# The warden's farewell

*Mr Harding, warden of an almshouse for old men, resigned after a newspaper campaign wrongly accused him of deliberately drawing too large a salary. The old people – with the exception of loyal Bunce – turned against him too. Mr Harding was vindicated but was still the victim of political manoeuvrings. He said farewell to his former charges:*

When they were all in their places, Mr Harding rose to address them; and then finding himself not quite at home on his legs, he sat down again. 'My dear old friends,' said he, 'you all know that I am going to leave you.'

There was a sort of murmur ran round the room, intended, perhaps, to express regret at his departure; but it was but a murmur, and might have meant that or anything else.

'There has been lately some misunderstanding between us. You have thought, I believe, that you did not get all that you were entitled to, and that the funds of the hospital have not been properly disposed of. As for me, I cannot say what should be the disposition of these moneys, or how they should be managed, and I have therefore thought it best to go.'

'We never wanted to drive your reverence out of it,' said Handy.

'No, indeed, your reverence,' said Skulpit, 'we never thought it would come to this...'

'No,' continued Mr Harding; 'I am sure you did not wish to turn me out; but I thought it best to leave you. I am not a very good hand at a lawsuit, as you may all guess; and when it seemed necessary that our ordinary quiet mode of living should be disturbed, I thought it better to go. I am neither angry nor offended with any man in the hospital... If any man has been wrong – and I don't say that any man has – he has erred through wrong advice... Some gentleman will probably take my place here very soon, and I strongly advise you to be prepared to receive him in a kindly spirit, and to raise no further question among yourselves as to the amount of his income. Were you to succeed in lessening what he has to receive, you would not increase your own allowance.'...

'It's all true, your reverence,' said Skulpit; 'we sees it all now.'

'Yes, Mr Harding,' said Bunce, opening his mouth for the first time;

'I believe they do understand it now, now that they've driven from under the same roof with them such a master as not one of them will ever know again – now that they're like to be in sore need of a friend.'

'Come, come, Bunce,' said Mr Harding, blowing his nose and manoeuvring to wipe his eyes.

'Oh, as to that,' said Handy, 'we none of us never wanted to do Mr Harding any harm; if he's going now, it's not along of us; and I don't see for what Mr Bunce speaks up agen us that way.'

'You've ruined yourselves, and you've ruined me too, and that's why,' said Bunce.

'Nonsense, Bunce,' said Mr Harding; 'there's nobody ruined at all. I hope you'll let me leave you all friends. I hope you'll all drink a glass of wine in friendly feeling with me and with one another.'...

Mr Harding filled all the glasses, and himself handed each a glass to the men round him, and raising his own, said –

'God bless you all! You have my heartfelt wishes for your welfare. I hope you may live contented, and die trusting in the Lord Jesus Christ, and thankful to Almighty God for the good things he has given you. God bless you, my friends!' and Mr Harding drank his wine.

From *The Warden*, 1855

## Maya Angelou (Marguerite Johnson) (b. 1928)

# 'When I lay my burden down'

*Maya Angelou told the story of her childhood life with her grandmother ('Momma'), who kept a store in the black area of Stamps, Arkansas. The only white people that Maya saw in Stamps were scruffy children labelled by black people as 'powhitetrash'.*

One summer morning, after I had swept the dirt yard of leaves, spearmint-gum wrappers and Vienna-sausage labels… I put the rake behind the Store and came through the back of the house to find Grandmother on the front porch in her big, wide white apron. The apron was so stiff by virtue of the starch that it could have stood alone. Momma was admiring the yard, so I joined her… At just about the same time we saw a troop of the powhitetrash kids marching over the hill and down by the side of the school.

I looked to Momma for direction… When the children reached halfway down the hill, halfway to the Store, she said without turning, 'Sister, go on inside.'

I wanted to beg her, 'Momma, don't wait for them. Come on inside with me. If they come to the Store, you go to the bedroom, and let me wait on them…' But of course I couldn't say anything, so I went in and stood behind the screen door.

Before the girls got to the porch I heard their laughter crackling and popping like pine logs in a cooking-pot. I suppose my lifelong paranoia was born in those cold, molasses-slow minutes. They came finally to stand on the ground in front of Momma. At first they pretended seriousness. Then one of them wrapped her right arm in the crook of her left, pushed out her mouth and started to hum. I realised that she was aping my grandmother. Another said, 'Naw, Helen, you ain't standing like her. This here's it.' Then she lifted her chest, folded her arms and mocked that strange carriage that was Annie Henderson. Another laughed, 'Naw, you can't do it. Your mouth ain't pooched out enough. It's like this.'…

Through the fly-specked screen-door I could see that the arms of Momma's apron jiggled from the vibrations of her humming. But her knees seemed to have locked as if they would never bend again.

She sang on. No louder than before, but no softer either. No slower or faster.

The dirt of the girls' cotton dresses continued on their legs, feet, arms and faces to make them all of a piece. Their greasy uncoloured hair hung down, uncombed, with a grim finality. I knelt to see them better, to remember them for all time. The tears that had slipped down my dress left unsurprising dark spots, and made the front yard blurry and even more unreal...

The girls had tired of mocking Momma and turned to other means of agitation. One crossed her eyes, stuck her thumbs in both sides of her mouth and said, 'Look here, Annie.' Grandmother hummed on and the apron strings trembled. I wanted to throw a handful of black pepper in their faces... but I knew I was as clearly imprisoned behind the scene as the actors outside were confined to their roles.

One of the smaller girls did a kind of puppet dance while her fellow clowns laughed at her. But the tall one, who was almost a woman, said something very quietly, which I couldn't hear. They all moved backward from the porch, still watching Momma. For an awful second I thought they were going to throw a rock at Momma, who seemed (except for the apron strings) to have turned into stone herself. But the big girl turned her back, bent down and put her hands flat on the ground – she didn't pick up anything. She simply shifted her weight and did a handstand.

Her dirty bare feet and long legs went straight for the sky. Her dress fell down around her shoulders, and she had on no drawers...

Momma changed her song to 'Bread of Heaven, bread of Heaven, feed me till I want no more.'

I found that I was praying too. How long could Momma hold out? What new indignity would they think of to subject her to?...

Then they were moving out of the yard, on their way to town. They bobbed their heads and shook their slack behinds and turned, one at a time:

''Bye, Annie.'

''Bye, Annie.'

''Bye, Annie.'

Momma never turned her head or unfolded her arms, but she stopped singing and said, ''Bye, Miz Helen, 'bye, Miz Ruth, 'bye Miz Eloise.'

I burst. A firecracker July-the-Fourth burst. How could Momma call them Miz? The mean nasty things. Why couldn't she have come inside the sweet, cool Store when we saw them breasting the hill? What did she prove? And then, if they were dirty, mean and impudent, why did Momma have to call them Miz?

She stood another whole song through and then opened the screen door to look down on me crying in rage. She looked until I looked up. Her face was a brown moon that shone on me. She was beautiful. Something had happened out there, which I couldn't completely understand, but I could see that she was happy. Then she bent down and touched me as mothers of the church 'lay hands on the sick and the afflicted' and I quieted.

'Go wash your face, Sister.' And she went behind the candy counter and hummed, 'Glory, glory, hallelujah, when I lay my burden down.'

From *I Know Why the Caged Bird Sings*, 1969

## George Eliot (Mary Ann Evans) (1819–80)

# *A good wife*

*Nicholas Bulstrode – successful and influential banker and business man – was a fervent Nonconformist. But dishonest and self-seeking action in the past came to light, threatening his reputation and life-style. His wife elicited the whole shameful story from her brother:*

When she got home she was obliged to say to her daughter, 'I am not well, my dear; I must go and lie down. Attend to your papa. Leave me in quiet. I shall take no dinner.'

She locked herself in her room. She needed time to get used to her maimed consciousness, her poor lopped life, before she could walk steadily to the place allotted her. A new searching light had fallen on her husband's character, and she could not judge him leniently: the twenty years in which she had believed in him and venerated him by virtue of his concealments came back with particulars that made them seem an odious deceit. He had married her with that past bad life hidden behind him and she had no faith left to protest his innocence of the worst that was imputed to him. Her honest ostentatious nature made the sharing of a merited dishonour as bitter as it could be to any mortal.

But this imperfectly taught woman, whose phrases and habits were an odd patchwork, had a loyal spirit within her. The man whose prosperity she had shared through nearly half a life, and who had unvaryingly cherished her – now that punishment had befallen him it was not possible to her in any sense to forsake him. There is a forsaking which still sits at the same board and lies on the same couch with the forsaken soul, withering it the more by unloving proximity. She knew, when she locked her door, that she should unlock it ready to go down to her unhappy husband and espouse his sorrow, and say of his guilt, I will mourn and not reproach. But she needed time to gather up her strength; she needed to sob out her farewell to all the gladness and pride of her life. When she had resolved to go down, she prepared herself by some little acts which might seem mere folly to a mere onlooker; they were her way of expressing to all spectators visible or invisible that she had begun a new life in which she embraced humiliation. She took off all her ornaments and put on a plain black gown, and instead of wearing her much-adorned cap and large bows of hair, she brushed her hair down and put on a plain bonnet-cap, which made her look suddenly like an early Methodist.

Bulstrode, who knew that his wife had been out and had come in saying that she was not well, had spent the time in an agitation equal to hers. He had looked forward to her learning the truth from others, and had acquiesced in that probability, as something easier to him than any confession. But now that he imagined the moment of her knowledge come, he awaited the result in anguish... He felt himself perishing slowly in unpitied misery. Perhaps he should never see his wife's face with affection in it again. And if he turned to God there seemed to be no answer but the pressure of retribution.

It was eight o'clock in the evening before the door opened and his wife entered. He dared not look up at her. He sat with his eyes bent down, and as she went towards him she thought he looked smaller – he seemed so withered and shrunken. A movement of new compassion and old tenderness went through her like a great wave, and putting one hand on his which rested on the arm of the chair, and the other on his shoulder, she said, solemnly, but kindly –

'Look up, Nicholas.'

He raised his eyes with a little start and looked at her half amazed for a moment: her pale face, her changed, mourning dress, the trembling about her mouth, all said, 'I know;' and her hands and eyes rested gently on him. He burst out crying and they cried together, she sitting at his side. They could not yet speak to each other of the shame which she was bearing with him, or of the acts which had brought it down on them. His confession was silent, and her promise of faithfulness was silent. Open-minded as she was, she nevertheless shrank from the words which would have expressed their mutual consciousness as she would have shrunk from flakes of fire. She could not say, 'How much is slander and suspicion?' and he did not say, 'I am innocent.'

From *Middlemarch*, 1871–72

**Peter Ackroyd (b. 1949)**

# 'Chancellor More is chancellor no more'

*More (1478–1535) was a loyal servant to King Henry VIII but recognised an even higher allegiance as the servant of God. When he refused to sanction Henry's actions, he was dismissed from his office as chancellor and imprisoned in the Tower of London. Later he was tried in Westminster Hall:*

After the sentence had been pronounced against him he was led away from the bar of the King's Bench and escorted from Westminster Hall. The constable of the Tower, Sir William Kingston, was in charge of the guard which accompanied the prisoner from Westminster Stairs towards the Tower; the swift tides made it impossible to cross beneath London Bridge and instead the armed party disembarked from the barge at Old Swan Stairs. Here William Kingston began to cry as he took his leave of him, but More comforted him by saying, 'Good master Kingston, trouble not yourself but be of good cheer; for I will pray for you, and my good Lady your wife, that we may meet in heaven together, where we shall be merry for ever and ever.' Kingston reported this to More's son-in-law a little while after, and added, 'In good faith, master Roper, I was ashamed at myself that, at my departing from your father, I found my heart so feeble, and his so strong, that he was fain to comfort me which should rather have comforted him.' More was taken up Old Swan Lane and then turned right into Thames Street, which would lead him back to the Tower; he was walking, according to report, in a coarse woollen gown.

From *The Life of Thomas More*, 1998

## Ellis Peters (Edith Pargeter) (1913–95)

# *Judgement and mercy*

*In this medieval whodunnit, Brother Cadfael recognized Meurig
as the guilty man, in spite of the arrest of another for the crime.
The murderer secretly accosted Cadfael in the barn where he had
herded the sheep for the night and put a knife to his throat:*

'Are you not afraid of death?' asked Meurig, barely above a whisper.

'I've brushed elbows with him before. We respect each other. In any
case there's no evading him for ever, we all come to it, Meurig... We have
to die, everyone of us, soon or late. But we do not *have* to kill. You and I
both made a choice, you only a week or so ago, I when I lived by the
sword. Here am I, as you willed it. Now take what you want of me.'

He did not take his eyes from Meurig's eyes, but he saw at the edge of
vision the tightening of the strong brown fingers and the bracing of the
muscles in the wrist to strike home. But there was no other movement. All
Meurig's body seemed suddenly to writhe in an anguished attempt to
thrust, and still he could not... He cast the knife out of his hand to whine
and stick quivering in the beaten earth of the floor, and flung up both
arms to clasp his head, as though all his strength of body and will could
not contain or suppress the pain that filled him to overflowing. Then... he
was crouched in a heap at Cadfael's feet, his face buried in his arms
against the hay-rack...

'Oh, God that I could so face my death... for I owe it, I owe it, and
I dare not pay. If I were clean... Give me help! Help me... Help me to
be fit to die...' He raised himself suddenly, and looked up at Cadfael,
clutching with one hand at the skirts of his habit. 'Brother, those things
you said of me... never meant to be a murderer, you said...'

'Have I not proved it?' said Cadfael. 'I live, and it was not fear that
stayed your hand.'

'Mere chance that led me, you said... Great pity it is, you said! Pity...
Did you mean all those things, brother? Is there pity?'

'I meant them,' said Cadfael, 'every word. Pity, indeed, that ever you
went so far aside from your own nature, and poisoned yourself as surely
as you poisoned your father.'... Meurig... lifted a tormented face into the
soft light of the lantern. 'Brother, you have been conscience to other men

in your time, for God's sake do as much for me... Hear all my evil!'

'Child,' said Cadfael, shaken... 'I am not a priest, I cannot give absolution, I cannot appoint penance...'

'Ah, but you can, you can, none but you, who found out the worst of me! Hear me my confession, and I shall be better prepared, and then deliver me to my penalty, and I will not complain.'

'Speak then, if it gives you ease,' said Cadfael heavily.

From *Monk's Hood*, 1980

## Laura Ingalls Wilder (1867–1957)

# *Indian beads*

*Laura Ingalls Wilder tells of visiting a deserted Indian camp with her father and older sister, Mary, when the family lived as settlers in the prairies:*

Suddenly Laura shouted, 'Look! Look!' Something bright blue glittered in the dust. She picked it up, and it was a beautiful blue bead. Laura shouted with joy.

Then Mary saw a red bead, and Laura saw a green one, and they forgot everything but beads. Pa helped them look. They found white beads and brown beads and more and more red and blue beads. All that afternoon they hunted for beads in the dust of the Indian camp. Now and then Pa walked to the edge of the hollow and looked towards home, then he came back and helped to hunt for more beads. They looked all the ground over carefully.

When they couldn't find any more, it was almost sunset. Laura had a handful of beads, and so did Mary. Pa tied them carefully in his handkerchief, Laura's beads in one corner and Mary's in another corner. He put the handkerchief in his pocket and they started home.

Home was a long way off and Pa carried Laura when she was very tired.

Supper was cooking on the fire, Ma was setting the table, and Baby Carrie played with pieces of wood on the floor. Pa tossed the handkerchief to Ma.

'I'm later than I meant, Caroline,' he said. 'But look what the girls found.' He took the milk bucket and went quickly to bring Pet and Patty from their picket-lines and to milk the cow.

Ma untied the handkerchief and exclaimed at what she found. The beads were even prettier than they had been in the Indian camp.

Laura stirred her beads with her finger and watched them sparkle and shine. 'These are mine,' she said.

Then Mary said, 'Carrie can have mine.'

Ma waited to hear what Laura would say. Laura didn't want to say anything. She wanted to keep those pretty beads. Her chest felt all hot inside, and she wished with all her might that Mary wouldn't always be such a good little girl. But she couldn't let Mary be better than she was.

So she said, slowly, 'Carrie can have mine, too.'

'That's my unselfish, good little girls,' said Ma...

Mary and Laura sat side by side on their bed, and they strung those pretty beads on the thread that Ma gave them... They didn't say anything. Perhaps Mary felt good and sweet inside, but Laura didn't. When she looked at Mary she wanted to slap her. So she dared not look at Mary again.

The beads made a beautiful string. Carrie clapped her hands and laughed when she saw it. Then Ma tied it around Carrie's little neck, and it glittered there. Laura felt a little better. After all, her beads were not enough to make a whole string, and neither were Mary's, but together they made a whole string for Carrie.

When Carrie felt the beads on her neck, she grabbed at them. She was so little that she did not know any better than to break the string. So Ma untied it, and she put the beads away until Carrie should be old enough to wear them. And often after that Laura thought of those pretty beads and she was still naughty enough to want those beads for herself.

But it had been a wonderful day. She could still think about that long walk across the prairie, and about all they had seen at the Indian camp.

From *The Little House on the Prairie*, 1935

**Geoffrey Chaucer (c. 1343–1400)**

# The country parson

*Many of the professional religious in Chaucer's* Prologue *to the* Canterbury Tales *are hypocrites or scoundrels but Chaucer depicts the country parson and his brother the ploughman in kind and glowing terms as genuinely good people.*

One of our pilgrims was a parish priest, a poor man who was rich in goodness, both in his thoughts and his deeds. He was a scholar, a truly learned man, but he preached Christ's gospel in simple sincerity and taught his parishioners with honesty and truth. He was kindly, extremely conscientious, and very patient when things went badly, as he clearly showed on many occasions. He hated having to excommunicate anyone because they had not paid their tithes; in fact there's no doubt that he much preferred to give to the poor members of his parish – using money from voluntary offerings he received or even out of his own meagre stipend; he himself was happy to subsist on very little. His parish was large and scattered but, come rain come shine, he never put off visiting the furthest flung home, whatever the trouble was, great or small. He went everywhere on foot with his staff in his hand. He set his flock a fine example by practising goodness himself before he preached it to others. He went by what the Gospel teaches on the subject, adding his own proverb: 'If gold begins to rust, what will happen to iron?' And it's true enough that if the priest we trust is evil, we shouldn't be surprised if the ordinary person gets tarred with the same brush. It's a crying shame – as priests should recognise – to see an unclean shepherd leading a clean flock! A priest should set his sheep an example of how to live by his own purity of life.

This parish priest never hired out his living, leaving his flock stuck in the mud, so that he could run off to St Paul's in London to be paid a lot to sing masses for the dead or earn a fat fee as chaplain to a guild. He stayed at home and guarded his flock so that they would not be led astray by any wolf in sheep's clothing. He was a true shepherd, not a hireling. Though he was so good and holy himself, he never looked down on sinful people, and he was never offhand or difficult to approach when he talked with them. He was wise and kindly in the way he taught. His chief aim was to attract folk to heaven by his honest life and good example. But if any one were obstinate and stubborn, he would tick him off sharply, whatever his station in life might be. I don't believe there is a better priest anywhere around! He did not expect fuss or fine talk and he was never touchy. He faithfully preached the teaching of Christ and the twelve apostles – but first and foremost he followed it himself.

A free translation from *The Prologue to the Canterbury Tales*, 1387

# REACHING OUT TO OTHERS

## A plea for justice

*Amos is the first Hebrew prophet whose message was recorded at length. He came from the south of the country and insisted that he was not a professional prophet; he kept sheep and it was possibly on business trips to the north of Israel that he witnessed the injustice and dishonesty practised in Israel and spoke out against it in God's name.*

The Lord says, 'The people of Israel have sinned again and again, and for this I will certainly punish them. They sell into slavery honest men who cannot pay their debts, poor men who cannot repay even the price of a pair of sandals. They trample down the weak and helpless and push the poor out of the way. A man and his father have intercourse with the same slave-girl, and so profane my holy name. At every place of worship men sleep on clothing they have taken from the poor as security for debts. In the temple of their God they drink wine which they have taken from those who owe them money.'...

Listen to this, you women of Samaria, who grow fat like the well-fed cows of Bashan, who ill-treat the weak, oppress the poor, and demand that your husbands keep you supplied with liquor! As the Sovereign Lord is holy, he has promised, 'The days will come when they will drag you away with hooks; every one of you will be like a fish on a hook. You will be dragged to the nearest break in the wall and thrown out.'...

Listen to this, you that trample on the needy and try to destroy the poor of the country. You say to yourselves, 'We can hardly wait for the holy days to be over so that we can sell our corn. When will the Sabbath end, so that we can start selling again? Then we can overcharge, use false measures, and tamper with the scales to cheat our customers. We can sell worthless wheat at a high price. We'll find a poor man who can't pay his debts, not even the price of a pair of sandals, and we'll buy him as a slave.'

The Lord, the God of Israel, has sworn, 'I will never forget their evil deeds. And so the earth will quake, and everyone in the land will be in distress... I will turn your festivals into funerals and change your glad songs into cries of grief.'

From Amos 2, 4, 8

## The Venerable Bede (c. 673–735)

# *The fearsome task of converting the English*

*In AD 596 Pope Gregory sent Augustine from Rome, with a band of monks, to convert the English.*

In the year of our Lord 582, Maurice, the fifty-fourth from Augustus, ascended the throne, and reigned twenty-one years. In the tenth year of his reign, Gregory, a man renowned for learning and behaviour, was promoted to the apostolical see of Rome, and presided over it thirteen years, six months and ten days. He, being moved by Divine inspiration, in the fourteenth year of the same emperor, and about the one hundred and fiftieth after the coming of the English into Britain, sent the servant of God, Augustine, and with him several other monks, who feared the Lord, to preach the word of God to the English nation. They having, in obedience to the pope's command, undertaken that work, were, on their journey, seized with a sudden fear, and began to think of returning home, rather than proceed to a barbarous, fierce, and unbelieving nation, to whose very language they were strangers; and this they unanimously agreed was the safest course. In short, they sent back Augustine, who had been appointed to be consecrated bishop in case they were received by the English, that he might, by humble entreaty, obtain of the holy Gregory, that they should not be compelled to undertake so dangerous, toilsome, and uncertain a journey. The pope, in reply, sent them a hortatory epistle, persuading them to proceed in the work of the Divine word, and rely on the assistance of the Almighty. The purport of which letter was as follows: –

'Gregory, *the servant of the servants of God, to the servants of our Lord.* Forasmuch as it had been better not to begin a good work, than to think of desisting from that which has been begun, it behoves you, my beloved sons, to fulfil the good work, which, by the help of our Lord, you have undertaken. Let not, therefore, the toil of the journey, nor the tongues of evil speaking men, deter you; but with all possible earnestness and zeal perform that which, by God's direction, you have undertaken; being assured, that much labour is followed by an eternal reward... Almighty God protect you with his grace, and grant that I may, in the heavenly country, see the fruits of your labour... God keep you safely, my beloved sons.'

> *On the same day, Gregory sent a letter to the bishop of Arles, asking him to give hospitality and help to the band of monks on their way to England.*

Augustine, thus strengthened by the confirmation of the blessed Father Gregory, returned to the work of the word of God, with the servants of God, and arrived in Britain.

From *Ecclesiastical History of the English People*, 731

## Charles Kingsley (1819–75)

# *The little chimney-sweep*

*Kingsley was a clergyman and a Christian Socialist with deep practical concern for the lot of the working classes of his time. The Water Babies, a children's fairy tale, is also an exposure of the way young children were being exploited.*

Once upon a time there was a little chimney-sweep, and his name was Tom. That is a short name, and you have heard it before, so you will not have much trouble in remembering it. He lived in a great town in the North country, where there were plenty of chimneys for Tom to sweep, and plenty of money for Tom to earn and his master to spend. He could not read nor write, and did not care to do either; and he never washed himself, for there was no water up the court where he lived. He had never been taught to say his prayers. He had never heard of God, or of Christ, except in words which you have never heard, and which it would have been well if he had never heard. He cried half his time, and laughed the other half. He cried when he had to climb the dark flues, rubbing his poor knees and elbows raw; and when the soot got into his eyes, which it did every day in the week; and when his master beat him, which he did every day in the week; and when he had not enough to eat, which happened every day in the week likewise. And he laughed the other half of the day, when he was tossing halfpennies with the other boys, or playing leapfrog over the posts, or bowling stones at the horses' legs as they trotted by, which last was excellent fun, when there was a wall at hand behind which to hide. As for chimney-sweeping, and being hungry, and being beaten, he took all that for the way of the world, like the rain and the snow and the thunder.

From *The Water Babies*, 1863

## Harriet Beecher Stowe (1811–96)

# 'What country have I?'

*George Harris, an escaping slave, encounters Mr Wilson, for whom he once worked:*

Mr Wilson, a good-natured but extremely fidgety and cautious old gentleman, ambled up and down the room... divided between his wish to help George, and a certain confused notion of maintaining law and order: so, as he shambled about, he delivered himself as follows:

'Well, George, I s'pose you're running away – leaving your lawful master, George – (I don't wonder at it) – at the same time, I'm sorry, George, – yes, decidedly – I think I must say that, George – it's my duty to tell you so.'

'Why are you sorry, sir?' said George, calmly.

'Why, to see you, as it were, setting yourself in opposition to the laws of your country.'

'*My* country!' said George, with a strong and bitter emphasis; 'what country have I, but the grave, – and I wish to God that I was laid there!'

'Why, George, no – no – it won't do; this way of talking is wicked – unscriptural.'...

'Don't quote Bible at me in that way, Mr Wilson,' said George, with a flashing eye, 'don't! for my wife is a Christian, and I mean to be, if ever I get to where I can; but to quote Bible to a fellow in my circumstances, is enough to make him give it up altogether. I appeal to God Almighty; – I'm willing to go with the case to him, and ask him if I do wrong to seek my freedom...

'See here now, Mr Wilson... look at me, now. Don't I sit before you, every way, just as much a man as you are? Look at my face, – look at my hands, – look at my body,' and the young man drew himself up proudly; 'why am I *not* a man as much as anybody?... I had a father – one of your Kentucky gentlemen – who didn't think enough of me to keep me from being sold with his dogs and horses, to satisfy the estate, when he died. I saw my mother put up at sheriff's sale, with her seven children. They were sold before her eyes, one by one, to different masters; and I was the youngest. She came and kneeled down before old Mas'r, and begged him to buy her with me, that she might have at least one child with her; and he kicked her away with his heavy boot. I saw him do it; and the last that

I heard was her moans and screams, when I was tied to his horse's neck, to be carried off to his place...

'When I was a little fellow, and laid awake whole nights and cried, it wasn't the hunger, it wasn't the whipping, I cried for. No, sir, it was for *my mother* and *my sisters*, – it was because I hadn't a friend to love me on earth... Then, sir, I found my wife; you've seen her, – you know how beautiful she is... and, sir, she is as good as she is beautiful. But now what? Why, now comes my master, takes me right away from my work and my friends, and all I like, and grinds me down into the very dirt! And why? Because, he says, I forgot who I was; he says, to teach me that I am only a nigger! After all, and last of all, he comes between me and my wife, and says I shall give her up and live with another woman. And all this your laws give him power to do, in spite of God or man... Do you call these the laws of *my* country? Sir, I haven't any country, any more than I have any father. But I'm going to have one. I don't want anything of *your* country, except to be let alone – to go peaceably out of it...'

From *Uncle Tom's Cabin*, 1852

## Charles Dickens (1812–70)

# *Coketown*

*In* Hard Times *Dickens wrote powerfully about the evils that came with the Industrial Revolution in England. He went to Preston in 1854 to research the conditions in big industrial cities and to discover the changes brought about in the lives of employers and 'hands' alike.*

The streets were hot and dusty on the summer day, and the sun was so bright that it even shone through the heavy vapour drooping over Coketown, and could not be looked at steadily. Stokers emerged from low underground doorways into factory yards, and sat on steps, and posts, and palings, wiping their swarthy visages, and contemplating coals. The whole town seemed to be frying in oil. There was a stifling smell of hot oil everywhere. The steam-engines shone with it, the dresses of the Hands were soiled with it, the mills throughout their many stories oozed and trickled it. The atmosphere of those Fairy palaces was like the breath of the simoom; and their inhabitants, wasting with heat, toiled languidly in the desert. But no melancholy made the melancholy mad elephants more mad or more sane. Their wearisome heads went up and down at the same rate, in hot weather and cold, wet weather and dry, fair weather and foul. The measured motion of their shadows on the walls, was the substitute Coketown had to show for the shadows of rustling woods; while, for the summer hum of insects, it could offer, all the year round, from the dawn of Monday to the night of Saturday, the whirr of shafts and wheels.

Drowsily they whirred all through this sunny day, making the passenger more sleepy and more hot as he passed the humming walls of the mills. Sun-blinds, and sprinklings of water, a little cooled the main streets and the shops; but the mills, and the courts and alleys, baked at a fierce heat. Down upon the river that was black and thick with dye, some Coketown boys who were at large – a rare sight there – rowed a crazy boat, which made a spumous track upon the water as it jogged along, while every dip of an oar stirred up vile smells. But the sun itself, however beneficent generally, was less kind to Coketown than hard frost, and rarely looked intently into any of its closer regions without engendering more death than life. So does the eye of Heaven itself become an evil eye, when incapable or sordid hands are interposed between it and the things it looks upon to bless.

From *Hard Times*, 1854

**George Orwell (Eric Arthur Blair) 1903–50)**

# Tea and prayers

*In* Down and Out in Paris and London, *Orwell describes his first-hand experiences on the road. In London he meets up with an Irish tramp; the 'spike' was a casual ward of a workhouse, where tramps could get a night's lodging.*

We stayed talking for an hour or two. The Irishman was a friendly old man, but he smelt very unpleasant, which was not surprising when one learned how many diseases he suffered from. It appeared (he described his symptoms fully) that taking him from top to bottom he had the following things wrong with him: on his crown, which was bald, he had eczema; he was shortsighted and had no glasses; he had chronic bronchitis; he had some undiagnosed pain in the back; he had dyspepsia; he had urethritis; he had varicose veins, bunions and flat feet. With this assemblage of diseases he had tramped the streets for fifteen years.

At about five the Irishman said, 'Could you do wid a cup o' tay? De spike don't open till six.'

'I should think I could.'

'Well, dere's a place where dey gives you a free cup o' tay and a bun. *Good* tay it is. Dey makes you say a lot o' bloody prayers after; but hell! It all passes de time away. You come wid me.'

He led the way to a small tin-roofed shed in a side-street, rather like a village cricket pavilion. About twenty-five other tramps were waiting. A few of them were dirty old habitual vagabonds, the majority decent-looking lads from the north, probably miners or cotton operatives out of work. Presently the door opened and a lady in a blue silk dress, wearing gold spectacles and a crucifix, welcomed us in...

Uncomfortably we took off our caps and sat down. The lady handed out the tea, and while we ate and drank she moved to and fro, talking benignly. She talked upon religious subjects – about Jesus Christ always having a soft spot for poor rough men like us, and about how quickly the time passed when you were in church, and what a difference it made to a man on the road if he said his prayers regularly. We hated it. We sat against the wall fingering our caps (a tramp feels indecently exposed with his cap off), and turning pink and trying to mumble something when the lady addressed us. There was no doubt that she meant it all kindly...

Tea ended, and I could see the tramps looking furtively at one another. An unspoken thought was running from man to man – could we possibly make off before the prayers started? Someone stirred in his chair – not getting up actually, but with just a glance at the door, as though half suggesting the idea of departure. The lady quelled him with one look. She said in a more benign tone than ever:

'I don't think you need go *quite* yet. The casual ward doesn't open till six, and we have time to kneel down and say a few words to our Father first. I think we should all feel better after that, shouldn't we?...

Bare-headed, we knelt down among the dirty teacups...

The prayers lasted half an hour, and then, after a handshake at the door, we made off. 'Well,' said somebody, as soon as we were out of hearing, 'the trouble's over. I thought them prayers was never goin' to end.'

'You 'ad your bun,' said another; 'you got to pay for it.'

'Pray for it, you mean. Ah, you don't get much for nothing. They can't even give you a twopenny cup of tea without you go down on your knees for it.'

There were murmurs of agreement. Evidently the tramps were not grateful for their tea. And yet it was excellent tea, as different from coffee-shop tea as good Bordeaux is from the muck called colonial claret, and we were all glad of it. I am sure too that it was given in a good spirit, without any intention of humiliating us; so in fairness we ought to have been grateful – still, we were not.

From *Down and Out in Paris and London*, 1933

**Daniel Defoe (1660–1731)**

# *Religious instruction for Friday*

*After 'breaking loose' from his parents and their instructions in moral living, Robinson Crusoe joins a ship's crew and is shipwrecked on a desert island. After serious moral reform and many years of solitude he is delighted to have a fellow-man, whom he names Friday; he is Crusoe's loyal servant in gratitude for his new master's having rescued him from cannibals.*

During the long time that Friday had now been with me, and that he began to speak to me and understand me... I began to instruct him in the knowledge of the true God... He listened with great attention, and received with pleasure the notion of Jesus Christ being sent to redeem us, and of the manner of making our prayers to God...

I found it was not easy to imprint right notions in his mind about the Devil... and the poor creature puzzled me once in such a manner, by a question merely natural and innocent, that I scarce knew what to say to him. I had been talking a great deal to him of the power of God, His omnipotence, His dreadful aversion to sin, His being a consuming fire to the workers of iniquity...

After this, I had been telling him how the Devil was God's enemy in the hearts of men, and used all his malice and skill to defeat the good designs of Providence... 'Well,' says Friday, 'you say God is so strong, so great; is He not much strong, much might as the Devil?' 'Yes, yes,' says I, 'Friday, God is stronger than the Devil, God is above the Devil...' 'But,' says he again, 'if God much strong, much might as the Devil, why God no kill the Devil, to make him no more wicked?'

I was strangely surprised at his question... And at first could not tell what to say; so I pretended not to hear him, and asked him what he said. But he was too earnest for an answer to forget his question; so that he repeated it in the very same broken words as before. By this time I had recovered myself a little, and I said, 'God will at last punish him severely, he is reserved for the judgement, and is to be cast into the bottomless pit, to dwell with everlasting fire.' This did not satisfy Friday, but he returns upon me, repeating my words, '"Reserve at last," me no understand; but why not kill the Devil now, not kill great ago?' 'You may as well ask me,' said I, 'why God does not kill you and I, when we do wicked things here that offend Him. We are preserved to repent and be pardoned.'

He muses awhile at this. 'Well, well,' says he, mighty affectionately, 'that well; so you, I, Devil, all wicked, all preserve, repent, God pardon all.' Here I was run down again by him to the last degree... I therefore diverted the present discourse between me and my man, rising up hastily, as upon some sudden occasion of going out; then sending him for something a good way off, I seriously prayed to God that He would enable me to instruct savingly this poor savage, assisting by His Spirit the heart of the poor ignorant creature to receive the light of the knowledge of God in Christ.

From *Robinson Crusoe*, 1719

Elizabeth Gaskell (1810–65)

# North and South

*Margaret Hale and her parents are forced to move from the
south to the industrial north where the local mill-owner, John
Thornton, becomes her father's pupil, She is shocked by his
views on the rights of master over worker. Industrial strikes and
the illness and death of Mrs Hale would eventually affect and
modify both John's and Margaret's attitudes:*

The medicines and treatment that Dr Donaldson had ordered for Mrs
Hale did her so much good at first that, not only she herself, but Margaret
began to hope that he might have been mistaken and that she could
recover permanently...

They needed this gleam of brightness indoors, for out-of-doors, even to
their uninstructed eyes, there was a gloomy, brooding appearance of
discontent. Mr Hale had his own acquaintances among the working-men,
and was depressed with their earnestly told tales of suffering and long
endurance. They would have scorned to speak of what they had to bear
to any one who might, from his position, have understood it without their
words. But here was this man, from a distant country, who was perplexed
by the workings of the system into the midst of which he was thrown; and
each was eager to make him a judge, and to bring witness of his own
causes for irritation. Then Mr Hale brought all his budget of grievances,
and laid it before Mr Thornton, for him, as a master, to arrange them, and
explain their origin; which he always did, on sound economical principles;
showing that, as trade was conducted, there must always be a waxing and
waning of commercial prosperity; and that in the waning a certain number
of masters, as well as of men, must go down into ruin, and be no more
seen among the ranks of the happy and prosperous... Of course, speaking
so of the fate that, as a master, might be his own in the fluctuations of
commerce, he was not likely to have more sympathy with that of the
workmen, who were passed by in the swift merciless improvement or
alteration...

Margaret's whole soul rose up against him while he reasoned in this way
– as if commerce were everything and humanity nothing. She could hardly
thank him for the individual kindness, which brought him that evening to

offer her... every convenience for illness... which, as he learnt from Dr Donaldson, Mrs Hale might possibly require. His presence... set Margaret's teeth on edge, as she looked at him, and listened to him. What business had he to be the only person, except Dr Donaldson and Dixon, admitted to the awful secret, which she held shut up in the most dark and secret recess of her heart – not daring to look at it, unless she invoked heavenly strength to bear the sight – that, some day soon, she should cry aloud for her mother, and no answer would come out of the blank, dumb darkness? Yet he knew all. She saw it in his pitying eyes. She heard it in his grave and tremulous voice. How reconcile those eyes, that voice, with the hard, reasoning, dry, merciless way in which he laid down axioms of trade, and serenely followed them out to their full consequences? The discord jarred upon her inexpressibly.

From *North and South*, 1855

## Lady Mary Wortley Montagu (1689–1762)

# *Dealing with distempers*

*When her husband was appointed English ambassador to the Porte, Lady Mary accompanied him to Turkey – a country little known about in England at that time. She wrote letters home about her experiences, and through her enthusiasm for the Turkish custom of 'ingrafting' or inoculating against smallpox, she encouraged the practice to be adopted in England. The exact date of this letter is uncertain, but it was written between 1716 and 1718.*

*To Mrs S.C. Adrianople, 1 April*
… Those dreadful stories you have heard of the *plague* have very little foundation in truth. I own I have much ado to reconcile myself to the sound of a word which has always given me such terrible ideas, though I am convinced there is little more in it than in a fever. As a proof of this, let me tell you that we passed through two or three towns most violently infected. In the very next house where we lay (in one of those places) two persons died of it. Luckily for me, I was so well deceived that I knew nothing of the matter…

*À propos* of distempers, I am going to tell you a thing that will make you wish yourself here. The small-pox, so fatal, and so general amongst us, is here entirely harmless by the invention of *ingrafting*, which is the term they give it. There is a set of old women who make it their business to perform the operation every autumn, in the month of September, when the great heat is abated. People send to one another to know if any of their family has a mind to have the small-pox: they make parties for this purpose, and when they are met (commonly fifteen or sixteen together), the old woman comes with a nut-shell full of the matter of the best sort of small-pox, and asks what vein you please to have opened. She immediately opens up that you offer to her with a large needle (which gives you no more pain than a common scratch), and puts into the vein as much matter as can lie upon the head of her needle, and after that binds up the little wound with a little bit of shell; and in this manner opens four or five veins… The children or young patients play together all the rest of the day, and are in perfect health to the eighth. Then the fever begins to seize them and they keep their beds two days, very seldom three. They have very rarely above twenty or thirty in their faces, which never mark; and in eight days' time they are as well as before their illness... There is no example of any that one that has died of it; and you may believe I am well satisfied with the safety of this experiment, since I intend to try it on my dear little son.

I am patriot enough to take pains to bring this useful invention into fashion in England; and I should not fail to write to some of our doctors very particularly about it, if I knew any of them that I thought·had virtue enough to destroy such a considerable branch of their revenue for the good of mankind. But that distemper is too beneficial to them, not to expose to all their resentment the hardy wight that should undertake to put an end to it. Perhaps, if I live to return, I may, however, have courage to war with them. Upon this occasion admire the heroism in the heart of your friend, etc, etc.

From a letter to Mrs S.C.

# FOIBLES AND VICES

## Get rid of evil

*The apostle Paul wrote to the Christians at Colossae describing their old lifestyle then the new kind of life that, as Christians, they should live.*

You must put to death, then, the earthly desires at work in you, such as sexual immorality, indecency, lust, evil passions and greed (for greed is a form of idolatry). Because of such things God's anger will come upon those who do not obey him. At one time you yourselves used to live according to such desires, when your life was dominated by them.

But now you must get rid of all these things: anger, passion, and hateful feelings. No insults or obscene talk must ever come from your lips. Do not lie to one another, for you have taken off the old self with its habits and have put on the new self. This is the new being which God, its Creator, is constantly renewing in his own image, in order to bring you to a full knowledge of himself.

From Colossians 3

Jane Austen (1775–1817)

# Unkindness

*Emma Woodhouse was young, 'clever, handsome and rich'. She was also kind but sharp-witted. Miss Bates 'had no intellectual superiority... Her middle of life was devoted to the care of a failing mother, and the endeavour to make a small income go as far as possible. And yet she was... interested in everybody's happiness, quick-sighted to everybody's merits... She was a great talker upon little matters.'*

*An outing to Box Hill was arranged; Emma, Mr Knightley, and Miss Bates were among those who went. Frank Churchill, an eligible and handsome bachelor, decided to liven up proceedings and announced to the picnic party:*

'Ladies and gentlemen – I am ordered by Miss Woodhouse to say, that... she only demands from each of you either one thing very clever, be it prose or verse, original or repeated or two things moderately clever or three things very dull indeed, and she engages to laugh heartily at them all.'

'Oh! very well,' exclaimed Miss Bates, 'then I need not be uneasy. "Three things very dull indeed." That will just do for me, you know. I shall be sure to say three dull things as soon as ever I open my mouth, shan't I? – (looking round with the most good-humoured dependence on every body's assent) – Do not you all think I shall?'

Emma could not resist.

'Ah! ma'am, but there may be a difficulty. Pardon me – but you will be limited as to number – only three at once.'

Miss Bates, deceived by the mock ceremony of her manner, did not immediately catch her meaning; but, when it burst on her, it could not anger, though a slight blush showed that it could pain her.

'Ah! – well – to be sure. Yes, I see what she means (turning to Mr Knightley), and I will try to hold my tongue. I must make myself very disagreeable, or she would not have said such a thing to an old friend.'

*Later, Mr Knightley talked privately to Emma:*

'Emma... how could you be so unfeeling to Miss Bates?... I had not thought it possible.'

Emma recollected, blushed, was sorry, but tried to laugh it off... 'It was not so very bad. I daresay she did not understand me.'

'I assure you she did. She felt your full meaning. She has talked of it since... Were she a woman of fortune, I would leave every harmless absurdity to take its chance, I would not quarrel with you for any liberties of manner. Were she your equal in situation – but, Emma, consider how far this is from the case. She is poor; she has sunk from the comforts she was born to... Her situation should secure your compassion. It was badly done, indeed! – You, whom she had known from an infant, whom she had seen grow up from a period when her notice was an honour, to have you now, in thoughtless spirits, and the pride of the moment, laugh at her, humble her... This is not pleasant to you, Emma – and it is far from pleasant to me; but I must, I will, – I will tell you truths while I can, satisfied with proving myself your friend by very faithful counsel.'

From *Emma*, 1816

**Beatrix Potter (1866–1943)**

# *Disobedience*

Once upon a time there were four little Rabbits, and their names were –
Flopsy, Mopsy, Cotton-tail, and Peter.

They lived with their Mother in a sand-bank, underneath the roots of
a very big fir-tree.

'Now, my dears,' said old Mrs Rabbit one morning, 'you may go into
the fields or down the lane, but don't go into Mr McGregor's garden: your
Father had an accident there; he was put in a pie by Mrs McGregor.

'Now run along, and don't get into mischief. I am going out.'

Then old Mrs Rabbit took a basket and her umbrella, and went through
the wood to the baker's. She bought a loaf of brown bread and five
currant buns.

Flopsy, Mopsy, and Cotton-tail, who were good little bunnies, went
down the lane to gather blackberries:

But Peter, who was very naughty, ran straight away to Mr McGregor's
garden, and squeezed under the gate!

First he ate some lettuces and some French beans; and then he ate some
radishes;

And then, feeling rather sick, he went to look for some parsley.

*But round the end of a cucumber frame, whom should he meet but Mr
McGregor!*

Mr McGregor was on his hands and knees planting out young cabbages,
but he jumped up and ran after Peter, waving a rake and calling out, 'Stop
thief!'

Peter was most dreadfully frightened; he rushed all over the garden, for
he had forgotten the way back to the gate.

From *The Tale of Peter Rabbit*, 1901

## Samuel Pepys (1633–1703)

# *Lust and jealousy*

*Pepys's love affair with his wife's maid, Deb Willett, is the only serious one he records in his diary. It led to much distress to his wife Elizabeth and continued temptation for Pepys. The following extracts detail the beginnings of the sad affair, whose more intimate moments Pepys describes with a euphemistic shorthand of his own.*

*27 September 1667*
While I was busy at the office, my wife sends for me to come home, and what was it but to see the pretty girl which she is taking to wait upon her; and although she seems not altogether so great a beauty as she had before told me, yet endeed she is mighty pretty; and so pretty, that I find I shall be too much pleased with it, and therefore could be contented as to my judgement, though not to my passion, that she might not come, lest I may be found too much minding her, to the discontent of my wife. She is to come next week... To the office again, my [mind] running on this pretty girl.

*1 October 1667*
Home by coach; and there to sing and sup with my wife and look upon our pretty girl, and so to bed.

*22 December 1667. Lord's Day*
Up and then to dress myself and down to my chamber to settle some papers; and thither came to me Willett with an errand from her mistress, and this time I did first give her a little kiss, she being a very pretty-humoured girl, and so one that I do love mightily.

*25 October 1668. Lord's Day*
At night, W. Batelier comes and sups with us; and after supper, to have my head combed by Deb, which occasioned the greatest sorrow to me that ever I knew in this world; for my wife, coming up suddenly, did find me imbracing the girl con my hand sub su coats. I was at a wonderful loss upon it, and the girl also; and I endeavoured to put it off, but my wife was

struck mute and grew angry, and as her voice came to her, grew quite out of order; and I do say little, but to bed; and my wife said little also, but could not sleep all night; but about 2 in the morning waked me and cried... she went on from one thing to another, till at last it appeared plainly her trouble was at what she saw; but yet I did not know how much she saw and therefore said nothing to her. But after her much crying and reproaching me with inconstancy and preferring a sorry girl before her, I did give her no provocations but did promise all fair usage to her, and love, and foreswore any hurt that I did with her – till at last she seemed to be at ease again; and so toward morning, a little sleep; and so I, with some little repose and rest, rose, and up and by water to Whitehall, but with my mind mightily troubled for the poor girl, whom I fear I have undone by this, my [wife] telling me that she would turn her out of door.

Entries from Pepys's diary, 1667–68

**Arnold Bennett (1867–1931)**

# *Miserliness*

*Henry Earlforward kept a second-hand bookshop in London, off the King's Cross Road. His 'thrift' was in fact obsessive miserliness and led to the tragic end of his marriage to Violet, which had promised such happiness.*

In the darkened bedroom Violet leaned over from her side of the bed and placed her lips on Henry's in a long, anxious, loving kiss, and felt the responsive pressure of his rich, indolent lips. They were happy together, these two, so far as the dreadful risks of human existence would allow. Never a cross word! Never a difference!

'How are you?' she murmured.

'I'm all right, Vi.'

'You've got a heavy day in front of you.'

'Yes. Fairly. I'm all right.'

'Darling, I want you to do something for me, to please me. I know you will.'

'I expect I shall.'

'*I want you to eat a good breakfast before you start. I don't like the idea of you –*'

'Oh! *That!*' he interrupted her negligently. 'I always eat as much as I want. Nothing much the matter with me.'

'*No, of course there isn't. But I don't like –*'

'I say,' he interrupted her again. 'I tore the seat of my grey trousers on Sunday. I wish you'd just mend it – now. It won't show, anyhow. You can do it in a minute or two.'

'You never told me.'... Then she rose and slipped an old mantle over her night-dress.

'Oh, Harry,' she cried, near the window, examining the trousers. 'I can't possibly mend this now. It will take me half the morning. You must put on your blue trousers.'

'To go to an auction? No, I can't do that. You'll manage it well enough.'

'But you've got seven pairs of them, and six quite new.'

Years ago he had bought a job lot of blue suits, which fitted him admirably, for a song. Yes, for a song! At the present rate of usage some of them would go down unworn to his heirs. He had had similar luck with a parcel of flannel shirts. On the other hand, the expensiveness and the mortality of socks worried him considerably.

'I don't think I'll wear the blue,' he insisted blandly. 'They're too good, those blue ones are.'

'Well, I shall mend it in bed,' said Violet, brightly yielding. 'There must have been a frost in the night.'

She got back into bed with the trousers and stitching gear, and lit the candle which saved the fantastic cost of electric light. As soon as she had done so, Mr Earlforward arose and drew up the blind.

'I think you won't want that,' said he, indicating the candle.

'No, I shan't,' she agreed, and extinguished the candle.

'You're a fine seamstress,' observed Mr Earlforward with affectionate enthusiasm, 'and I like to see you at it.'

Violet laughed, pleased and flattered. Simple souls, somehow living very near the roots of happiness – though precariously!

From *Riceyman Steps*, 1923

**George Eliot (Mary Ann Evans) 1819–80**

# *Lost gold*

*In* Silas Marner, *a poor weaver leaves home after being wrongly
accused of theft, thereby forfeiting his good name and the woman
he was to wed. In* Raveloe, *where he is unknown, he sets up as
a weaver again, concentrating all his affection and efforts on the
gold he earns. But one day while he is suffering a cataleptic fit
his gold is stolen:*

The light of his faith quite put out, and his affections made desolate, he
had clung with all the force of his nature to his work and his money; and
like all objects to which a man devotes himself, they had fashioned him
into correspondence with themselves. His loom, as he wrought in it
without ceasing, had in its turn wrought on him, and confirmed more and
more the monotonous craving for its monotonous response. His gold, as
he hung over it and saw it grow, gathered his power of loving together into
a hard isolation like its own.

As soon as he was warm, he began to think it would be a long while to
wait till after supper before he drew out his guineas, and it would be
pleasant to see them on the table before him as he ate his unwonted feast.
For joy is the best of wine, and Silas's guineas were a golden wine of that
sort.

He rose and placed his candle unsuspectingly on the floor near his
loom, swept away the sand without noticing any change, and removed
the bricks. The sight of the empty hole made his heart beat violently, but
the belief that his gold was gone could not come at once – only terror,
and the eager effort to put an end to the terror. He passed his trembling
hand all about the hole, trying to think it possible that his eyes had
deceived him; then he held the candle in the hole and examined it
curiously, trembling more and more. At last he shook so violently that he
let fall the candle, and lifted his hands to his head, trying to steady
himself, that he might think. Had he put his gold somewhere else, by a
sudden resolution last night, and then forgotten it? A man falling into
dark water seeks a momentary footing even on sliding stones; and Silas,
by acting as if he believed in false hopes, warded off the moment of
despair. He searched in every corner, he turned his bed over, and shook

it, and kneaded it; he looked in his brick oven where he laid his sticks.

When there was no other place to be searched, he kneeled down again and felt once more all round the hole. There was no untried refuge left for a moment's shelter from the terrible truth.

From *Silas Marner*, 1861

## Samuel Butler (1835–1902)

# *Temptation*

*Ernest had grown up in a clergy family where religion consisted of outward observance and pious words. Later, at university, when he was taken to hear an enthusiastic evangelist, he believed that his life had been transformed:*

Ernest seemed likely to develop – as indeed he did for a time – into a religious enthusiast.

In one matter only, did he openly backslide. He had, as I said above, locked up his pipes and tobacco, so that he might not be tempted to use them. All day long on the day after Mr Hawke's sermon he let them lie in his portmanteau bravely; but this was not very difficult, as he had for some time given up smoking till after hall. After hall this day he did not smoke till chapel time, and then went to chapel in self-defence. When he returned he determined to look at the matter from a common-sense point of view. On this he saw that, provided tobacco did not injure his health – and he really could not see that it did – it stood on much the same footing as tea or coffee.

Tobacco had nowhere been forbidden in the Bible, but then it had not yet been discovered, and had probably only escaped proscription for this reason. We can conceive of St Paul or even our Lord himself drinking a cup of tea, but we cannot imagine either of them smoking a cigarette or a churchwarden. Ernest could not deny this, and admitted that Paul would almost certainly have condemned tobacco in good round terms if he had known of its existence. Was it not then taking a rather mean advantage of the Apostle to stand on his not having actually forbidden it? On the other hand, it was possible that God knew Paul would have forbidden smoking and purposely arranged the discovery of tobacco for a period at which Paul should be no longer living. This might seem rather hard on Paul, considering all he had done for Christianity, but it would be made up to him in other ways.

These reflections satisfied Ernest that on the whole he had better smoke, so he sneaked to his portmanteau and brought out his pipes and tobacco again. There should be moderation he felt in all things, even in virtue; so for that night he smoked immoderately. It was a pity, however, that he had bragged to Dawson about giving up smoking. The pipes had better be kept in a cupboard for a week or two, till in other and easier respects Ernest should have proved his steadfastness. Then they might steal out little by little – and so they did.

From *The Way of All Flesh*, 1903 (published posthumously)

## William Langland (c. 1332–c. 1400)

# *Gluttony*

*Langland's allegorical* Piers the Ploughman *was written in Middle English alliterative verse and describes a journey taken by the poet in a dream, on a quest for the meaning of life and for truth and charity. In the prologue, the poet sees the seven deadly sins personified and the scenes overflow with exuberance and humour as well as mordant wit, depicting fourteenth-century England in vibrant colours.* Piers the Ploughman *is finally transformed to become Christ.*

And then Gluttony set out to go to Confession. But as he sauntered along to the church, he was hailed by Betty, the ale-wife, who asked him where he was going.

'To Holy Church,' he replied, 'to hear Mass and go to Confession; then I shan't commit any more sins.'

*'I've got some good ale here, Glutton,' she said. 'Why don't you come and try it, ducky?'*

'Have you got spices in your bag?'

'Yes, I've got pepper, and peony seeds, and a pound of garlic – or would you rather have a ha'porth of fennel seed, as it's a fish-day?'

So Glutton entered the pub, and Great Oaths followed him. He found Cissie the shoemaker sitting on the bench, and Wat the gamekeeper with his wife, and Tim the tinker with two of his apprentices, and Hick the hackneyman, and Hugh the haberdasher, and Clarice, the whore of Cock Lane, with the parish clerk, and Davy the ditcher, and Father Peter of Prie-Dieu Abbey, with Peacock the Flemish wench, with a dozen others, not to mention a fiddler, and a rat-catcher, and a Cheapside scavenger, a rope-maker and a trooper. Then there was Rose the pewterer, Godfrey of Garlick-hithe, Griffiths the Welshman, and a crew of auctioneers. Well, there they all were, early in the morning, ready to give Glutton a good welcome and start him off with a pint of beer...

There were scowls and roars of laughter and cries of 'Pass round the cup!' And so they sat shouting and singing till time for vespers. By that time, Glutton had put down more than a gallon of ale, and his guts were beginning to rumble like a couple of greedy sows. Then, before you had time to say the Our Father, he had pissed a couple of quarts, and blown such a blast on the round horn of his rump, that all who heard it had to hold their noses, and wished to God he would plug it with a bunch of gorse!

He could neither walk nor stand without his stick. And once he got going, he moved... sometimes sideways, sometimes backwards. And when he drew near to the door, his eyes grew glazed, and he stumbled on the threshold and fell flat on the ground. Then Clement the cobbler seized him round the middle to lift him up, and got him onto his knees. But Glutton was a big fellow, and he took some lifting; and to make matters worse, he was sick in Clement's lap...

At last, after endless trouble, his wife and daughter managed to carry him home and get him into bed...[He] slept throughout Saturday and Sunday. Then at sunset on Sunday he woke up, and as he wiped his bleary eyes, the first words he uttered were,

'Who's had the tankard?'

From the prologue to *Piers the Ploughman*, begun in 1362

**Rose Macaulay (1881–1958)**

# *Adultery*

The Towers of Trebizond, *Rose Macaulay's last novel, describes a trip to Turkey and the Black Sea, on which Laurie, the narrator, accompanies her Aunt Dot and Father Chantry-Pigg, who are exploring, among other things, the possibility of setting up an Anglo-Catholic mission there. Aunt Dot's camel goes too.*

*Laurie stood on deck as they steam down the Black Sea, looking for a first sight of Trebizond. Father Chantry-Pigg joined her:*

He came and stood by me and said, 'How much longer are you going on like this, shutting the door against God?'

This question always disturbed me; I sometimes asked it of myself, but I did not know the answer...

'I don't know,' I said.

'It's your business to know... do you mean to drag on for years more in deliberate sin, refusing grace, denying the Holy Spirit? And when it ends, what then? It will end; such things always end. What then? Shall you come back, when it is taken out of your hands, and it will cost you nothing? When you will have nothing to offer to God but a burnt-out fire and a fag-end? Oh, he'll take it, he'll take anything we offer. It is you who will be impoverished for ever by so poor a gift. Offer now what will cost you a great deal, and you'll be enriched beyond anything you can imagine... You may leave this world without grace, go into the next stage in the chains you won't break now. Do you ever think of that, or have you put yourself beyond caring?'

Not quite, never quite. I had tried, but never quite. From time to time I knew what I had lost. But nearly all the time, God was a bad second, enough to hurt but not to cure, to hide from but not to seek, and I knew that when I died I should hear him saying, 'Go away, I never knew you,' and that would be the end of it all, the end of everything, and after that I never should know him, though then to know him would be what I should want more than anything, and not to know him would be hell. I sometimes felt this even now, but not often enough to break my life to bits...

He left me, and I stayed there at the rail, looking at the bitter Black Sea and its steep forested shores by which the Argonauts had sailed and where presently Trebizond would be seen...

I was a religious child... I was an agnostic through school and university, then, at twenty-three, took up with the Church again; but the Church met its Waterloo a few years later when I took up with adultery; (curious how we always seem to see Waterloo from the French angle and count it a defeat) and this adultery lasted on and on, and I was still in it now, steaming down the Black Sea to Trebizond, and I saw no prospect of it ending except with death – the death of one of three people, and perhaps it would be my own.

From *The Towers of Trebizond*, 1956

# TRUTH AND PRETENCE

## Message of truth

*The night before his death, Jesus said to his disciples:*

'I have much more to tell you but you cannot bear it now. Yet when that one I have spoken to you about comes – the Spirit of truth – he will guide you into everything that is true. For he will not be speaking of his own accord but exactly as he hears, and he will inform you about what is to come. He will bring glory to me for he will draw on my truth and reveal it to you. Whatever the Father possesses is also mine; that is why I tell you that he will draw on my truth and will show it to you.'

From John 16

## Living truthfully

Here, then, is the message which we heard from him, and now proclaim to you: *God is light* and no shadow of darkness can exist in him. Consequently, if we were to say that we enjoyed fellowship with him and still went on living in darkness, we should be both telling and living a lie. But if we really are living in the same light in which he eternally exists, then we have true fellowship with each other, and the blood which his son Jesus shed for us keeps us clean from all sin. If we refuse to admit that we are sinners, then we live in a world of illusion and truth becomes a stranger to us. But if we freely admit that we have sinned, we find him reliable and just – he forgives our sins and makes us thoroughly clean from all that is evil. For if we say 'we have not sinned', we are making him a liar and cut ourselves off from what he has to say to us.

From 1 John 1

## William Makepeace Thackeray (1811–63)

# *Practising deception*

*In* Vanity Fair, *set in the period of the Napoleonic Wars,
Thackeray brilliantly creates his anti-heroine, Becky Sharpe.
She is an impoverished pupil at Miss Pinkerton's Academy in
Chiswick, where she teaches French to other pupils to pay for her
keep. Her friend, Amelia Sedley, innocent, trusting and adored
by well-to-do parents, invites Rebecca home for a fortnight after
they both leave the Academy for the last time:*

You may be sure that she showed Rebecca over every room of the house,
and everything in every one of her drawers; and her books, and her piano,
and her dresses, and all her necklaces, brooches, laces, and gimcracks. She
insisted upon Rebecca accepting the white cornelian and the turquoise
rings, and a sweet sprigged muslin, which was too small for her now,
though it would fit her friend to a nicety; and she determined in her heart
to ask her mother's permission to present her white Cashmere shawl to
her friend. Could she not spare it? – and had not her brother Joseph
brought her two from India?

When Rebecca saw the two magnificent Cashmere shawls which Joseph
Sedley had brought home to his sister, she said, with perfect truth, 'that
it must be delightful to have a brother,' and easily got the pity of the
tender-hearted Amelia, for being alone in the world, an orphan without
friends or kindred.

'Not alone,' said Amelia; 'you know, Rebecca, I shall always be your
friend, and love you as a sister – indeed I will.'

'Ah, but to have parents, as you have – kind, rich, affectionate parents,
who give you everything you ask for; and their love, which is more
precious than all! My poor papa could give me nothing, and I had but two
frocks in all the world! And then to have a brother, a dear brother! Oh,
how you must love him!'

Amelia laughed.

'What! *don't* you love him? you, who say you love everybody?'

'Yes, of course, I do – only –'

'Only what?'

'Only Joseph doesn't seem to care much whether I love him or not. He

gave me two fingers to shake when he arrived after ten years' absence!...
I think he loves his pipe a great deal better than his...' but here Amelia
checked herself, for why should she speak ill of her brother? 'He was very
kind to me as a child,' she added, 'I was but five years old when he went
away.'

'Isn't he very rich?' said Rebecca. 'They say all Indian nabobs are
enormously rich.'

'I believe he has a very large income.'

'And is your sister-in-law a nice pretty woman?'

'La! Joseph is not married,' said Amelia, laughing again.

Perhaps she had mentioned the fact already to Rebecca, but that young
lady did not appear to have remembered it; indeed vowed and protested
that she expected to see a number of Amelia's nephews and nieces. She
was quite disappointed that Mr Sedley was not married; she was sure
Amelia had said he was, and she doted so on little children.

'I think you must have had enough of them at Chiswick,' said Amelia,
rather wondering at the tenderness on her friend's part; and indeed in
later days Miss Sharpe would never have committed herself so far as to
advance opinions the untruth of which would have been so easily
detected. But we must remember that she is but nineteen as yet, unused
to the art of deceiving, poor innocent creature! and making her own
experience in her own person. The meaning of the above series of queries,
as translated in the heart of this ingenious young woman, was simply this:
– 'If Mr Joseph Sedley is rich and unmarried, why should I not marry
him? I have only a fortnight, to be sure, but there is no harm in trying.'
And she determined within herself to make this laudable attempt.

From *Vanity Fair*, first published in parts by *Punch*, beginning in January 1847

## Lewis Carroll (Charles Dodgson) (1832–98)

# *What's in a word?*

*In the course of her adventures through the looking-glass, Alice buys an egg, which turns into the Humpty Dumpty of the nursery rhyme, sitting, true to the original, on a high and narrow wall:*

'What a beautiful belt you've got on!' Alice remarked... 'At least,' she corrected herself on second thoughts, 'a beautiful cravat, I should have said – no, a belt, I mean – I beg your pardon!' she added in dismay...

'It's a cravat, child, and a beautiful one, as you say. It's a present from the White King and Queen. There now!... They gave it me... – for an un-birthday present.'

'I beg your pardon?' Alice said, with a puzzled air.

'I'm not offended,' said Humpty Dumpty.

'I mean what *is* an un-birthday present?'

'A present given when it isn't your birthday, of course.'

Alice considered a little. 'I like birthday presents best,' she said at last.

'You don't know what you're talking about!' cried Humpty Dumpty. 'How many days are there in a year?'

'Three hundred and sixty-five,' said Alice.

'And how many birthdays have you?'

'One.'

'And if you take one from three hundred and sixty-five, what remains?'

'Three hundred and sixty-four, of course...'

'And that shows that there are three hundred and sixty-four days when you might get un-birthday presents –'

'Certainly,' said Alice.

'And only *one* for birthday presents, you know. There's glory for you!'

'I don't know what you mean by "glory,"' Alice said.

Humpty Dumpty smiled contemptuously. 'Of course you don't – till I tell you. I meant "there's a nice knock-down argument for you!"'

'But "glory" doesn't mean "a nice knock-down argument,"' Alice objected.

'When I use a word,' Humpty Dumpty said in rather a scornful tone, 'it means just what I choose it to mean – neither more nor less.'

'The question is,' said Alice, 'whether you *can* make words mean so many different things.'

'The question is,' said Humpty Dumpty, 'which is to be master – that's all... They've a temper, some of them... however, *I* can manage the whole lot of them. Impenetrability! that's what *I* say!'

'Would you tell me, please,' said Alice, 'what that means?'...

'I meant by "impenetrability" that we've had enough of that subject, and it would be just as well if you'd mention what you mean to do next, as I suppose you don't mean to stop here all the rest of your life.'

'That's a great deal to make one word mean,' Alice said in a thoughtful tone.

From *Through the Looking-Glass, and What Alice Found There*, 1872

**Tom Wolfe (b. 1931)**

# New York party chic

*The Bonfire of the Vanities, his best-selling novel first*
*published in 1987, satirises the New York of the 1980s.*
*    Sherman McCoy, 'Wall Street bond-trader with a salary like*
*a telephone number', and his wife Judy ascended in the*
*mahogany-panelled elevator with other guests to the vestibule of*
*the Bavardages' apartment where the party was in full swing:*

There was an open doorway... a rich and rosy glow... the sound of a hive
of excited voices...

They went through the doorway, into the apartment's entry gallery.
Such voices! Such delight! Such laughter! Sherman faced catastrophe in
his career, catastrophe in his marriage – and the police were circling – and
yet the hive – the hive! – the hive! – the sonic waves of the hive made his
innards vibrate. Faces full of grinning, glistening, boiling teeth! How
fabulous and fortunate we are, we few, to be in these upper rooms together
with our radiant and incarnadine glows!...

He surveyed the crowd and immediately sensed a pattern... *presque vu!*
*presque vu!* almost seen!... And yet he couldn't have put it into words. That
would have been beyond him. All the men and women in this hall were
arranged in clusters, conversational bouquets, so to speak. There were no
solitary figures, no strays... There were no men under thirty-five and
precious few under forty. The women came in two varieties. First, there
were women in their late thirties and in their forties and older (women 'of
a certain age'), all of them skin and bones (starved to near perfection). To
compensate for the concupiscence missing from their juiceless ribs and
atrophied backsides, they turned to the dress designers... These were the
social X-rays, to use the phrase that had bubbled up into Sherman's own
brain. Second, there were the so-called Lemon Tarts. These were women
in their twenties or early thirties, mostly blonde (the Lemon in the Tarts)
who were the second, third, or fourth wives or live-in girlfriends of men
over forty or fifty or sixty (or seventy), the sort of women that men refer
to, quite without thinking, as *girls*. This season the Tart was able to flaunt
the natural advantages of youth by showing her legs from well above the
knee and emphasizing her round bottom (something no X-ray had). What

was entirely missing from *chez* Bavardage was that manner of woman who is neither very young nor very old, who has laid in a lining of subcutaneous fat, who glows with plumpness and a rosy face that speaks, without a word, of home and hearth and hot food ready at six and stories read aloud at night and conversations while seated on the edge of the bed, just before the Sandman comes. In short, no one ever invited... Mother.

From *The Bonfire of the Vanities*, 1987

**Beatrix Potter (1866–1943)**

# *Jemima Puddle-duck*

*Jemima's eggs are always taken from her by the farmer's wife, to be hatched by a more reliable hen. Jemima is determined to hatch her own eggs, so flies away from the farm to the woods.*

Jemima alighted rather heavily, and began to waddle about in search of a convenient dry nesting-place. She rather fancied a tree-stump amongst some tall fox-gloves.

But – seated upon the stump, she was startled to find an elegantly dressed gentleman reading a newspaper.

He had black prick ears and sandy coloured whiskers.

'Quack?' said Jemima Puddle-duck, with her head and her bonnet on one side –

'Quack?'

The gentleman raised his eyes above his newspaper and looked curiously at Jemima. 'Madam, have you lost your way?' said he. He had a long bushy tail which he was sitting upon, as the stump was somewhat damp.

Jemima thought him mighty civil and handsome. She explained that she had not lost her way, but that she was trying to find a convenient dry nesting-place.

'Ah! is that so? Indeed!' said the gentleman with sandy whiskers, looking curiously at Jemima. He folded up the newspaper, and put it in his coat-tail pocket.

Jemima complained of the superfluous hen.

'Indeed! How interesting! I wish I could meet with that fowl. I would teach it to mind its own business!

'But as to a nest – there is no difficulty: I have a sackful of feathers in my wood-shed. No, my dear madam, you will be in nobody's way. You may sit there as long as you like,' said the bushy long-tailed gentleman.

He led the way to a very retired, dismal-looking house amongst the fox-gloves.

It was built of faggots and turf, and there were two broken pails, one on top of the other, by way of a chimney.

'This is my summer residence; you would not find my earth – my winter house – so convenient,' said the hospitable gentleman.

There was a tumble-down shed at the back of the house, made of old soap-boxes. The gentleman opened the door and showed Jemima in.

The shed was almost quite full of feathers – it was almost suffocating; but it was comfortable and very soft.

Jemima Puddle-duck was rather surprised to find such a vast quantity of feathers. But it was very comfortable; and she made a nest without any trouble at all.

From *The Tale of Jemima Puddle-Duck,* 1908

Dorothy L. Sayers (1893–1957)

# Advertising 'truth' in the 1930s

*In* Murder Must Advertise, *Lord Peter Wimsey took a job in an advertising agency in order to investigate, unobtrusively, the suspicious death of a member of staff. He adopted the pseudonym of Death Bredon (his own middle names):*

To Lord Peter Wimsey, the few weeks of his life spent in unravelling the Problem of the Iron Staircase possessed an odd dreamlike quality... the very work that engaged him... wafted him into a sphere of dim platonic archetypes, bearing a scarcely recognizable relationship to anything in the living world. Here those strange entities, the Thrifty Housewife, the Man of Discrimination, the Keen Buyer and the Good Judge, for ever young, for ever handsome, for ever virtuous, economical and inquisitive, moved to and fro upon their complicated orbits, comparing prices and values, making tests of purity, asking indiscreet questions about each other's ailments, household expenses, bed-springs, shaving cream, diet, laundry work and boots, perpetually spending to save and saving to spend, cutting out coupons and collecting cartons... occupied from morning to night in washing, cooking, dusting, filing, saving their children from germs, their complexions from wind and weather, their teeth from decay and their stomachs from indigestion, and yet adding so many hours to the day by labour-saving appliances that they always had leisure... Where, Bredon asked himself, did the money come from that was to be spent so variously and so lavishly?... If all the advertising in the world were to shut down tomorrow, would people still go on buying... or would the whole desperate whirligig slow down, and the exhausted public relapse upon plain grub and elbow-grease? He did not know. Like all rich men, he had never before paid any attention to advertisements. He had never realized the enormous commercial importance of the comparatively poor. Not on the wealthy, who buy only what they want when they want it, was the vast superstructure of industry founded and built up, but on those who, aching for a luxury beyond their reach and for a leisure for ever denied them, could be bullied or wheedled into spending their few hardly won shillings on whatever might give them, if only for a moment, a leisured and luxurious illusion.

From *Murder Must Advertise*, 1933

## T.S. Eliot (1888–1965)

# *Truth or 'spin'?*

Murder in the Cathedral *was written for the Canterbury Festival of 1935 and first performed in the cathedral. Having murdered Thomas Becket in cold blood, the four knights made speeches to justify their action to the audience:*

*Third Knight*

I am afraid I am not anything like such an experienced speaker as my old friend Reginald Fitz Urse would lead you to believe. But there is one thing I should like to say, and I might as well say it at once. It is this: in what we have done, and whatever you may think of it, we have been perfectly disinterested. [*the other* Knights: 'Hear! Hear!']

*We* are not getting anything out of this. We have much more to lose than to gain. We are four plain Englishmen who put our country first. I dare say that we didn't make a very good impression when we came in just now. The fact is that we knew we had taken on a pretty stiff job; I'll only speak for myself, but I had drunk a good deal – I am not a drinking man ordinarily – to brace myself up for it. When you come to the point, it does go against the grain to kill an Archbishop, especially when you have been brought up in good Church traditions. So if we seemed a bit rowdy, you will understand why it was; and for my part I am awfully sorry about it. We realized this was our duty, but all the same we had to work ourselves up to it. And, as I said, *we* are not getting a penny out of this. We know perfectly well how things will turn out. King Henry – God bless him – will have to say, for reasons of state, that he never meant this to happen; and then there is going to be an awful row; and at the best we shall have to spend the rest of our lives abroad. And even when reasonable people come to see that the Archbishop *had* to be put out of the way – and personally I had a tremendous admiration for him – you must have noticed what a good show he put up at the end – they won't give *us* any glory. No, we have done for ourselves, there's no mistake about that. So, as I said at the beginning, please give us at least the credit for being completely disinterested in this business. I think that is about all I have to say.

From *Murder in the Cathedral*, 1935

# WAR AND PEACE

## No more war

*Both Isaiah and Micah – prophets who spoke out God's message in the second half of the eighth century BC – include this oracle, perhaps the work of some third, unknown prophet.*

In days to come,
   the mountain of the Lord's house
shall be established as the highest of the mountains,
   and shall be raised up above the hills.
Peoples shall stream to it,
   and many nations shall come and say:
'Come, let us go up to the mountain of the Lord,
   to the house of the God of Jacob;
that he may teach us his ways
   and that we may walk in his paths.'
For out of Zion shall go instruction,
   and the word of the Lord from Jerusalem.
He shall judge between many peoples,
   and shall arbitrate between strong nations far away;
they shall beat their swords into ploughshares,
   and their spears into pruning-hooks;
nation shall not lift up sword against nation,
   neither shall they learn war any more;
but they shall all sit under their own vines and under
      their own fig trees,
   and no one shall make them afraid;
   for the mouth of the Lord of hosts has spoken.

From Micah 4

# The glory has departed

*Before the days of the monarchy in Israel, there were constant battles against the Philistines, who had settled along the coastal strip of Canaan. Hoping for victory, the Israelites took with them into battle the sacred Ark of God, as a lucky talisman. Eli, the old priest of the shrine at Shiloh, and guardian of the Ark, waited in trepidation for news of the battle in which his two reprobate sons were also fighting.*

The Philistines fought, and Israel was smitten, and they fled every man into his tent: and there was a very great slaughter; for there fell of Israel thirty thousand footmen. And the ark of God was taken; and the two sons of Eli, Hophni and Phinehas, were slain.

And there ran a man of Benjamin out of the army, and came to Shiloh the same day with his clothes rent, and with earth upon his head. And when he came, lo, Eli sat upon a seat by the wayside watching: for his heart trembled for the ark of God. And when the man came into the city, and told it, all the city cried out. And when Eli heard the noise of the crying, he said, What meaneth the noise of this tumult? And the man came in hastily, and told Eli. Now Eli was ninety and eight years old; and his eyes were dim, that he could not see. And the man said unto Eli, I am he that came out of the army, and I fled to day out of the army. And he said, What is there done, my son? And the messenger answered and said, Israel is fled before the Philistines, and there hath been also a great slaughter among the people, and thy two sons also, Hophni and Phinehas, are dead, and the ark of God is taken. And it came to pass, when he made mention of the ark of God, that he fell from off the seat backward by the side of the gate, and his neck brake, and he died: for he was an old man, and heavy. And he had judged Israel forty years.

And his daughter in law, Phinehas's wife, was with child, near to be delivered: and when she heard the tidings that the ark of God was taken, and that her father in law and her husband were dead, she bowed herself and travailed; for her pains came upon her. And about the time of her death the women that stood by her said unto her, Fear not; for thou hast born a son. But she answered not, neither did she regard it. And she named the child Ichabod, saying, The glory is departed from Israel: because the ark of God was taken, and because of her father in law and her husband. And she said, The glory is departed from Israel: for the ark of God is taken.

From 1 Samuel 4

## Wilfred Owen (1893–1918)

# *The poet and war*

*In this letter from hospital on the Somme in the First World War, Owen outlined his creed about war:*

Already I have comprehended a light which will never filter into the dogma of any national church: namely, that one of Christ's essential commands was: Passivity at any price! Suffer dishonour and disgrace, but never resort to arms. Be bullied, be outraged, be killed; but do not kill. It may be a chimerical and an ignominious principle, but there it is. It can only be ignored; and I think pulpit professionals are ignoring it very skilfully and successfully indeed... And am I not myself a conscientious objector with a very seared conscience?... Christ is literally in 'no man's land'. There men often hear his voice: Greater love hath no man than this, that a man lay down his life for a friend. Is it spoken in English only and French? I do not believe so. Thus you see how pure Christianity will not fit in with pure patriotism.

> *Owen's war poems express the horror and the pity of war. In a hastily written preface to the volume of poems he planned to publish, Owen explained their raison d'être:*

This book is not about heroes. English Poetry is not yet fit to speak of them. Nor is it about deeds, or lands, nor anything about glory, honour, might, majesty, dominion or power, except War.

Above all, I am not concerned with Poetry.

My subject is War, and the pity of War.

The Poetry is in the pity.

Yet these elegies are to this generation in no sense consolatory. They may be to the next. All a poet can do to-day is warn. That is why the true Poets must be truthful.

(If I thought the letter of this book would last, I might have used proper names; but if the spirit of it survives – survives Prussia – my ambition and those names will have achieved themselves fresher fields than Flanders...)

From the memoir and preface to *Poems*, 1931

## Abraham Lincoln (1809–65)

# *The fruits of war*

*On 19 November 1863 Abraham Lincoln, president of the United States, delivered his famous Gettysburg Address at the dedication of a cemetery for the 3,600 Union soldiers who had died there in one of the worst battles of the Civil War. Two years later, in April 1865, he was assassinated.*

Four score and seven years ago our fathers brought forth on this continent a new nation, conceived in Liberty, and dedicated to the proposition that all men are created equal.

Now we are engaged in a great civil war, testing whether that nation, or any nation so conceived and so dedicated, can long endure. We are met on a great battle-field of that war. We have come to dedicate a portion of that field as a final resting place for those who here gave their lives that that nation might live. It is altogether fitting and proper that we should do this.

But, in a larger sense, we cannot dedicate – we cannot consecrate – we cannot hallow – this ground. The brave men, living and dead, who struggled here, have consecrated it, far above our poor power to add or detract. The world will little note, nor long remember, what we say here, but it can never forget what they did here. It is for us the living, rather, to be dedicated here to the unfinished work which they who fought here have thus far so nobly advanced. It is rather for us to be here dedicated to the great task remaining before us – that from these honoured dead we take increased devotion to that cause for which they gave the last full measure of devotion – that we here highly resolve that these dead shall not have died in vain – that this nation, under God, shall have a new birth of freedom – and that government of the people, by the people, for the people, shall not perish from the earth.

'The Gettysburg Address', 1863

# War and reason

*In the country of the Houyhnhnms (or horses) Gulliver discovered that normal patterns were reversed; Yahoos (humans) were servants and Houyhnhnms the masters. Gulliver's Houyhnhnm master was puzzled by the practice of lying among Gulliver's people and also asked him to explain war and the reasons for war among the Yahoos in his countries.*

In obedience therefore to his Honour's commands, I related to him the Revolution under the Prince of Orange, the long war with France entered into by the said Prince... and which still continued: I computed, at his request, that about a million of Yahoos might have been killed in the whole progress of it, and perhaps a hundred or more cities taken, and five times as many ships burnt or sunk.

He asked what were the usual causes or motives that made one country go to war with another. I answered they were innumerable, but I should only mention a few of the chief. Sometimes the ambition of princes, who never think they have land or people enough to govern: sometimes the corruption of ministers, who engage their master in a war in order to stifle or divert the clamour of the subjects against their evil administration. Difference in opinion hath caused many millions of lives: for instance, whether *flesh* be *bread*, or *bread* be *flesh*; whether the juice of a certain berry be *blood* or *wine*... with many more. Neither are any wars so furious or bloody, or of so long continuance, as those occasioned by difference in opinion, especially if it be in things indifferent.

Sometimes the quarrel between two princes is to decide which of them shall dispossess a third of his dominions, where neither of them pretend to any right. Sometimes one prince quarrelleth with another, for fear the other should quarrel with him... It is a very justifiable cause of war to invade a country after the people have been wasted by famine, destroyed by pestilence, or embroiled by factions among themselves... If a prince sends forces into a nation where the people are poor and ignorant, he may lawfully put half of them to death, and make slaves of the rest, in order to civilise and reduce them from their barbarous way of living...

For these reasons the trade of a *soldier* is held the most honourable of all others: because a *soldier* is a Yahoo hired to kill in cold blood as many of his own species, who have never offended him, as possibly he can.

From *Gulliver's Travels*, 1726

Sebastian Faulks (b. 1953)

# *Peace and reconciliation*

*In the First World War, Allied and German soldiers dug tunnels into no-man's-land, to provide listening posts near enemy lines. The war was all but over when Captain Stephen Wraysford was sent underground to check for enemy activity. In explosions that followed, both Stephen's companions and German soldiers were killed. One of the German soldiers was Joseph, and his brother Levi, along with Lamm, worked urgently to release the trapped men. Levi knew he would find alive either his beloved brother Joseph – or the enemy who killed him.*

It was Levi's work, not Lamm's, that had loosened the earth sufficiently at the end of Stephen's coffin for him to be able to crawl out of it...

On hands and knees he moved back among the debris his own explosion had made. About a yard further along he could see where the tunnel was still intact. It was here that Lamm had broken through. Levi pushed Lamm back and climbed into the British tunnel himself. Tricked by the echo of Stephen's tapping, he turned the wrong way, and began to walk away from him.

Gurgling and spitting earth from his mouth, Stephen clawed his way forward, shouting as he went. He could see light from some lantern swaying in the tunnel ahead of him. There was air. He could breathe.

Levi heard him. He turned and walked back.

As the tunnel roof lifted, Stephen moved up into a crouch and called out again. The lantern was on him.

He looked up and saw the legs of his rescuer. They were clothed in the German feldgrau, the colour of his darkest dream.

He staggered to his feet and his hand went to pull out his revolver, but there was nothing there, only the torn, drenched rags of his trousers.

He looked into the face of the man who stood in front of him and his fists went up from his sides like those of a farm boy about to fight.

At some deep level, far below anything his exhausted mind could reach, the conflicts of his soul dragged through him like waves grating on the packed shingle of a beach. The sound of his life calling to him on a distant road; the faces of the men who had been slaughtered... his scalding hatred of the enemy, of Max and all the men who had brought him to this moment; the flesh and love of Isabelle, and the eyes of her sister.

Far beyond thought, the resolution came to him and he found his arms, still raised, begin to spread and open.

Levi looked at this wild-eyed figure, half-demented, his brother's killer. For no reason he could tell, he found that he had opened his own arms in turn, and the two men fell upon each other's shoulders, weeping at the bitter strangeness of their human lives.

From *Birdsong*, 1993

# A king in war

*In his biography of King George V, Churchill wrote glowingly
of the king's conduct both before and during the First World
War:*

Suddenly, out of what, to ordinary folk, appeared to be a summer sky,
rushed the thunderbolts of world war.

This is not the place to argue whether a more precise declaration by
Great Britain might have postponed the German onslaught. It must have
been with great compunction that King George, by the advice of Sir
Edward Grey, signed his non-committal reply to the impassioned appeal
of President Poincaré. Certainly he understood as well as any of his
Ministers the vital need of bringing the British Empire unitedly into the
struggle. Certainly also that love of peace – though not peace at any price
– which his whole reign evinced, led him to avoid the formidable danger
of moving in such a terrible business in advance of public opinion. The
reserve, and even apparent hesitancy, of Britain were part of the price we
had to pay for being a free Constitutional Democracy. But we gained it
back tenfold by the surge of national and Imperial resolve and inflexible
determination, wearing down the will-power of every antagonist, lasting
unquenched over fifty-two fearful months, with which the nation once
convinced entered the struggle…

The King and his devoted Queen threw themselves into every form of
war work and set an example to all. Tirelessly the King inspected and
reviewed the growing armies, alas for many months without weapons.
Day by day he encouraged and assisted his ministers in their various
tasks. As soon as his eldest son reached the minimum age he allowed him
to go to the Front, where that Prince – afterwards King Edward VIII –
was repeatedly under shell and rifle fire in the trenches as a junior officer
of the Guards… But his second son, now King George VI, was also in
danger. He served afloat and was present at the battle of Jutland, the
largest of all naval encounters. King George himself frequently visited
the war zone, and the photographs of him in his steel helmet attest the
numerous occasions when he came under or within the fire of the enemy.
On one of these visits of inspection an unlucky accident occurred. His

horse, startled by the loud cheers of the troops, reared up and fell backwards, crushing and mangling the King in a most grievous manner. When some months later I took leave of him, on resigning from the Cabinet, I was shocked at his shattered condition and evident physical weakness, which had of course been hidden from the world.

From *Great Contemporaries*, 1937

## John Betjeman (1906–84)

# *War's silver lining*

*From 1940 to 1945, during the dark days of the Second World War, John Betjeman was commissioned by the BBC to give talks that would cheer and encourage the British public, who already knew and loved him:*

The title of this talk might lead you to think that I was going to make some sort of political comment. But I'm afraid you will be disappointed. I don't know anything about politics. Instead I am going to talk about some of the pleasant things I have discovered as a result of this war, and observations about things, scenery and people in these islands...

For instance, the country, which people who don't live in it call 'the countryside'. It used to be the thing to say, 'Oh, the country's all right in the summer, but I should go mad if I had to live in it all the year round.' By now, many thousands of town people will have spent a winter in the country for the first time. They will have seen that the country in winter is as full of life as in the summer. They will have noticed how willows burn red in the meadows before they bud and how oaks turn gold with early leaf. They will have known the pleasure of feeling rain on the face and retreating to a warm cottage and the comfortable feeling of listening to the storm outside...

For those of us who live in the country, the war has increased our love of it. I used for ever to be on the rush, even in the country. Hedges and fields swirled by from the windows of cars and trains. Then when my activity was slowed down, I started to see again and to feel... I stood on bridges and watched water beetles and water boatmen scudding about on the surface, mud-coloured fish lurking in the depths below. One garden wall, one stream, one tree, one tiny little bed of earth, became something to watch and enjoy, whereas before I had taken them for granted and hurried on in pursuit of that fussy grab for money called 'business'...

The time came for me to leave my family in the country and take up work in a big town. And the town instead of being the roaring hell of the past, that I dreaded visiting, had submitted itself to a decent discipline with comparatively few motors on the road. Now the buildings stand out and I have time to see them – decent Georgian terraces built of brick with windows neatly graded in height; fanciful and often beautiful Victorian churches with their tall spires and towers... Luxuriant plane trees hanging over squares, that healthy smell of tar melting in the sun instead of the blue petrol vapours of the past...

Yes, the war has wakened my wits a bit and showed me the beauty of England, in all sorts of places where I did not expect to find it. It has done something else. It has made me see that possessions don't matter and that what really does matter is people, not their possessions. As the result of billeting and various war occupations I have had to meet all sorts of strangers and as a result, I like to think that I have made a lot of new friends... War brings out the best in people; dithery old fusspots suddenly cease to fuss: the most unexpected people show great courage and pessimists become cheerful. War divides us into where we really belong. Class nonsense and incomes and possessions become of no importance. The cake is cut at right angles to the way it was cut before... War sorts us all out and the process is sad and painful, very sad and very painful for some of us. But also it teaches us to look at the world about us and gives us new interests. Better still, it teaches us to consider other people and to value a man not according to his income but according to his heart.

From *Some Comments in Wartime*, broadcast on the BBC Home Service, 4 July 1940

## Richard Baxter (1615–91)

# *No promised peace*

*Baxter was deeply grieved by 'our sad divisions and unchristianlike quarrels with one another'. In the seventh edition of* The Saints' Everlasting Rest, *Baxter added a marginal note to the extract that follows: 'this was written upon the war in Scotland... and an Ordinance for the sequestering of all Ministers who would not go to God on their Errand, in Fasting and Prayer, or in Thanksgiving for their successes.'*

O what sweet Idolizing thoughts of our future state, had we in time of Wars! What full content did I promise my soul! when I should enjoy Peace, and see the Gospel set up in power and plenty, and all the ordinances in purity, and true Discipline exercised in the Churches, and ignorance cured, and all persecution ceased, and the mouths of railers stopped, who kept men from Christ by filling the world with prejudice against him! And now where is the Rest which I promised my soul? even that is my greatest grief from which I expected most Content. Instead of Peace we have more bloodshed: and such as is confessed to be the blood of Saints: the two nations that were bound in an oath of Union, and where so great a part of the Interest of Christ on earth is contained... are dashing each other in pieces, and the souls of multitudes let out of their bodies, by those that look to rejoyce with them for ever in Heaven.

From *The Saints' Everlasting Rest*, 1650

### Leo Tolstoy (1828–1910)

# Sharing the pains of war

*In* War and Peace, *Tolstoy centred events on Napoleon's war with Russia through which his main characters – Natasha Rostov, Prince Andrew Bolkonsky and Pierre Bezukov – change and mature. Pierre, taken prisoner at one point, was now with Princess Mary and Natasha in the 'large, brightly lit dining-room':*

'And did you really see and speak to Napoleon, as we have been told?' said Princess Mary.

Pierre laughed.

'No, never once! Everybody seems to imagine that being taken prisoner means being Napoleon's guest. Not only did I never see him, But I heard nothing about him – I was in much lower company!'

Supper was over, and Pierre, who at first declined to speak about his captivity, was gradually led on to do so...

At first he spoke with the amused and mild irony now customary with him towards everybody and especially towards himself, but when he came to describe the horrors and sufferings he had witnessed he was unconsciously carried away, and began speaking with the suppressed emotion of a man re-experiencing in recollection strong impressions he has lived through.

Princess Mary with a gentle smile looked now at Pierre and now at Natasha. In the whole narrative she saw only Pierre and his goodness. Natasha, leaning on her elbow, the expression of her face constantly changing with the narrative, watched Pierre with an attention that never wandered – evidently herself experiencing all that he described. Not only her look, but her exclamations and the brief questions she put, showed Pierre that she understood just what he wished to convey. It was clear that she understood not only what he said, but what he wished to, but could not, express in words. The account Pierre gave of the incident with the child and the woman for protecting whom he was arrested, was this: 'It was an awful sight – children abandoned, some in the flames... One was snatched out before my eyes... and there were women who had their things snatched off and their ear-rings torn out...' he flushed and grew confused. 'Then a patrol arrived and all the men – all those who were not looting that is – were arrested, and I among them.'...

He told of his adventures as he had never yet recalled them. He now, as it were, saw a new meaning in all he had gone through... Natasha, without knowing it, was all attention: she did not lose a word, no single quiver in Pierre's voice, no look, no twitch of a muscle in his face, or a single gesture. She caught the unfinished word in its flight and took it straight into her open heart, divining the secret meaning of all Pierre's mental travail.

From *War and Peace*, 1863–69

PART FIVE

# THE CYCLE
# OF LIFE

# BIRTH, CHILDHOOD
# AND YOUTH

## God's handiwork

*Lord... it was you who formed my inward parts;*
  *you knit me together in my mother's womb.*
*I praise you, for I am fearfully and wonderfully made.*
  *Wonderful are your works;*
*that I know very well.*
  *My frame was not hidden from you,*
*when I was being made in secret,*
  *intricately woven in the depths of the earth.*
*Your eyes beheld my unformed substance.*
*In your book were written*
  *all the days that were formed for me,*
  *when none of them as yet existed.*

From Psalm 139

## God's children

Some people brought their little children for Jesus to bless. But when his disciples saw them doing this, they told the people to stop bothering him. So Jesus called the children over to him and said, 'Let the children come to me! Don't try to stop them. People who are like these children belong to God's kingdom. You will never get into God's kingdom unless you enter it like a child!'

From Luke 18

## Tim Winton (b. 1960)

# *A neighbourhood birth*

*A pair of newlyweds moved into a neighbourhood full of European migrants. He was writing a thesis on the twentieth-century novel while she went out to work. Life was very different from the suburbs both had grown up in, where neighbours were seen but not heard. Then, unexpectedly, the young wife became pregnant:*

Before long the young couple realized that the whole neighbourhood knew of the pregnancy. People smiled tirelessly at them. The man in the deli gave her small presents of chocolates and him packets of cigarettes, that he stored at home, not being a smoker. In the summer, Italian women began to offer names. Greek women stopped the young woman in the street, pulled her skirt up and felt her belly, telling her it was bound to be a boy. By late summer the woman next door had knitted the baby a suit... The young woman felt flattered, claustrophobic, grateful, peeved...

Labour came abruptly. The young man abandoned the twentieth-century novel for the telephone. His wife began to black the stove. The midwife came and helped her finish the job while he ran about making statements that sounded like queries. His wife hoisted her belly about the house, supervising his movements. Going outside for more wood, he saw in the last light of day, the faces at each fence. He counted twelve faces. The Macedonian family waved and called out what sounded like their best wishes.

As the night deepened, the young woman dozed between contractions, sometimes walking, sometimes shouting. She had a hot bath and began to eat ice and demand liverwurst. Her belly rose, uterus flexing downward. Her sweat sparkled, the gossamer highlit by movement and firelight. The night grew older. The midwife crooned. The young man rubbed his wife's back, fed her ice and rubbed her lips with oil.

And then came the pushing. He caressed and stared and tried not to shout. The floor trembled as the young woman bore down in a squat. He felt the power of her, the sophistication of her. She strained. Her face mottled. She kept at it, push after push, assaulting some unseen barrier, until suddenly it was smashed and she was through. It took his wind away to see the look on the baby's face as it was suddenly passed up to the breast. It had one eye on him. It found the nipple. It trailed cord and vernix smears and its mother's own sweat. She gasped and covered the tiny buttocks with a hand. A boy, she said. For a second, the child lost the nipple and began to cry. The young man heard shouting outside. He went to the back door. On the Macedonian side of the fence, a small queue of bleary faces looked up, cheering, and the young man began to weep. The twentieth-century novel had not prepared him for this.

From 'Neighbours', *Scission and Other Stories*, 1985

### E.M. Forster (1879–1970)

# *Virgin and child*

*When Lilia – member of a conventional English family – and her friend Caroline Abbott visit Italy, Lilia falls in love and marries a handsome young Italian. Her family is appalled and when Lilia dies giving birth to a son, both Miss Abbott and members of Lilia's family set off for Italy independently to rescue the baby, bring him to England and give him a 'respectable' upbringing. Miss Abbott visits Carlo, who tells her of his plans to marry again to provide a mother for the baby:*

'He is troublesome, but I must have him with me. I will not even have my father and mother too. For they would separate us.'

'How?'

'They would separate our thoughts.'

She was silent... The horrible truth, that wicked people are capable of love, stood naked before her, and her moral being was abashed. It was her duty to rescue the baby, to save it from contagion, and she still meant to do her duty. But the comfortable sense of virtue left her...

Forgetting that this was an interview, he had strolled back into the room... 'Wake up!' he cried to the baby, as if it was some grown-up friend. Then he lifted his foot and trod lightly on its stomach.

Miss Abbott cried, 'Oh, take care!' She was unaccustomed to this method of awakening the young...

The baby gave a piercing yell.

'Oh, do take care!' begged Miss Abbott. 'You are squeezing it.'

'It is nothing... He thinks I am going to wash him, and he is quite right.'

'Wash him?' she cried, 'You? Here?' The homely piece of news seemed to shatter all her plans...

He walked sternly to the loggia and drew from it a large earthenware bowl. It was dirty inside; he dusted it with a tablecloth. Then he fetched the hot water, which was in a copper pot. He poured it out. He added cold. He felt in his pocket and brought out a piece of soap. Then he took up the baby, and, holding his cigar between his teeth, began to unwrap it.

'But why are you going? Excuse me if I wash him while we talk.'

'I have nothing more to say,' said Miss Abbott...

'Oh, but stop a moment!' he cried. 'You have not seen him yet.'

'I have seen as much as I want, thank you.'

The last wrapping slid off. He held out to her in his two hands a little kicking image of bronze.

'Take him!'

She would not touch the child.

'I must go at once,' she cried; for the tears – the wrong tears – were hurrying to her eyes...

'Ah, but how beautiful he is! And he is mine; mine for ever. Even if he hates me he will be mine. He cannot help it; he is made out of me; I am his father.'

It was too late to go. She could not tell why, but it was too late...

'May I help you to wash him?' she asked humbly.

He gave her his son without speaking, and they knelt side by side, tucking up their sleeves. The child had stopped crying, and his arms and legs were agitated by some overpowering joy...

'I am ready for a soft towel now,' said Miss Abbott, who was strangely exalted by the service.

'Certainly! Certainly!' He strode in a knowing way to a cupboard. He had no idea where the soft towel was. Generally he dabbed the baby on the first dry thing he found...

She sacrificed her own clean handkerchief. He put a chair for her on the loggia... and he placed the dripping baby on her knee. It shone now with health and beauty; it seemed to reflect light, like a copper vessel. Just such a baby Bellini sets languid on his mother's lap, or Signorelli flings wriggling on pavements of marble, or Lorenzo di Credi, more reverent but less divine, lays carefully among flowers, with his head upon a wisp of straw. For a time Gino contemplated them standing. Then, to get a better view, he knelt by the side of the chair, with his hands clasped before him.

So they were when Philip entered, and saw, to all intents and purposes, The Virgin and Child, with Donor.

From *Where Angels Fear to Tread*, 1905

## L.P. Hartley (1895–1972)

# *At the beach*

*Eustace and his older sister, Hilda, have been on the beach at Anchorstone, banking up the sand to make a pond – a favourite pursuit of local children, which is approached by Hilda with professional determination:*

Hilda, who possessed a watch, announced that it was dinner-time. Collecting their spades and buckets they made their way across the sand and shingle to the concrete flight of steps which zigzagged majestically up the red sandstone cliffs... Their ascent was slow because Eustace had formed a habit of counting the steps. Their number appealed to his sense of grandeur, and though they usually came to the same total, a hundred and nineteen, he tried to think he had made a mistake and that one day they would reach a hundred and twenty, an altogether more desirable figure. He had grounds for this hope because, at the foot of the stairs, six inches deep in sand, there undoubtedly existed another step. Eustace could feel it with his spade. A conscientious scruple forbade him to count it with the rest, but – who could tell? – some day a tidal wave might come and lay it bare... When they reached the top... they surveyed the sands below. There lay the pond... but – horrors! – it was completely dry... a gaping hole in the retaining wall must be the work of an enemy. A small figure was walking away from the scene of demolition with an air of elaborate unconcern. 'That's Gerald Steptoe,' said Hilda. 'I should like to kill him!'

'He's very naughty... he doesn't pay any attention to Nancy,' remarked Eustace, hoping to mollify his sister.

'She's as bad as he is! I should like to –' Hilda looked around her...

'What would you do?' asked Eustace fearfully.

'I should tie them together and throw them off the cliff!'

Eustace tried to conceal the pain he felt.

'Oh, but Nancy sent you her love!'

'She didn't mean it. Anyhow I don't want to be loved by her... I should like to be loved by somebody great and good.'...

She... started at a great pace up the chalky footpath. Eustace followed more slowly... searching for a lover who should fulfil his sister's requirements. But he could think of no one but God or Jesus and he didn't like to mention their names except in church or at his prayers or during Scripture lessons. Baffled, he hurried after Hilda… but he had small hope of catching up with her, and the start she had gained would be enough to make her in time for dinner and him late.

From *The Shrimp and the Anemone*, 1944

**Maxim Gorky (Aleksei Maximovich Peshkov) (1868–1936)**

# Death to the frogs

*The child Aleksei is taken to the see the body of his father, dead from cholera.*

By the window of a small, darkened room Father lay on the floor, dressed in white, and looking terribly long. His feet were bare and his toes were strangely splayed out. His gentle fingers, now peacefully resting on his chest, were also distorted, and the black discs of copper coins firmly sealed his once shining eyes. His kind face had darkened and its nastily bared teeth frightened me.

Mother, half naked in a red skirt, was kneeling beside him, combing his long soft hair down from the forehead to the nape of his neck with the black comb I loved to use as a saw for melon rinds. She kept muttering something in a hoarse, deep voice. Her grey eyes were swollen and seemed to be dissolving in a flood of tears.

Grandmother was holding me by the hand. She was a fat, round woman with a large head, enormous eyes and a funny, puffy nose. She was crying as well, her voice pitched differently from Mother's but in a way that perfectly harmonised with it. Shaking all over, she pulled and pushed me over to Father. I stubbornly resisted and tried to hide behind her, for I felt frightened and out of place there.

I'd never seen grown-ups crying before and couldn't make head or tail of the words Grandmother repeated again and again:

'Say good-bye to your father. You won't ever see him again, dear. He died too young, before his time...'

Another vivid experience that stands out in my memory is a rainy day in a deserted corner of a cemetery. I stood on a slippery heap of sticky mud and looked down into the pit where my father's coffin had been lowered. At the bottom was a lot of water, and a few frogs. Two of them had succeeded in climbing onto the yellow coffin lid. My grandmother, myself, a policeman who looked soaked to the skin, and two men with spades who were evidently in a very bad mood, had gathered round the grave. A warm rain, as fine as delicate beads, began to fall gently on us.

'Fill it in,' said the policeman as he walked away.

Grandmother burst into tears and hid her face in her shawl. The gravediggers, bent double, began piling the earth into the grave at great speed. Water squelched. The frogs jumped off the coffin and tried to escape up the sides, but were thrown back by clods of earth.

'Let's go now, Lenya,' said Grandmother, as she put her hand on my shoulder. Reluctant to leave, I slipped out of her grasp.

'God help us,' she grumbled, not at me, or even at God, and she stood by the grave for a long time, quite silent. Even when the grave had been levelled off she still stood there.

The gravediggers smacked their spades against the mud, which made them ring out with a hollow sound. A sudden gust of wind drove away the rain.

Grandmother took my hand and led me to a distant church surrounded by a great number of dark crosses.

'Why don't you cry?' she asked when we left the cemetery. 'You *ought* to cry.'

'I don't want to,' I replied.

'Well, you'd better not if you don't want to,' she said softly...

Afterwards we drove in a droshky along a broad and very muddy street lined with houses painted deep red. I asked Grandmother:

'Will the frogs get out?'

'No, they don't stand a chance, God help them!'

Neither my mother nor my father ever mentioned the name of God so often and with such familiarity.

From *My Childhood*, 1913

## Daisy Ashford (1881–1972)

# *Family ancestors and family prayers*

*Mr Salteena ('not quite a gentleman, but you would hardly
notice it') and Ethel visit Bernard Clark, in his 'sumpshous'
ancestral home. While Mr Salteena is away at the Crystal
Palace learning how to be a gentleman, Bernard and Ethel fall
in love. So Ethel rejects Mr Salteena's proposal of marriage –
who laments: 'My life will be sour grapes and ashes without
you.' A fine society wedding between Ethel and Bernard takes
place, followed by a honeymoon in Egypt for a 'merry six weeks
of bliss' from which they return with a son and 'hair'.*

*After dinner on the first evening of their visit, Bernard shows
the visitors round his domain:*

They strolled into the gloomy hall.

I see you have a lot of ancesters said Mr Salteena in a jelous tone, who
are they.

Well said Bernard they are all quite correct. This is my aunt Caroline
she was rarther excentrick and quite old.

So I see said Mr Salteena and he passed on to a lady with a very tight
waist and quearly shaped. That is Mary Ann Fudge my grandmother
I think said Bernard she was very well known in her day.

Why asked Ethel who was rarther curious by nature.

Well I dont quite know said Bernard but she was and he moved away
to the next picture. It was of a man with a fat smiley face and a red ribbon
round him and a lot of medals. My great uncle Ambrose Fudge said
Bernard carelessly.

He looks a thourough ancester said Ethel kindly.

Well he was said Bernard in a proud tone he was really the Sinister son
of Queen Victoria.

Not really cried Ethel in excited tones but what does that mean.

Well I dont quite know said Bernard Clark it puzzles me very much but
ancesters do turn quear at times.

Peraps it meant god son said Mr Salteena in an inteligent voice.

Well I dont think so said Bernard but I mean to find out.

It is very grand anyhow said Ethel.

It is that replied her host geniully.

Who is this said Mr Salteena halting at a picture of a lady holding up some grapes and smiling a good deal.

Her name was called Minnie Pilato responded Bernard she was rarther far back but a real relation and she was engaged to the earl of Tullyvarden only it did not quite come off.

What a pity crid Ethel...

Here Mr Salteena thourght he had better go to bed as he had had a long jornney. Bernard always had a few prayers in the hall and some whiskey afterwards as he was rarther pious but Mr Salteena was not very adicted to prayers so he marched up to bed. Ethel stayed as she thourght it would be a good thing. The butler came in as he was a very holy man and Bernard piously said the Our Father and a very good hymm called I will keep my anger down and a Decad of the Rosary. Ethel chimed in quiutly and Francis Minnit was most devout and Ethel thourght what a good holy family she was stopping with. So I will end my chapter.

From *The Young Visiters*, 1919

## Anton Chekhov (1860–1904)

# *Little Jack*

Jack Jukoff was a little boy of nine who, three months ago, had been apprenticed to Aliakin, the shoemaker. On Christmas Eve he did not go to bed. He waited until his master and the foreman had gone out to church, and then fetched a bottle of ink and a rusty pen from his master's cupboard, spread out a crumpled sheet of paper before him, and began to write. Before he had formed the first letter he had more than once looked fearfully round at the door, glanced at the icon, on each side of which were ranged shelves laden with boot-lasts, and sighed deeply. The paper lay spread on the bench, and before it knelt Little Jack.

Dear Grandpa – Constantine Makaritch (he wrote), I am writing you a letter. I wish you a merry Christmas and I hope God will give you all sorts of good things. I have no papa or mama, and you are all I have.

Little Jack turned his eyes to the dark window, on which shone the reflection of the candle, and vividly pictured to himself his grandfather, Constantine Makaritch: a small, thin, but extraordinarily active old man of sixty-five, with bleary eyes and a perpetually smiling face; by day sleeping in the kitchen or teasing the cook; by night, muffled in a huge sheepskin coat, walking about the garden beating his watchman's rattle...

At this moment, no doubt, grandfather is standing at the gate, blinking at the glowing red windows of the village church, stamping his felt boots, and teasing the servants. His rattle hangs at his belt...

Little Jack sighed, dipped his pen in the ink, and went on:

I had a dragging yesterday. My master dragged me into the yard by my hair and beat me with a stirrup because I went to sleep without meaning to while I was rocking the baby... The foreman laughs at me and sends me for vodka, makes me steal cucumbers... And I have nothing to eat. I get bread in the morning, and porridge for dinner, and bread for supper. My master and mistress drink up all the tea and soup... Dear Grandpa, please take me away from here, home to the village. I can't stand it. I beg you on my knees; I will pray to God for you all my life. Take me away from here, or else I shall die...

Little Jack's mouth twisted; he rubbed his eyes with a grimy fist and sobbed...

Dear Grandpa, I can't stand it; I shall die. I wanted to run away to the village on foot, but I haven't any boots, and it is so cold. And when I am big I will always take care of you and not allow anyone to hurt you at all...

Dear Grandpa, when they have the Christmas tree at the big house, keep some gold nuts for me and put them away in the green chest. Ask Miss Olga for them and say they are for Little Jack.

Little Jack heaved a shuddering sigh and stared at the window again. He remembered how his grandfather used to go to the forest for the Christmas tree... then drag the fallen fir tree up to the big house, and there they would all set to work trimming it. The busiest of all was Miss Olga, Jack's favourite. While Jack's mother, Pelagea, was still alive and a housemaid at the big house Miss Olga used to give Little Jack candy, and because she had nothing better to do had taught him to read and write...

When Pelagea died the little orphan was banished to the kitchen, where his grandfather was, and from there he was sent to Moscow, to Aliakin, the shoemaker.

Do come, dear grandpapa (Little Jack went on). Please come; I beg you for Christ's sake to come and take me away... It's so lonely – I can't tell you how lonely it is. I cry all day long... Give my love to Nelly and one-eyed Gregory and to the coachman, and don't let anyone use my accordion.

Your grandson,

John Jukoff

Dear Grandpapa, do come.

Little Jack folded the paper in four and put it in an envelope which he had bought that evening for one kopeck. He reflected an instant, then dipped his pen in the ink and wrote the address:

To my Grandpapa in the Village.

Then he scratched his head, thought a moment, and added:

Constantine Makaritch...

The butcher, whom he had asked the evening before, had told him that one drops letters into the mail-boxes, and that from there they are carried all over the world in mail wagons with ringing bells, driven by drivers who are drunk. Little Jack ran to the nearest mailbox and dropped his letter in the opening.

An hour later he was sound asleep, lulled by the sweetest hopes. He dreamed he saw a stove. On the stove sat his grandfather swinging his bare legs and reading his letter to the cook.

'Little Jack', *Stories of Russian Life*, published in England in 1918

## Kenneth Grahame (1859–1932)

# *Uncles on trial*

*The children – the narrator, older sister Selina, brothers Edward and Harold, and youngest Charlotte – were brought up by aunts and uncles. These so-called 'Olympians', seemed to have absolute power combined with minimal imagination or understanding.*

In our small lives that day was eventful when another uncle was to come down from town, and submit his character and qualifications (albeit unconsciously) to our careful criticism. Earlier uncles had been weighed in the balance, and – alas! – found grievously wanting. There was Uncle Thomas – a failure from the first... his rooted conviction seemed to be that the reason for a child's existence was to serve as a butt for senseless adult jokes – or what, from the accompanying guffaws of laughter, appeared to be intended for jokes...

Uncle George – the youngest – was distinctly more promising. He accompanied us cheerily round the establishment – suffered himself to be introduced to each of the cows – held out the right hand of fellowship to the pig – and even hinted that a pair of pink-eyed Himalayan rabbits might arrive – unexpectedly – from town some day... when our governess appeared on the scene. Uncle George's manner at once underwent a complete and contemptible change... And though Miss Smedley's ostensible purpose was to take Selina for her usual walk, I can vouch for it that Selina spent the morning ratting, along with the keeper's boy and me; while if Miss Smedley walked with any one, it would appear to have been with Uncle George...

Uncle George had fallen from grace, and was unanimously damned. And the non-arrival of the Himalayan rabbits was only another nail in his coffin. Uncles, therefore, were just then a heavy and lifeless market, and there was little inclination to deal. Still it was agreed that Uncle William, who had just returned from India, should have as fair a trial as the others.

Selina had just kicked my shins – like the girl she is! – during a scuffle in the passage, and I was still rubbing them with one hand when I found that the uncle-on-approbation was half-heartedly shaking the other. A florid, elderly man, quite unmistakably nervous, he let drop one grimy paw after another, and, turning very red, with an awkward simulation of heartiness, 'Well, h'are y'all?' he said, 'Glad to see me, eh?' As we could hardly, in justice, be expected to have formed an opinion of him at that early stage, we could but look at each other in silence; which scarce served to relieve the tension of the situation. Indeed, the cloud never really lifted during his stay...

When at last the atmosphere was clear of his depressing influence, we met in the potato-cellar – all of us, that is, but Harold, who had been told off to accompany his relative to the station; and the feeling was unanimous that, as an uncle, William could not be allowed to pass. Selina roundly declared him a beast... and indeed there seemed little to do but pass sentence. We were about to put it to the vote, when Harold appeared on the scene; his red face, round eyes, and mysterious demeanour, hinting at awful portents. Speechless he stood a space: then, slowly drawing his hand from the pocket of his knickerbockers, he displayed on a dirty palm one – two – three – four half-crowns! We could but gaze... Never had any of us seen, in the aggregate, so much bullion before. Then Harold told his tale.

'I took the old fellow to the station,' he said, and as we went along I told him all about the stationmaster's family, and how I had seen the porter kissing our housemaid, and what a nice fellow he was, with no airs or affectation about him, and anything I thought would be of interest; but he didn't seem to pay much attention... and once I thought – I'm not certain, but I *thought* I heard him say, "Well, thank God, that's over!" When we got to the station he stopped suddenly, and said, "Hold on a minute!" Then he shoved these into my hand in a frightened sort of way, and said, "Look here, youngster! These are for you and the other kids. Buy what you like – make little beasts of yourselves – only don't tell the old people, mind! Now cut away home!" So I cut.'

A solemn hush fell on the assembly, broken at first by... Charlotte. 'I didn't know,' she observed dreamily, 'that there were such good men anywhere in the world. I hope he'll die tonight, for then he'll go straight to heaven!' But the repentant Selina bewailed herself with tears and sobs, refusing to be comforted; for that in her haste she had called this white-souled relative a beast.

'I'll tell you what we'll do,' said Edward, the master-mind... 'we'll christen the piebald pig after him – the one that hasn't got a name yet...'

'I – I christened that pig this morning,' Harold guiltily confessed, 'I christened it after the curate... He came and bowled to me after you others had been sent to bed early...'

'Oh, but that doesn't count,' said Edward hastily; 'because we weren't all there. We'll take that christening off and call it Uncle William. And you can save up the curate for the next litter!'

From *The Golden Age*, 1895

**Dorothy L. Sayers (1893–1957)**

# Growing up

'Except,' said Christ, 'ye become as little children' – and the words are sometimes quoted to justify the flight into infantilism. Now, children differ in many ways, but they have one thing in common. Peter Pan – if indeed he exists otherwise than in the nostalgic imagination of an adult – is a case for the pathologist. All normal children (however much we discourage them) look forward to growing up. 'Except ye become as little children,' except you can wake on your fiftieth birthday with the same forward-looking excitement and interest in life that you enjoyed when you were five, 'ye cannot see the kingdom of God.' One must not only die daily, but every day one must be born again.

From *Strong Meat*, 1939

## Dennis Potter (1935–94)

# 'Blue remembered hills'

*In April 1994, two months before he died, Dennis Potter spoke poignantly on television to Melvyn Bragg about his impending death as well as his early years in the Forest of Dean:*

In *Blue Remembered Hills*, for example, I used adult actors to play children in order to make them like a magnifying glass, to show what it's like. Because if you look at a child – talk about the present tense, that's all a small child lives in. So a wet Tuesday afternoon, for example, can actually be years long, and childhood is full to the brim of fear, horror, excitement, joy, boredom, love, anxiety... I remember losing a pen once, and the sleeplessness, the anxiety: 'I've lost my pen. Oh my god, I've lost my pen.' The pen-ness of that pen, and the lostness of that loss, is so great to a child. Maybe you kind of revert to that in a way.

But my Forest of Dean childhood, well – it is a strange and beautiful place, with a people who were as warm as anywhere else, but they seemed warmer to me, and the accent is so strong it's almost like a dialect. And up the hill twice, usually on a Sunday sometimes three times – to Salem Chapel, and those little floppy, orange-covered hymn-books. The numbers would be slotted up on the board. There's one chorus – it's funny, I can think of the number before I can think of the chorus. I can see it as clear as though it were written in front of me on the slat – hymn number 787. 'Will there be any stars, any stars, in my crown when the evening sun goes down? When I wake with the blessed in the mansion of rest, will there be any stars in my crown?' And of course, it makes me laugh, and yet it tugs at me, and I see those little kids' faces singing, and countless numbers of such things.

And for me of course the language of the New Testament in particular, but the Bible in general, was actually, as it is to a child – I suppose even to a child brought up in Pinner or Wembley Park, it must be something similar – it *was* the Holy Land. I knew that Cannock Ponds, by the pit where Dad worked, was where Jesus walked on the water; I knew the Valley of the Shadow of Death was that lane with the overhanging trees. As I said, I was a coward – at dusk I'd whistle, going down that particular lane.

But I'm grateful for that language, that dialect and also that time...

From an edited transcript of Melvyn Bragg's interview on Channel 4, 5 April 1994

# AGE

## Old age will come

*The author of Ecclesiastes calls himself 'Qoheleth' – an almost untranslatable Hebrew word that could be rendered as 'The Preacher', 'The Speaker', 'The President', 'The Spokesman', 'The Philosopher' or even 'The Professor'. He writes of experimenting with everything money can buy or learning can achieve and reckons it all 'Vanity of vanities!' or 'Utter futility!' In this last section he describes old age and coming death using various metaphors to describe failing faculties and desires.*

Remember now thy Creator in the days of thy youth, while the evil days come not, nor the years draw nigh, when thou shalt say, I have no pleasure in them; While the sun, or the light, or the moon, or the stars, be not darkened, nor the clouds return after the rain: In the day when the keepers of the house shall tremble, and the strong men shall bow themselves, and the grinders cease because they are few, and those that look out of the window be darkened, And the doors shall be shut in the streets, when the sound of the grinding is low, and he shall rise up at the voice of the bird, and all the daughters of musick shall be brought low; Also when they shall be afraid of that which is high, and fears shall be in the way, and the almond tree shall flourish, and the grasshopper shall be a burden, and desire shall fail: because man goeth to his long home, and the mourners go about the streets: Or ever the silver cord be loosed, or the golden bowl be broken, or the pitcher be broken at the fountain, or the wheel broken at the cistern. Then shall the dust return to the earth as it was: and the spirit shall return unto God who gave it.

Vanity of vanities, saith the preacher; all is vanity.

Ecclesiastes 12

Barbara Pym (1913–80)

# *Growing old*

*Letty, Norman, Edwin and Marcia Ivory are in their sixties and work in the same office. They communicate superficially but each exists in a private world. The two women retire and Marcia continues living in her dead parents' house:*

Although he had been dead for some years, Marcia still missed the old cat, Snowy, and one evening she found herself particularly reminded of him when she came across one of his dishes in the cupboard under the sink. She was surprised and a little upset to notice that it still had some dried up fragments of Kit-e-Kat adhering to it. Had she then not washed it up after his death? It would seem not. That might not have surprised an observer, but Marcia regarded herself as a meticulous housekeeper, and she had always been especially careful with Snowy's dishes, keeping them, in her own words, 'spotlessly clean'.

The finding of the dish gave her a desire to visit the cat's grave which was somewhere at the bottom of the garden. When Snowy had died, Mr Smith, who had lived next door before Nigel and Priscilla came, had dug a grave and Marcia had laid Snowy in it, his body wrapped in a piece of her old blue ripple-cloth dressing gown which he used to sleep on... She had not marked the grave in any way, but she remembered where it was, for when she walked down the path she would think, Snowy's grave; but as time went on she forgot the exact spot... Then it occurred to her that if she were to dig in that bit of garden, she would surely come upon the grave...

She went to the shed and found a spade, but it was very heavy, and if she had ever wielded it in the past, she was certainly unable to now...

It was thus that Priscilla saw her, crouched at the bottom of the garden. What was she *doing*, trying to dig with that heavy spade? It was worrying and upsetting, for the old – especially Miss Ivory – were perpetually nagging at her conscience... Of course, Nigel had asked Miss Ivory if she wanted her lawn cut but she had preferred it the way it was and one couldn't bully the elderly, their independence was their last remaining treasure and must be respected. All the same, one could perhaps offer a little gardening assistance, digging, for example... but not *now*, when

Priscilla had people coming to dinner, the avocados to prepare and mayonnaise to make. Perhaps it was a fine enough evening to have drinks out on the little patio they had made, but the view of the neglected garden next door would detract from the elegance of the occasion, and if Miss Ivory was going to go on digging in this disturbing way something would have to be done about it. But now, to Priscilla's relief, she was going back towards the house, dragging the heavy spade behind her. One had to cling to the hope that she knew what she was doing.

From *Quartet in Autumn*, 1977

Muriel Spark (b. 1918)

# Offering up old age

*Miss Taylor, one-time companion to the now elderly novelist
Charmian Piper, has been consigned to the Maud Long Medical
Ward ('aged people, female') because of severe arthritis. She was
one of a dozen elderly women from various walks in life, aged
from seventy to ninety-three:*

These twelve old women were known variously as Granny Roberts,
Granny Duncan, Granny Taylor, Grannies Barnacle, Trotsky, Green,
Valvona, and so on.

Sometimes, on being first received into her bed, the patient would be
shocked and feel rather let down by being called Granny. Miss or Mrs
Reewes-Duncan threatened for a whole week to report anyone who called
her Granny Duncan. She threatened to cut them out of her will and to
write to her M.P. The nurses provided writing-paper and a pencil at her
urgent request. However, she changed her mind about informing her M.P.
when they promised not to call her Granny any more. 'But,' she said, 'you
shall never go back into my will.'...

Miss Jean Taylor mused upon her condition and upon old age in
general. Why do some people lose their memories, some their hearing?
Why do some talk of their youth and some of their wills?...

A year ago, when Miss Taylor had been admitted to the ward, she had
suffered misery when addressed as Granny Taylor, and she thought she
would rather die in a ditch than be kept alive under such conditions. But
she was a woman practised in restraint; she never displayed her
resentment. The lacerating familiarity of the nurses' treatment merged in
with the arthritis, and she bore them both as long as she could without
complaint. Then she was forced to cry out with pain during a long
haunted night when the dim ward lamp made the beds into grey-white
lumps like terrible bundles of laundry which muttered and snored
occasionally. A nurse brought her an injection.

The arthritic pain subsided, leaving the pain of desolate humiliation, so
that she wished rather to endure the physical nagging again.

After the first year she resolved to make her suffering a voluntary affair.
If this is God's will then it is mine. She gained from this state of mind a

decided and visible dignity, at the same time as she lost her stoical resistance to pain. She complained more, called often for the bed-pan, and did not hesitate, on one occasion when the nurse was dilatory, to wet the bed as the other grannies did so frequently.

Miss Taylor spent much time considering her position. The doctor's 'Well, how's Granny Taylor this morning? Have you been making your last will and test–' would falter when he saw her eyes, the intelligence. She could not help hating these visits, and the nurses giving her a hair-do, telling her she looked like sixteen, but she volunteered mentally for them, as it were, regarding them as the Will of God. She reflected that everything could be worse.

From *Memento Mori*, 1959

**The Brothers Grimm: Jacob Ludwig Carl Grimm (1785–1863)
and Wilhelm Carl Grimm (1786–1859)**

# Old age comes to all

There was once an old man, whose eyes had become dim, his ears dull of hearing, his knees trembled, and when he sat at table he could hardly hold the spoon, and spilt the broth upon the table-cloth, or let it run out of his mouth. His son and his son's wife were disgusted at this, so the old grandfather at last had to sit in the corner behind the stove and they gave him his food in an earthenware bowl, and not even enough of it. And he used to look towards the table with his eyes full of tears. Once, too, his trembling hands could not hold the bowl, and it fell to the ground and broke. The young wife scolded him, but he said nothing and only sighed. Then they bought him a wooden bowl for a few half-pence, out of which he had to eat.

They were once sitting thus when the little grandson of four years old began to gather together some bits of wood upon the ground. 'What are you doing there?' asked the father. 'I'm making a little trough,' answered the child, 'for father and mother to eat out of when I am big.'

The man and his wife looked at each other for a while, and presently began to cry. Then they took the old grandfather to the table, and henceforth always let him eat with them, and likewise said nothing if he did spill a little of anything.

From 'The Old Man and His Grandson', *Grimm's Fairy Tales*, 1812, 1815, 1822

### Ivan Turgenev (1818–83)

# *Old love*

*Fathers and Sons describes the relationships between the generations. Bazarov, a young nihilist doctor, represents the spirit of revolution. His elderly parents, conservative and religious, adore but fail to understand their brilliant son.*

*Bazarov – with his friend Arkady – have been staying only three days with his father, Vasili Ivanitch and his mother, Arina Vlasievna, when Bazarov asks his father to have the horses ready for the two friends to leave next day:*

'I – I will, I will,' the old man stuttered... 'Only, only – is there any particular reason for this change of plan?'

'There is. I am engaged to pay Arkady a short visit. That done, I will return to you.'

'Only to be a short visit? Good!' And Vasili Ivanitch pulled out his handkerchief and blew his nose... 'Well, well! Things shall be as you desire. Yet we had hoped that you would have stayed with us a little longer. Three days only! Three days after three years of absence! Ah, that is not much, Evgenii – it is not much.'

'But I tell you I intend to return soon. You see, I *must* go.'

'You have no choice, eh? Very well, very well. Of course, engagements must be kept... Naturally, Arina and I had not altogether looked for this...'

A sudden break occurred in his voice and he made for the door.

'I promise you that we will return soon, my father, I give you my word of honour upon that.'

But Vasili Ivanitch did not look round – he just waved his hand and departed. Mounting to the bedroom, he found Arina asleep, so started to say his prayers in an undertone, for fear of awaking her. But at once she opened her eyes.

'Is that you, Vasili Ivanitch?' she asked.

'Yes, mother.'

'Have you just left Eniusha? Do you know, I am anxious about him. Does he sleep comfortably on the sofa?...'

'Do not fret, mother dear. He is quite comfortable. "Lord, pardon us sinners.'" And Vasili Ivanitch went on with his prayers. Yet his heart was full of an aching compassion for his old companion; nor did he want to tell her overnight of the sorrow which was awaiting her on the morrow.

Next day, therefore, Arkady and Bazarov departed. From earliest morn an air of woe pervaded the household... As for Vasili Ivanitch, he fussed about, and made a brave show – he talked in loud tones and stamped his feet upon the floor as he walked; but his face had suddenly fallen in, and his glance could not meet that of his son. Meanwhile Arina Vlasievna indulged in quiet weeping. Indeed, but for the fact that her husband had spent two hours that morning in comforting her, she would have broken down completely, and lost all self-control.

But at last, when, after reiterated promises to return within, at most, a month, Bazarov had freed himself from the arms which sought to detain him... when the old couple found themselves alone in a house which seemed suddenly to have grown as dishevelled and as decrepit as they – then, ah, then did Vasili Ivanitch... sink into a chair, and drop his head on his breast.

'He has gone for ever, he has gone for ever,' he muttered. 'He has gone because he found life here tedious, and once more I am as lonely as the sand in the desert!'

These words he kept repeating again and again; and, each time that he did so, he raised his hand, and pointed into the distance.

But presently Arina Vlasievna approached him, and, pressing her grey head to his, said:

'Never mind, my Vasia. True, our son has broken away from us; he is like a falcon – he has flown hither, he has flown thither, as he willed: but you and I, like lichen in a hollow tree, are still side by side, we are not parted... And ever I shall be the same to you, as you will be the same to me.'

Taking his hands from his face, Vasili Ivanitch embraced his old comrade, his wife, as never – no, not even during the days of his courtship – he had done before. And thus she comforted him.

From *Fathers and Sons*, 1862

Margaret Forster (b. 1938)

# *Enduring love*

*In* Have the Men Had Enough? *Margaret Forster poses questions about how we should deal with old age. Every member of Mrs McKay's family responds to her differently. Bridget returns from holiday to find that her mother has been moved into an old people's home, following a stroke. Bridget and Hannah – her niece – go to the Home, where Bridget confronts Sister:*

It is game, set and match to Sister. She implies, without saying a single word, that Bridget is deluding herself, that she really knows she will never take Grandma home. And *she* isn't in the least worried at what Bridget implies, that Grandma is somehow being ill-treated, or at least not supervised carefully enough. Bridget, I'm sure, expected Sister to be on the defensive but she isn't, not a bit. She doesn't give a damn what Bridget thinks. She wanders off, doling out sweets... Bridget stands fuming. She makes a decision. She pursues Sister. I hear her ask if there is a wheelchair. Sister nods, points. Bridget gets the wheelchair and we try to get Grandma into it. We fail. Sister saunters over. She puts an arm lock on Grandma and has her into the wheelchair in no time. She tells Bridget there's a knack, that nursing the senile demented is a specialised skill. And she smirks. She knows Bridget doesn't possess it. We wheel Grandma away, but where to? I don't know, Bridget doesn't know. Sister comes to the rescue. She says we can use the office, she won't be in there for half an hour. Bridget is obliged to thank her... The office is quite pleasant. There are posters, plants, and a few old, but quite attractive, chintz-covered chairs. It's obviously Sister's sanctum and we are privileged. I venture to point this out and Bridget snaps at me... I am startled to see tears in her eyes. Just as I'm wondering how to cope with this, Grandma speaks. She says, quite distinctly, 'Is there any tea left in that pot?' We both stare. There is a brown teapot on Sister's desk and Grandma is looking straight at it. Bridget bounds up, feels the pot, looks around for a mug, finds one, fills it, finds milk and sugar, and lovingly takes it to Grandma, who slurps thirstily. Bridget strokes her hair as she does so, crooning over her. When the mug has been drained, Grandma looks at Bridget as though seeing her for the first time. She says,

'You took your time, you hussy,' and shakes her fist at Bridget in the pretend-fierce way she used to. She smiles, Bridget smiles. They are beam-to-beam, their faces very close together, as Bridget bends down over the wheelchair. I feel an intruder. I should go away. This is private. They don't even notice me slip out or if Bridget does she makes no sign. And when I'm out, although still in the ward, I feel so relieved, like being really out, in the fresh air.

From *Have the Men Had Enough?*, 1989

## Christina Stead (1902–83)

# *In love*

Jenny was going to the hairdresser down the hill. Everything was in order, gloves, bag, key in purse, milk bottles to take down, fires out, time to go.

At the last, she held up the magnifying mirror to her face, checked in the bathroom mirror, wardrobe mirror for her skirt, shoes. She knew she would see him somewhere on the hill.

She came neatly downstairs, not to fall on the old ragged matting in the smeary brown hall. Up the street, fresh and bright: rosebush, white patch on stone fence, don't stare at it, it resembles a face; curtains in basement opposite, sort of crochet grid; flagged yard, hello to red-haired cleaner, garage to let: and so to the corner where the big church is and the red pillar-box where she posted so many letters.

Beside it, a seat for old people on sunny days. Once, even she and Gill had sat there. A wedding for a neighbour's daughter...

Jenny and Gill liked to look at weddings; marriage was in their minds. They had nothing but good to say of marriage. It was the best state for men and women; there was calm and thrilling joy, there was forgiveness, solace, peace, certain home and country, without passport, rent book, marching, petitions.

Otherwise, Jenny would not have sat on a bench; she had a horror of it, as a proof of old age, impotence, neglect...

Now, she was round the horseshoe bend of the churchyard and she started downhill, searching in the far distance for Gill, who might now be visible among the shopping crowds.

She stared carefully, not only to see him at the first moment possible, but to see him make the crossing, for it was a death spot, a traffic black spot down there, where three streets met, not to mention the station yard, hotel parking lot and parade. Gill was shortsighted...

There was Gill, a short square peg in a quadrilateral situation, streets, footpaths, flagged courtyards, low block buildings, trudging along...

Just where would they meet? It was always exciting; her heart beat a little faster. Not too soon – spin it out! Now he was across, looking left and right and over.

He began to pass the real estate agent's, the little alley, the dress-shop, the bingo parlour, once a cinema where they had seen foreign films; now he was at the auctioneer's.

Now they were close, they did not look any more. She glanced to one side... Now his big dark eyes were on her; she looked away. They met, their faces lighting up... They halted, their eyes fastened on each other...

They stood there, not knowing what to say, for there is nothing to express the emotion that brought them together the first time and now brought them together... They stood quiet, embarrassed, unable to move away...

'Well,' then a slight smile, a grin, too, 'All right –' 'I won't be long.' 'Okay.' Each takes a step to pass, hesitates... they take another step and turn, 'Goodbye.' 'Goodbye.'...

'I'll be home by twelve,' says Jenny. 'I'll be waiting for you,' says Gill.

For the fact is, though this took place every time they met... Jenny and Gill were husband and wife and had spent nearly forty years together...

Jenny and Gill are no longer there... but very often I now meet on the hill another couple... and by the air they carry with them, and the look of gold, I know that is how they feel too.

From 'Street Idyll', in *Festival and Other Stories*,
edited by Brian Buckley and Jim Hamilton, 1974

**Anne Tyler (b. 1941)**

# *Faithful love*

*Barnaby Gaitlin works for a firm called Rent-a-Back which hires out their employees to do for old people the jobs they can no longer manage. He works alongside Martine and they talk as they clear Mrs Cartwright's spare room for an expected guest:*

We were dragging an unbelievably heavy footlocker out to the hall when I asked Martine, 'have you ever thought of changing jobs?'

'Why? Am I doing something wrong?'

'I mean, doesn't this job get you down? Don't you think it's a kind of a *sad* job?'

She straightened up from the footlocker to consider. 'Well,' she said, 'I know once when I was taking Mrs Gordoni to visit her father... Did you ever meet her father? He'd been in some kind of accident years before and ended up with this peculiar condition where he didn't have any short term memory. Not a bit. He forgot everything that happened from one minute to the next... so he was living in this special-care facility, and I had to drive Mrs Gordoni there once when her car broke down. And her father gave her a big hello, but then when Mrs Gordoni stepped out to speak to a nurse, he asked me, 'Do you happen to be acquainted with my daughter? She never visits! I can't think what's become of her!'

'See what I mean?' I said.

'*That* kind of got me down.'

'Right.'

'But then you have to look on the other side of it,' Martine said.

'What other side, for God's sake?'

'Well, it's kind of encouraging that Mrs Gordoni still came, don't you think? She certainly didn't get *credit* for coming, beyond the very moment she was standing in her father's view. Just for that moment, her father was happy. Not one instant longer. But Mrs Gordoni went even so, every day of the week.'

'Well,' I said. Then I said, 'Yeah, okay.'

From *A Patchwork Planet*, 1998

# DEATH AND DYING

## The death of Stephen

*Stephen – the first Christian martyr – was one of seven appointed by the early Church to look after the social needs of widows. He had a particularly clear-sighted understanding of the way in which the rituals and holy places of Judaism were outdated by the Gospel of Jesus Christ. When some of the strict Jewish leaders made trouble for him, he was called before the Sanhedrin – or Jewish council – to defend himself. His apologia stirred up further conflict and downright fury; Stephen accused them:*

'How stubborn you are, heathen still at heart and deaf to the truth! You always resist the Holy Spirit!... You received the Law given by God's angels and yet you have not kept it.'

This touched them on the raw, and they ground their teeth with fury. But Stephen, filled with the Holy Spirit, and gazing intently up to heaven, saw the glory of God, and Jesus standing at God's right hand. 'Look!' he said, 'I see the heavens opened and the Son of Man standing at the right hand of God.' At this they gave a great shout, and stopped their ears; they made a concerted rush at him, threw him out of the city, and set about stoning him... As they stoned him, Stephen called out, 'Lord Jesus, receive my spirit.' He fell on his knees and cried aloud, 'Lord, do not hold this sin against them,' and with that he died...

Stephen was given burial by devout men, who made a great lamentation for him.

From Acts 7, 8

### Cuthbert, Abbot of Wearmouth and Jarrow (c. 673–735)

# The death of the Venerable Bede

*One of Bede's monks called Cuthbert (not St Cuthbert of Lindisfarne) later became Abbot of Wearmouth and Jarrow. He wrote about Bede's death, which he had witnessed.*

When the Tuesday before the Lord's Ascension came, his breathing became much worse and a small swelling appeared in his feet.

None the less he continued his teaching all that day and dictated cheerfully; among other things he said several times: 'Learn quickly now, for I do not know how long I shall live, nor whether after a short time my Maker shall take me.' But he seemed to us to know very well when his end would come. And so he spent all that night awake in thanksgiving.

At day break on Wednesday he told us to finish the writing which we had begun. We did this until the third hour...

There was one of us with him who said: 'Beloved master, there is still one chapter missing from the book you were dictating, but it seems to me difficult to ask you for more.' But he answered: 'It is easy. Take your pen and prepare it and write quickly.' And this he did.

At the ninth hour he said to me: 'I have a few treasures in my little box: pepper, handkerchiefs and incense. Run quickly and fetch the priests of our monastery to me, so that I can distribute to them these little gifts which God has given me.' This I did with some trembling. When they came he spoke to them, urgently asking them to say masses and prayers for him with diligence; this they gladly promised. But they were all very sad and they all wept, because they would not see his face much longer in this world.

But they rejoiced about one thing he had said: 'It is time, if it so please my Maker, that I should be released from the body and come now to him who formed me from nothing when I did not exist... my soul longs to see Christ my king in all his beauty.'...

Then the boy of whom I spoke, Wilbur by name, said again: 'Beloved master, there is still one sentence left, not yet written down.' He answered: 'Write it then.' After a short time the boy said: 'Now it is written.' And he replied: 'Good. It is finished. You have spoken the truth. Take my head in your hands, for it pleases me very much to sit opposite

my holy place where I used to pray, so that as I sit there I may call upon
my Father.' And thus, on the floor of his cell singing: 'Glory be to the
Father and to the Son and to the Holy Spirit' and the rest, he breathed
out his spirit from his body...

Here ends the letter of Cuthbert on the death of the venerable Bede,
the priest.

Probably written, and widely circulated, soon after 735, the year in which Bede died

## John Bunyan (1628–88)

# *The celestial city*

*In the second part of* Pilgrim's Progress, *Bunyan describes Christiana's journey with her family from the City of Destruction. To enter the Celestial City the river of death must first be crossed. For some the river is deep and threatening; for others the crossing is easy. But all who have truly loved and followed the king arrive safely.*

After this it was noised abroad that Mr Valiant-for-Truth was taken with a summons... When he understood it, he called for his friends, and told them of it. Then said he, 'I am going to my fathers, and though with great difficulty I am got hither, yet now I do not repent me of all the trouble I have been at to arrive where I am. My sword, I give to him that shall succeed me in my pilgrimage, and my courage and skill, to him that can get it. My marks and scars I carry with me, to be a witness for me that I have fought his battles who will now be my rewarder.' When the day that he must go hence was come many accompanied him to the River side, into which, as he went, he said, *Death, where is thy sting?* And as he went down deeper, he said, *Grave, where is thy victory?* So he passed over, and the trumpets sounded for him on the other side.

Then there came forth a summons for Mr Standfast... When Mr Standfast had thus set things in order, and the time being come for him to haste him away; he also went down to the River. Now there was a great calm at that time in the River, wherefore Mr Standfast, when he was about half way in, he stood a while and talked to his companions that had waited upon him thither. And he said,

'This River has been a terror to many, yea the thoughts of it also have often frighted me. But now methinks I stand easy... The waters indeed are to the palate bitter, and to the stomach cold; yet the thoughts of what I am going to, and of the conduct that waits for me on the other side, doth lie like a glowing coal at my heart.

'I see myself now at the end of my journey, my toilsome days are ended. I am going now to see that head that was crowned with thorns, and that face that was spit upon, for me.

'I have formerly lived by hear-say and faith, but now I go where I shall live by sight, and shall be with him, in whose company I delight myself.

'I have loved to hear my Lord spoken of, and wherever I have seen the print of his shoe in the earth, there I have coveted to set my foot too...'

Now while he was thus in discourse his countenance changed, his strong men bowed under him, and after he had said, 'Take me, for I come unto thee,' he ceased to be seen.

But glorious it was, to see how the open region was filled with horses and chariots, with trumpeters and pipers, with singers, and players on stringed instruments, to welcome the pilgrims as they went up and followed one another in at the beautiful Gate of the City.

From *Pilgrim's Progress*, part 2, 1684

## Francis Bacon (1561–1626)

# *Death*

Men fear death, as children fear to go in the dark: and as that natural fear in children is increased with tales, so is the other. Certainly, the contemplation of death, as the wages of sin, and passage to another world, is holy and religious; but the fear of it, as a tribute due unto nature, is weak. Yet in religious meditations, there is sometimes mixture of vanity, and superstition. You shall read, in some of the friars' books of mortifications, that a man should think with himself, what the pain is, if he have but his finger's end pressed, or tortured; and thereby imagine, what the pains of death are, when the whole body is corrupted and dissolved; when many times, death passeth with less pain, than the torture of a limb: for the most vital parts are not the quickest of sense... Groans and convulsions, and a discoloured face, and friends weeping, and blacks, and obsequies, and the like, show death terrible. It is worthy the observing, that there is no passion in the mind of man so weak, but it mates and masters, the fear of death: and therefore death is no such terrible enemy, when a man hath so many attendants about him that can win the combat of him. Revenge triumphs over death; love slights it; honour aspireth to it; grief flieth to it; fear preoccupieth it; nay, we read, after Otho the Emperor, had slain himself, pity (which is the tenderest of affections) provoked many to die, out of mere compassion to their sovereign, and as the truest sort of followers... A man would die, though he were neither valiant, nor miserable, only upon a weariness to do the same thing so often, over and over...

It is as natural to die as to be born; and to a little infant, perhaps, the one is as painful as the other. He that dies in an earnest pursuit, is like one that is wounded in hot blood; who, for the time, scarce feels the hurt; and therefore, a mind fixed, and bent upon somewhat that is good, doth avert the dolours of death: but above all, believe it, the sweetest canticle is, *nunc dimittis*; when a man hath obtained worthy ends, and expectations. Death hath this also; that it openeth the gate to good fame, and extinguisheth envy.

From 'Of Death', *Essays*, 1601

James Boswell (1740–95)

# Dr Johnson faces death

The following particulars of his conversation, within a few days of his death, I give on the authority of Mr John Nichols: –

'He said, three or four days only before his death, speaking of the little fear he had of undergoing a chirugical operation, "I would give one of these legs for a year more of life, I mean of comfortable life, not such as that which I now suffer," – and lamented much his inability to read during his hours of restlessness. "I used formerly (he added), when sleepless in bed, *to read like a Turk*."

'Whilst confined in his last illness, it was his regular practice to have the church-service read to him, by some attentive and friendly Divine. The Reverend Mr [Samuel] Hoole performed this kind office in my presence for the last time, when, by his own desire, no more than the Litany was read; in which his responses were in the deep and sonorous voice which Mr Boswell has occasionally noticed, and with the most profound devotion that can be imagined. His hearing not being quite perfect, he more than once interrupted Mr Hoole, with "Louder, my dear Sir, louder, I entreat you, or you pray in vain!"'...

Amidst the melancholy clouds which hung over the dying Johnson, his characteristical manner shewed itself on different occasions.

When Dr Warren, in the usual style, hoped that he was better; his answer was, 'No, Sir; you cannot conceive with what acceleration I advance towards death.'

A man he had never seen before was employed one night to sit up with him. Being asked next morning how he liked his new attendant, his answer was, 'Not at all, Sir: the fellow's an idiot; he is as awkward as a turn-spit when first put into the wheel, and as sleepy as a dormouse.'

Mr Windham having placed a pillow conveniently to support him, he thanked him for his kindness, and said, 'That will do, – all that a pillow will do.'

As he opened a note which his servant brought to him, he said, 'An odd thought strikes me: we shall receive no letters in the grave.'

Johnson, with that native fortitude, which, amidst all his bodily distress and mental sufferings, never forsook him, asked Dr Brocklesby, as a man in whom he had confidence, to tell him plainly whether he could recover.

'Give me (said he,) a direct answer.' The Doctor having first asked him whether he could bear the whole truth, which way soever it might lead, and being answered that he could, declared that, in his opinion, he could not recover without a miracle. 'Then (said Johnson), I will take no more physick, not even my opiates; for I have prayed that I may render up my soul to God unclouded.' In this resolution he persevered...

Dr Brocklesby, who will not be suspected of fanaticism, obliged me with the following accounts: –

'For some time before his death, all his fears were calmed and absorbed by the prevalence of his faith, and his trust in the merits and *propitiation* of JESUS CHRIST.

'He talked often to me about the necessity of faith in the *sacrifice* of Jesus, as necessary, beyond all good works whatever, for the salvation of mankind.'

From *The Life of Samuel Johnson*, 1791

**John Updike (b. 1932)**

# 'His daughter is dead'

*In the* Rabbit *saga, John Updike chronicles the life of Harry Angstrom – known as Rabbit – living in middle America in the late twentieth century. His baby, June, has died and the black pastor, Eccles, is taking the funeral service:*

Eccles has arrived from some other entrance and from a far doorway beckons them. The seven of them file with Nelson into the room where the flowers wait, and take their seats on the front row. Black Eccles reads before the white casket. It annoys Rabbit that Eccles should stand between him and his daughter. It occurs to him, what no one has mentioned, the child was never baptized. Eccles reads: 'I am the resurrection and the life, saith the Lord: he that believeth in me, though he were dead, yet shall he live: and whosoever liveth and believeth in me, shall never die.'

The angular words walk in Harry's head like clumsy blackbirds; he feels their possibility. Eccles doesn't; his face is humourless and taut. His voice is false. All these people are false: except his dead daughter, the white box with gold trim.

'He shall feed his flock like a shepherd: he shall gather the lambs with his arms, and carry them in his bosom.'

Shepherd, lamb, arms: Harry's eyes fill with tears. It is as if at first the tears are everywhere about him, a sea, and that at last the saltwater gets into his eyes. His daughter is dead; June gone from him; his heart swims in grief, that had skimmed over it before, dives deeper and deeper into the limitless volume of loss. Never hear her cry again, never see her marbled skin again, never cup her faint weight in his arms again and watch the blue of her eyes wander in search of the source of his voice. Never, the word never stops, there is never a gap in its thickness.

They go to the cemetery. He and his father and Janice's father and the undertaker's man carry the white box to the hearse... They get into their cars and drive through the streets uphill... Up a crunching blue gravel lane the procession moves in second gear, its destination a meek green canopy smelling of earth and ferns. The cars stop; they get out. Beyond them at a distance stands a crescent sweep of black woods; the cemetery is high on the hill, between the town and the forest. Below their feet chimneys smoke. A man on a power lawnmower rides between the worn teeth of tombstones near the far hedge... The white coffin is artfully rolled on castors from the hearse's deep body onto crimson straps that hold it above the nearly square-mouthed but deep-dug grave. The small creaks and breaths of effort scratch on a pane of silence. Silence. A cough. The flowers have followed them; here they are, densely banked within the tent. Behind Harry's feet a neat mound of earth topped with squares of sod waits to be replaced and meanwhile breathes a deep word of earth. The undertaking men look pleased, their job nearly done, and fold their pink hands in front of their flies. Silence.

'The Lord is my shepherd; therefore can I lack nothing.'

Eccles' voice is fragile outdoors. The distant buzz of the power mower halts respectfully. Rabbit's chest vibrates with excitement and strength; he is sure his girl has ascended to Heaven. This feeling fills Eccles' recited words like a living body a skin. 'O God, whose most dear Son did take little children into his arms and bless them; Give us Grace, we beseech thee, to entrust the soul of this child to thy never-failing care and love, and bring us all to thy heavenly kingdom; through the same thy Son, Jesus Christ, our Lord. Amen.'

From *Rabbit, Run,* 1960

Peter Ackroyd (b. 1949)

# The death of John Fisher

*John Fisher (1469–1535), English prelate and humanist, became chancellor of Cambridge University and bishop of Rochester. He worked towards reformation within the Church. In 1527 he spoke out against Henry VIII's divorce from Catherine of Aragon. Just before his death he was created a cardinal by the pope, but as the historian Holinshed wrote: 'The hat came as far as Calais, but the head was off before the hat was on.'*

Three days later, John Fisher was put on trial for treason and condemned to death. He was no longer the Bishop of Rochester, having been stripped of his see by the king, and it was as 'Master Fisher' that he listened as Sir Thomas Audley ordered him to be hanged, drawn and quartered at Tyburn.

Five days later, John Fisher was led from the Tower. The king had been told that the prisoner was now so frail and thin that he would not survive the journey on a hurdle to Tyburn, and accordingly his sentence had been changed to that of beheading on Tower Hill. He had been woken at five o'clock in the morning with this news, and, when he was told that he would be led to his execution at nine o'clock, he asked to be allowed to sleep a little longer. He awoke at seven and asked his servant to lay out a clean white shirt and a furred tippet. It was, he said, his wedding day. He was too weak to walk to the scaffold and instead was carried in a chair the short distance to the infamous hill. He carried his New Testament with him and opening it at random came upon a passage from the gospel of St John. 'Now this is everlasting life,' he read, 'that they may know thee, the only true God, and him whom thou hast sent, Jesus Christ.' He climbed to the scaffold singing the *Te Deum*. When he took off his gown to prepare for death, the assembled crowd gasped at the sight of his gaunt and emaciated body. His head was off at the first blow and an extraordinary gush of blood issued from his neck: it seemed impossible that so much blood should come out of so skeletal a figure. His naked body was displayed at the place of execution, as the king had demanded; his head was then thrust upon a pike and placed in a small iron cage upon London Bridge. Here it grew 'ruddy and comely' and became such an object of wonder that Henry demanded that it be thrown into the river.

From *The Life of Thomas More*, 1998

**Evelyn Waugh (1903–66)**

# *Dressing for death*

*Dennis Barlow, poet and one-time employee of Hollywood's Megalopolitan Pictures, is deputed to visit Whispering Glades Memorial Park to arrange the funeral of Sir Francis Hinsley whom he discovered hanged. He is interviewed by the Mortuary Hostess:*

There came vividly into Dennis's mind that image which lurked there, seldom out of sight for long; the sack of body suspended and the face above it with eyes red and horribly starting from their sockets, the cheeks mottled in indigo like the mottled end-papers of a ledger and the tongue swollen and protruding like the end of a black sausage.

'Let us now decide on the casket.'

They went to the show-rooms where stood coffins of every shape and material…

'The two-piece lid is most popular for gentlemen Loved Ones. Only the upper part is then exposed to view.'

'Exposed to view?'

'Yes, when the Waiting Ones come to take leave.'

'But I say, I don't think that will quite do. I've seen him. He's terribly disfigured, you know.'

'If there are any special little difficulties in the case, you must mention them to our cosmeticians. You will be seeing one of them before you leave. They have never failed yet.'…

'You are sure that they will be able to make him presentable?'

'We had a Loved One last month who was found drowned. He had been in the ocean a month and they only identified him by his wrist-watch. They fixed that stiff,' said the hostess disconcertingly lapsing from the high diction she had hitherto employed, 'so he looked like it was his wedding-day. The boys up there surely know their job.'…

'That's very comforting.'

'I'll say it is.' And then slipping on her professional manner again as though it were a pair of glasses, she resumed, 'How will the Loved One be attired? We have our own tailoring section… You see, we can fit a Loved One out very reasonably as a casket-suit does not have to be designed for hard wear and in cases where only the upper part is exposed for leave-taking there is no need for more than jacket and vest...

Dennis was entirely fascinated...

The hostess led him to a set of sliding shelves like a sacristy chest where vestments are stored, and drawing one out revealed a garment such as Dennis had never seen before. Observing his interest she held it up for his closer inspection. It was in appearance like a suit of clothes, buttoned in front but open down the back; the sleeves hung loose, open at the seam; half an inch of linen appeared at the cuff and the V of the waistcoat was similarly filled; a knotted bowtie emerged from the opening of a collar which also lay as though slit from behind...

'A speciality of our own,' she said, 'though it is now widely imitated. The idea came from the quick-change artists in vaudeville. It enables one to dress the Loved One without disturbing the pose.'

'Remarkable. I believe that is just the article we require.'

'With or without trousers?'

From *The Loved One*, 1948

## The Brothers Grimm: Jacob Ludwig Carl Grimm (1785–1863) and Wilhelm Carl Grimm (1786–1859)

# *Inevitable death*

In ancient times a giant was once travelling on a great highway, when suddenly an unknown man sprang up before him, and said: 'Halt, not one step farther!'

'What!' cried the giant, 'a creature whom I can crush between my fingers, wants to block my way? Who are you that you dare to speak so boldly?' 'I am Death,' answered the other. 'No one resists me, and you also must obey my commands.'

But the giant refused, and began to struggle with Death. It was a long, violent battle, in which at last the giant got the upper hand, and struck Death down with his fist, so that he collapsed by a stone. The giant went his way, and Death lay there conquered, and so weak that he could not get up again.

'What will be done now,' said he, 'if I stay lying here in a corner? No one will die in the world, and it will get so full of people that they won't have room to stand beside each other.'

In the meantime a young man came along the road, who was strong and healthy, singing a song, and glancing around on every side. When he saw the half-fainting one, he went compassionately to him, raised him up, poured a strengthening draught out of his flask for him, and waited till he regained his strength.

'Do you know,' said the stranger, whilst he was getting up, 'who I am, and who it is you have helped on his legs again?'

'No,' answered the youth, 'I do not know you.'

'I am Death,' said he. 'I spare no one, and can make no exception with you, – but that you may see that I am grateful, I promise you that I will not fall on you unexpectedly, but will send my messengers to you before I come and take you away.'

'Well,' said the youth, 'it is something gained that I shall know when you come, and at any rate be safe from you for so long.'

Then he went on his way, and was light-hearted, and enjoyed himself, and lived without thought. But youth and health did not last long. Soon came sicknesses and sorrows, which tormented him by day, and took away his rest by night.

'Die, I shall not,' said he to himself, 'for Death will send his messengers before that, but I do wish these wretched days of sickness were over.'

As soon as he felt himself well again he began once more to live merrily. Then one day someone tapped him on the shoulder.

He looked round, and Death stood behind him, and said: 'Follow me, the hour of your departure from this world has come.'

'What,' replied the man, 'will you break your word? Did you not promise me that you would send your messengers to me before coming yourself? I have seen none!'

'Silence!' answered Death. 'Have I not sent one messenger to you after another? Did not fever come and smite you, and shake you, and cast you down? Has dizziness not bewildered your head? Has not gout twitched you in all your limbs? Did not your ears sing? Did not tooth-ache bite into your cheeks? Was it not dark before your eyes? And besides all that, has not my own brother Sleep reminded you every night of me? Did you not lie by night as if you were already dead?'

The man could make no answer. He yielded to his fate, and went away with Death.

'Death's Messengers', *Grimm's Fairy Tales*, 1812, 1815, 1822

**Muriel Spark (b. 1918)**

# *Burial or cremation?*

*In* Memento Mori, *Muriel Spark describes the lives of a group of elderly people facing death. In this extract Godfrey prepares to leave a funeral wake and return home to his wife Charmian:*

'What do you feel about the cremation service?'

'First rate,' said Godfrey, 'I've quite decided to be cremated when my turn comes. Cleanest way. Dead bodies under the ground only contaminate our water supplies...'

'I thought it was cold,' said Tempest, 'I do wish the minister had read out poor Lisa's obituary. The last cremation I was at – that was Ronald's poor brother Henry – they read out his obituary from the *Nottingham Guardian*, all about his war service and his work for SSAFA and Road Safety. It was so very moving. Now why couldn't they have read out Lisa's?'...

'I quite agree,' said Godfrey...

'I have been to Lisa Brooke's funeral,' he said to Charmian when he got home, 'or rather cremation... I have quite decided to be cremated when my time comes... It is the cleanest way... Cremation is best.'

'I do so agree with you,' said Charmian sleepily.

'No, you do *not* agree with me,' he said. 'R.C.s are not allowed to be cremated.'

'I mean I'm sure you're right, Eric dear.'

'I am not Eric,' said Godfrey. 'You are not sure I'm right. Ask Mrs Anthony, she'll tell you that R.C.s are against cremation.' He opened the door and bawled for Mrs Anthony.

'Mrs Anthony, you're a Roman Catholic, aren't you?' said Godfrey.

'That's right. I've got something on the stove.'

'Do you believe in cremation?'

'Well,' she said, 'I don't really much like the idea of being shoved away quick like that. I feel somehow it's sort of –'

'It isn't a matter of how you feel, it's a question of what your Church says you've not got to do. Your Church says you must not be cremated, that's the point.'

'Well, as I say, Mr Colston, I don't really fancy the idea –'

'*Fancy the idea*... It is not a question of what you fancy. You have no choice in the matter, do you see?'

'Well, I always like to see a proper burial, I always like –'

'It's a point of discipline in your Church that you mustn't be cremated. You women don't know your own system.'

'I see, Mr Colston. I've got something on the stove.'

'I believe in cremation, but you don't – Charmian, you disapp*rove* of cremation, you understand.'

'Very well, Godfrey.'

'And you too, Mrs Anthony.'

'O.K. Mr Colston.'

'On principle,' said Godfrey.

'That's right,' said Mrs Anthony, and disappeared.

From *Memento Mori*, 1959

## John Donne (1572–1631)

# *Inevitable death*

We are all conceived in close prison; in our mothers' wombs we are close prisoners all; when we are born, we are born but to the liberty of the house; prisoners still, though within larger walls; and then all our life is but a going out to the place of execution, to death. Now was there ever man seen to sleep in the cart, between Newgate and Tyburn? Between the prison and the place of execution, does any man sleep? And we sleep all the way; from the womb to the grave we are never thoroughly awake, but pass on with such dreams and imaginations as these – I may live as well as another, and why should I die rather than another? But awake and tell me, says this text, *Quis homo?* Who is that other that thou talkest of? *What man is he that liveth and shall not see death?*

From 'Sermon XXVII', preached 'to the Lords upon Easter Day at the communion, the King being dangerously sick at Newmarket', 28 March 1619

### Pope John XXIII (Angelo Roncalli) (1881–1963)

# *Ready for a good death*

I keep myself ready and prepared for death every day, and for a good death, desiring nothing else but the Lord's will... living in this way, every day being ready and prepared for a good death, ends by filling my heart with a profound and serene sense of peace, even greater than I had before, surely a foretaste of heaven where our dear ones are awaiting us.

From a letter to his sister, Maria, 8 January 1955

# Author Biographies

**ACKROYD, Peter (b. 1949)**
English novelist and highly successful biographer of T.S. Eliot, Dickens and Blake. He writes with affection and special understanding about London, where he lives.

**ALCOTT, Louisa May (1832–88)**
American author, served as a nurse in the Civil War and later published her letters home. Fame came with the publication of *Little Women*.

**ALIGHIERI, Dante (1265–1321)**
Italian poet, born in Florence of noble parents; the idealised love of his life was Beatrice, of whom little is known. She is his guide to Paradise in the *Divina Commedia*, his greatest work.

**ANDERSEN, Hans Christian (1805–75)**
Danish author, son of a poor shoemaker, whose education was paid for by generous friends. He is famous for his fairy stories for children.

**ANGELOU, Maya (Marguerite Johnson) (b. 1928)**
American activist and writer, brought up by her grandmother in the black community of Arkansas. She has been waitress, singer, dancer, actress, black activist, poet and writer, and is now a professor of American Studies.

**ASHFORD, Daisy (1881–1972)**
English child writer, who discovered in 1919 the manuscript of the book she had written when she was nine. It was published – with original spellings – and became a best-seller.

**AUSTEN, Jane (1775–1817)**
English novelist, the seventh child of a country parson, she led an uneventful life in Hampshire and Bath; her handful of novels arguably make her one of the greatest novelists.

**BACON, Francis (1561–1626)**
English statesman, philosopher and essayist, who contributed to scientific advancement. Created viscount of St Albans. Best remembered for his *Essays*, which he predicted would 'last as long as books last'.

*BAINBRIDGE, Beryl (b. 1934)*
English writer, born in Liverpool, now living in London, an actress before becoming a novelist and playwright. Several of her novels have been short-listed for the Booker Prize and she has gained other literary awards.

*BAXTER, Richard (1615–91)*
English Puritan clergyman during the Civil War, Restoration of the monarchy, the Great Plague and the Fire of London. Best known for *The Saints' Everlasting Rest*.

*BEDE, the Venerable (c. 673–735)*
British historian and lifelong monk at Jarrow in North-East England; studied widely and wrote – in Latin – an *Ecclesiastical History of the English People*, translated into Anglo-Saxon by (or at the command of) King Alfred.

*BENNETT, Alan (b. 1934)*
Northern English actor, director and playwright, appeared in *Beyond the Fringe* at the 1960 Edinburgh Festival; has written for television and stage. His *Talking Heads* monologues were first shown on television in 1988.

*BENNETT, Arnold (1867–1931)*
English novelist, grew up in the Pottery towns of Staffordshire, in which he set most of his novels. Began his career as a journalist living some years in Paris.

*BETJEMAN, John (1906–84)*
English poet, broadcaster and writer on architecture, high-church Anglican, became Poet Laureate in 1972 and was a much-loved public figure.

*BORROW, George (1803–81)*
English author and linguist, learned the language of gypsies and others among whom he lived; translated the Bible and travelled abroad for the Bible Society; he wrote colourful accounts of his experiences.

*BOSWELL, James (1740–95)*
Son of a Scottish judge, studied law but aspired to literary fame; famous for his biography of Samuel Johnson, to whom he was a loyal friend and travelling companion.

*BRAGG, Melvyn (b. 1939)*
English novelist, read history at Oxford and works extensively in television and radio; he has written some fifteen novels as well as works of non-fiction.

### BRUEGGEMANN, Walter (b. 1933)

A minister of the United Church of Christ and a widely published author. He is professor of Old Testament at Columbia Theological Seminary, Georgia, USA, and he has devoted his life to a passionate exploration of Old Testament theology.

### BUNYAN, John (1628–88)

English writer and preacher, son of a tinker. Converted after deep spiritual anguish and joined a Nonconformist congregation in Bedford; twice imprisoned for preaching without a licence. Best known for his allegorical *Pilgrim's Progress*.

### BUTLER, Samuel (1835–1902)

English writer, painter and musician, quarrelled with his clergyman father and went to New Zealand; returned to London, studied art, painted, wrote oratorios and translated Homer but is remembered for his autobiographical *The Way of All Flesh*.

### CARROLL, Lewis (Charles Dodgson) (1832–98)

The third of eleven children, a mathematician and Oxford lecturer. Alice, of *Alice's Adventures in Wonderland*, was the daughter of the dean of his college. He also wrote a mathematical work and other nonsense verse and prose.

### CERVANTES, Miguel de (1547–1616)

A devout Catholic, son of a poor doctor, had an adventurous career in the Spanish navy and army, was wounded, later taken prisoner, finally ransomed and returned to Spain. His comic epic, *Don Quixote* was an immediate and lasting success.

### CHAUCER, Geoffrey (c. 1343–1400)

English poet, courtier, diplomat and civil servant, best known for his *Canterbury Tales*, a collection of stories told by pilgrims travelling to the shrine of St Thomas à Becket. *The Prologue to the Canterbury Tales* describes the pilgrims themselves.

### CHEKHOV, Anton (1860–1904)

Russian playwright and writer, grandson of a Russian serf; qualified as a doctor in Moscow; he wrote magazine articles, then later plays and short stories. He died of tuberculosis soon after the premiere of *The Cherry Orchard*.

### CHESTERTON, G.K. (Gilbert Keith) (1874–1936)

English essayist, poet, novelist, critic, artist and biographer and staunch apologist for the Christian faith; became a Roman Catholic in 1922. Known popularly for his short stories of the detective-priest, Father Brown.

### CHURCHILL, Winston (1874–1965)

British statesman and charismatic leader of the country through the Second

World War, also an artist, brilliant orator and writer, best known for his *History of the English-Speaking Peoples*.

## COETZEE, J.M. (John Michael) (b. 1940)
South African novelist, educated there and in the United States as a computer scientist and linguist; became Professor of General Literature at the University of Cape Town. *Life and Times of Michael K* won the Booker Prize for 1983.

## CONRAD, Joseph (1857–1924)
Polish-born short-story writer and novelist, who served in the British merchant navy, later settled in England and became a British citizen.

## COWPER, William (1731–1800)
Elder son of a rector, his mother died when he was six. A great poet, he was dogged by severe depression and episodes of madness, and nursed back to health by two devoted women friends. He was also a close friend of John Newton; together they wrote the *Olney Hymns*.

## CUTHBERT, Abbot of Wearmouth and Jarrow (c. 673–735)
Not the St Cuthbert of whom Bede writes but a younger contemporary of the Venerable Bede. He witnessed Bede's death and later became abbot of Wearmouth and Jarrow.

## DEFOE, Daniel (1660–1731)
English author and adventurer, travelled widely on the Continent before setting up in business. His fiction reads like fact or an eyewitness account. *Robinson Crusoe* was based on the experience of a castaway, Alexander Selkirk.

## DICKENS, Charles (1812–70)
English writer of prolific output and creativity. His novels and stories entertain and expose the social evils of the time. He had a lifelong love of the theatre and his public readings from his books were hugely popular in the UK and the USA.

## DINESON, Isak (Karen Blixen) (1885–1962)
Danish writer; studied art in Copenhagen, Paris and Rome. She (at first with her husband), managed a coffee plantation in Kenya, returning to Denmark in 1931.

## DONNE, John (1572–1631)
English poet, courtier and cleric who became dean of St Paul's Cathedral. Metaphysical wit characterises his passionate love poems and illuminates the later religious sonnets; the greatest preacher of his time, crowds flocked to hear him.

## DOSTOEVSKY, Fyodor (1821–81)

Russian-born writer condemned to death and sent instead to Siberia for supposed involvement in a socialist plot; one of the greatest Russian novelists, he also portrayed some of the horrors of society of his time.

## ELIOT, George (Mary Ann Evans) (1819–80)

English novelist, born Mary Ann (Marion) Evans; she rejected early evangelical Christian beliefs but retained her strong sense of justice and compassion. She set up home with G.H. Lewes, who persuaded her to write fiction. *Middlemarch* is probably her greatest achievement.

## ELIOT, T.S. (Thomas Stearns) (1888–1965)

American-born poet, critic and dramatist; became a British subject and an Anglican. He studied at Harvard, Paris and Oxford. Encouraged by Ezra Pound, he published his ground-breaking poetry, the best known being *The Waste Land* and *Four Quartets*.

## FAULKS, Sebastian (b. 1953)

British writer, worked as a journalist for fourteen years before becoming a full-time writer in 1991. *Birdsong* – his fourth novel, a deeply moving story of love and the horrors of the First World War – made him widely known.

## FORSTER, E.M. (Edward Morgan) (1879–1970)

English novelist, mixed at Cambridge with members of the Bloomsbury circle. His novels give insight into the ethos of middle-class Britain before the First World War; he won literary prizes for perhaps his greatest novel – *A Passage to India*.

## FORSTER, Margaret (b. 1938)

English novelist and biographer, has achieved success with much-praised biographies and novels – each different and distinctive. She is married to writer and broadcaster Hunter Davies.

## FOXE, John (1516–87)

Staunch English Protestant whose *History of the Acts and Monuments of the Church*, usually known as *Foxe's Book of Martyrs*, was highly popular and influential. It tells the stories of the Protestant martyrs from the fourteenth century to Foxe's own day.

## GASKELL, Elizabeth (1810–65)

Northern England novelist, married a well-known Unitarian minister; she knew Dickens and Charlotte Brontë, whose biography she wrote. She worked tirelessly for the poor and wrote from a strong desire for social justice and reconciliation between the English classes.

## GOLDING, William (1911–93)
English writer, educated at Oxford, worked in the theatre, served in the Royal Navy during the Second World War. He taught before achieving international fame with *Lord of the Flies* in 1954. *Rites of Passage* won him the Booker Prize in 1980.

## GORKY, Maxim (Aleksei Maximovich Peshkov) (1868–1936)
Russian novelist and playwright; lived a nomadic early life, described in his autobiographical trilogy. His writing changed from romanticism to realism. He supported the Soviet regime.

## GOUDGE, Elizabeth (1900–84)
English novelist, daughter of a clergyman, spent her early years in Salisbury, Ely, Wells and Oxford – later settings for her gentle novels, where goodness triumphs. *Green Dolphin Country* was her first success.

## GRAHAME, Kenneth (1859–1932)
Scottish writer who grew up in England; he became secretary of the Bank of England, but retired in 1908 on health grounds. As well as his more famous *The Wind in the Willows*, he wrote about children in *The Golden Age* and *Dream Days*.

## GRAY, Thomas (1716–71)
English academic and poet, author of *Elegy Written in a Country Churchyard*, composed in the churchyard at Stoke Poges in Buckinghamshire, where he is buried. The poem has been considered near perfect of its kind.

## GREENE, Graham (1904–91)
English novelist, biographer, essayist, playwright. In 1926 he was received into the Roman Catholic Church, though his writing was not always considered orthodox by the Church. Many consider him the greatest novelist of his time.

## GRIMM, the Brothers: Jacob Ludwig Carl Grimm (1785–1863) and Wilhelm Carl Grimm (1786–1859)
German brothers, folklorists and philologists and professors in Berlin; Jacob Grimm produced a ground-breaking work on philology. They collected traditional folk stories and compiled three books of fairy stories which became the basis for the science of comparative folklore.

## GRISHAM, John (b. 1955)
American writer and international best-seller of suspense fiction. Many of his books have been made into films. He lives with his family in Virginia and Mississippi. He is a Christian belonging to the Southern Baptist Church.

## HARDY, Thomas (1840–1928)

English poet, novelist and dramatist, trained as an architect but turned to writing. He showed almost unremitting pessimism in the plotting of his novels, though *Under the Greenwood Tree* is a happy exception to this rule.

## HARTLEY, L.P. (Leslie Poles) (1895–1972)

An English writer of short stories with a macabre twist who later turned to novel-writing. *The Shrimp and the Anemone* is the first of a trilogy, but he is probably best known for *The Go-Between*, written in 1953, which has since been made into a film.

## HENRY, O. (William Sydney Porter) (1862–1910)

American writer, still considered one of the most popular American short-story writers. After a term of imprisonment for embezzling, he turned to writing. His stories are characterised by the unexpected 'twist in the tale'.

## HILL, Susan (b. 1942)

English writer and critic born in North Yorkshire; she has written novels and children's books – gaining literary awards – as well as biography. She broadcasts regularly and reviews fiction.

## HOWATCH, Susan (b. 1940)

British popular writer of international best-selling novels. She read law, lived in the USA but has returned to the UK. After conversion to Christian faith she continues to write highly readable best-sellers, exploring themes of truth, love, suffering and forgiveness. The Starbridge novels are centred on life in a cathedral city.

## HUXLEY, Aldous (1894–1963)

British writer, member of the famous scientific family, who changed from studying science to arts because of bad eyesight. He wrote essays, poetry, short stories and novels; one of which – *Brave New World* – describes a hellish Utopia created by science.

## IRVING, John (b. 1942)

Born in Exeter, New Hampshire, he published his first novel at the age of twenty-six. He is reckoned to be one of America's leading writers, and his highly successful and popular novels include *A Prayer for Owen Meany*, *The Cider House Rules* and *A Son of the Circus*. He lives in the USA and Canada.

## JAMES, P.D. (Phyllis Dorothy) (b. 1920)

British crime-writer, created Baroness James of Holland Park for her public and parliamentary duties. She worked in the Home Office, involved in the forensic science service, and the criminal law department before becoming a full-time writer.

### JOHN XXIII, Pope (Angelo Roncalli) (1881–1963)

Born the third of thirteen children to a family of farmers in northern Italy. In 1958, at nearly seventy-seven, he was elected as caretaker pope on the death of Pius XII. Instead, he initiated reforms through the Second Vatican Council, which had far-reaching effects on the Roman Catholic Church. He had a delightful sense of humour and was a gentle, loving and humble man of God.

### JOHNSON, Samuel (1709–84)

English writer, critic, lexicographer, born in Lichfield, where his father had a bookshop. He was a voracious reader, brilliant conversationalist and loyal friend. James Boswell portrays Johnson vividly in his biography of the great man.

### JULIAN of Norwich (c. 1342–after 1413)

English mystic and anchoress, lived in a cell outside the church of St Julian in Norwich. She wrote *The Revelations of Divine Love* – sixteen revelations, or 'showings', received after a near-fatal illness. It is probably the first book in English by a woman.

### KEMPE, Margery (c. 1373–c. 1440)

English mystic and eccentric; after several failed business ventures, and the birth of fourteen children, she devoted herself to pilgrimage and the spiritual life. She dictated her autobiography – the earliest in English – and the manuscript was discovered in 1934.

### KEMPIS, Thomas à (1379–1471)

German religious writer, entered an Augustinian convent in the Netherlands where he took holy orders, became sub-prior, then superior. His best-known writing is *The Imitation of Christ*, read and valued by Christians of all denominations.

### KILVERT, Francis (1840–79)

English clergyman and diarist, curate at Clyro in Radnorshire and later vicar of Bredwardine on the River Wye. His diaries – discovered in 1937 – give a vivid picture of country life in the Welsh Marches and Wiltshire where he assisted his clergyman father.

### KINGSLEY, Charles (1819–75)

English writer and cleric, a Christian Socialist who did much to improve social conditions both in his social novels and by his practical action. He was later made canon of Westminster and chaplain to Queen Victoria.

## KIPLING, Rudyard (1865–1936)

British poet and writer, born in India, where he later returned as a journalist. He is best remembered for his children's books – especially the *Jungle Books* and *Just So Stories*. He was awarded the Nobel Prize for Literature in 1907.

## LAMB, Charles (1775–1834)

English essayist, born in London; at Christ's Hospital School he formed a lasting friendship with the poet Coleridge. His essays were published under the pseudonym of Elia.

## LANGLAND, William (c. 1332–c. 1400)

English poet; his *Piers the Ploughman* describes a dream-journey to find truth in the course of which the poet bitterly attacks the church's hypocrisy and describes the people he meets with wit and exuberance.

## LAW, William (1686–1761)

William Law, cleric and writer, wrote *A Serious Call to a Devout and Holy Life* (usually known as *Law's Serious Call*) which has had profound influence. The Wesley brothers as well as Dr Johnson owed much to it.

## LESSING, Doris (b. 1919)

Zimbabwean novelist and short-story writer, came to England in 1949; briefly belonged to the Communist party and was declared a 'prohibited immigrant' by (as it then was) Rhodesia. Her writing mainly explores the political and social undercurrents in contemporary society.

## LEWIS, C.S. (Clive Staples) (1898–1963)

Irish-born academic and writer, popular communicator of the Christian faith. *Screwtape Letters* 'records' the letters of a senior devil to his young nephew; probably best remembered now for his *Narnia* series of children's stories.

## LINCOLN, Abraham (1809–65)

Sixteenth president of the USA; he defended the rights of slaves and successfully led the country to victory against the Confederates. Elected for a second term of office, but assassinated soon after.

## LIVELY, Penelope (b. 1933)

British writer, grew up in Egypt, settled in England after the Second World War and studied at Oxford. She won both the Carnegie Medal and the Whitbread Award for her children's books before writing for adults. *Moon Tiger* won the Booker Prize in 1987.

## LOFTING, Hugh (1886–1947)

English children's writer, author of the Dr Doolittle stories, which he also illustrated. They began as letters to his children from the trenches in the First World War, inspired by the part that horses played in the war.

## MACAULAY, Rose (1881–1958)

British novelist and essayist, daughter of a Cambridge academic. She read history at Oxford and wrote both travel books and novels. Her last novel, *The Towers of Trebizond*, won the James Tait Black Memorial Prize.

## MACDONALD, George (1824–1905)

Scottish poet and novelist, educated at Aberdeen University, became a Dissenting minister, then a university professor. He wrote allegorical novels but is best known for his children's books. C.S. Lewis acknowledged him as a great modern myth-maker.

## MELVILLE, Herman (1819–91)

American novelist with English and Dutch ancestry. At fifteen he went as a cabin boy and spent eighteen months on a whaling ship. He wrote adventure stories before his masterpiece, *Moby Dick*, which reveals his earnest search for a religious faith.

## MILNE, A.A. (Alan Alexander) (1882–1956)

English children's writer and essayist, became assistant editor of *Punch* but famous for his children's books of verse and the *Winnie-the-Pooh* books, written for his young son, Christopher Robin.

## MONTAGU, Lady Mary Wortley (1689–1762)

Daughter of the duke of Kingston, she moved all her life in aristocratic circles and was famous for her wit and beauty. She was well-read and a good linguist, and probably the most cultured woman of her time. When her husband, Edward Wortley Montagu, grandson of the earl of Sandwich, was appointed ambassador to the Ottoman court, she accompanied him to Turkey. She is remembered for her letters to her sister, daughter and friends.

## MORE, Thomas (1478–1535)

English statesman and scholar, he became chancellor to Henry VIII. When he refused to sanction Henry's actions, he was dismissed from office and imprisoned in the Tower of London; later tried, found guilty and beheaded.

## MUGGERIDGE, Malcolm (1903–90)

English journalist, sage and wit, one time editor of *Punch*; once a self-confessed rake, he became a Christian and in 1982 was received into the Roman Catholic Church. He excelled on television but criticised the medium bitterly.

## MURDOCH, Iris (1919–99)
Anglo-Irish academic and writer of novels, plays and works of philosophy; she wrote twenty-six novels and won numerous literary awards. She contracted Alzheimer's disease, and its tragic course was detailed in her husband's biography and the film *Iris*.

## MURRAY, Les (b. 1918)
Outstanding Australian poet, grew up in a Calvinist family in the Australian outback, later returned to Christian faith via Roman Catholicism. For him, poetry and faith go together. He writes pithy and provocative prose as well as poetry.

## NEWTON, John (1725–1807)
English seaman who was involved in the slave trade. After conversion he took holy orders, renounced slavery and was 'the letter writer *par excellence* of the Evangelical Revival'. His best-known hymn was *Amazing Grace*.

## ORWELL, George (Eric Arthur Blair) (1903–50)
English writer, born in Burma; he fought in the Spanish Civil War and was a war correspondent in the Second World War. He is best known for his bitter satire on Communist ideology in his novels *Animal Farm* and *Nineteen Eighty-Four*.

## OWEN, Wilfred (1893–1918)
English poet of the First World War, killed only days before the November armistice of 1918. His poems about the horror and pity of war became more generally known when Benjamin Britten used them in his *War Requiem*.

## PASCAL, Blaise (1623–62)
French mathematician, physicist, theologian, writer and man of letters. In 1654 he had a life-changing vision of God. Best remembered for his *Pensées* (*Thoughts*), scattered sentences about his faith, never revised before his untimely death.

## PATON, Alan (1903–88)
South African writer, teacher and principal of a reformatory. His experiences and his Christian conscience made him speak and write against apartheid. *Cry, the Beloved Country* (1948) brought him international fame.

## PEACOCK, Thomas Love (1785–1866)
English satirical novelist and poet, entered the East India company in 1819. Best known for *Nightmare Abbey* and *Crochet Castle*; as a man of reason, he disliked 'crochets'; he also caricatured the Romantic poets.

## PENN, William (1644–1718)

English reformer and colonialist, converted and became a Quaker at twenty-six, later imprisoned in the Tower of London for blasphemy; here he wrote *No Cross, No Crown*. Charles II granted him land in America on which he made the 'holy experiment' of Pennsylvania.

## PEPYS, Samuel (1633–1703)

English diarist, London born; rose from junior clerk at the exchequer to secretary to the admiralty and secretary to the king for naval affairs; famous for his diary which evokes his life and the period with zest and in great detail.

## PETERS, Ellis (Edith Pargeter) (1913–95)

English historical and crime writer, she created the popular sub-genre of medieval whodunnits with a twelfth-century 'detective', Brother Cadfael; her historical research was thorough. She also worked extensively for Czechoslovakian freedom and arts.

## PHILLIPS, J.B. (John Bertram) (1906–82)

British clergyman, writer and Bible translator; his translation of the Pauline epistles (1947) was the first lively, contemporary version to appear. He later translated the whole New Testament and wrote stimulating books of popular Christian apologetics.

## POPE, Alexander (1688–1744)

Leading English poet and critic of the eighteenth century, noted for his biting wit as well as his brilliant verse. Small and sickly, he referred to 'this long disease, my life'. He associated with many contemporary writers and was a loyal friend but a deadly enemy.

## POTTER, (Helen) Beatrix (1866–1943)

English writer and illustrator of children's stories, her first were written for the children of her former governess. She later farmed in the Lake District and married a farmer; she was a generous friend of the newly formed National Trust.

## POTTER, Dennis (1935–94)

Born in the Forest of Dean, the son of a miner and educated at Oxford; he worked as a journalist and toyed with politics. But it was as a television playwright that he demonstrated his brilliance, using the medium in new and innovative ways – as in *Pennies from Heaven* and *The Singing Detective*. He attracted criticism as well as praise for his brutally honest and frank exposure of the human condition.

### PROUST, Marcel (1871–1922)

French novelist, born in Paris; a semi-invalid, at thirty-four he retreated to a sound-proof flat after his mother's death. *Remembrance of Things Past* (translated into English by C.K. Scott-Moncrieff from *À la recherche du temps perdu* and published in twelve volumes in 1941) brought Proust international acclaim.

### PYM, Barbara (1913–80)

English novelist, an editorial secretary, wrote five novels in the fifties; in the late seventies Philip Larkin and Lord David Cecil nominated her one of the most underrated novelists of the century. *Quartet in Autumn* was shortlisted for the Booker Prize.

### READ, Piers Paul (b. 1941)

British writer born in Yorkshire, England, educated at Ampleforth (Roman Catholic public school) and Cambridge. He has written a number of novels and is a staunch defender of his Catholic Christian beliefs.

### RICHARDSON, Henry Handel (Ethel Robertson) (1870–1946)

Australian writer, daughter of a doctor, born in Melbourne and grew up in various Victorian towns. Most of her work is based on personal experience; the main character in her trilogy *The Fortunes of Richard Mahoney* is based on her father.

### SAYERS, Dorothy L. (Leigh) (1893–1957)

English writer, best known for her Lord Peter Wimsey detective novels, she also wrote stimulating Christian apologetics, a ground-breaking play cycle on the life of Christ, *The Man Born to Be King*, and she translated two parts of Dante's *Divine Comedy*.

### SCOTT, Paul (1920–78)

English novelist, served in the British and Indian army. His *Raj Quartet*, set in the India of 1939–47, gives a vivid picture of the end of the Raj. *Staying On*, which continues the story of two minor characters in the Quartet, won the Booker Prize.

### SEWELL, Anna (1820–78)

English author of *Black Beauty*, brought up a Quaker; she experienced a Christian conversion at twenty-five. Her book, written to promote good treatment of horses, became a best-seller, selling two million in two years in the United States.

### SHAKESPEARE, William (1564–1616)

English – and universal – playwright, poet, actor, born in Stratford-on-Avon, went to London, finding fame and fortune as a member of an acting company for whom he later wrote plays. He ended his days in Stratford. His sonnets and plays reflect the human condition and emotions in poetry unsurpassed in any age or culture.

## SHAW, George Bernard (1856–1950)

Born in Dublin of Irish Protestant parents, left Ireland in 1871 and spent years in poverty and literary struggle before success as a playwright with the new drama of ideas. Deeply influenced by Karl Marx, he was a staunch member of the Fabian Society.

## SOLZHENITSYN, Alexander (b. 1918)

Russian writer, Nobel Prize winner, arrested in 1945 for criticising Stalin and sent to a labour camp for eight years; released on Stalin's death but exiled after publication in the West of *The Gulag Archipelago*; he lived in the USA, later returning to Russia.

## SPARK, Muriel (b. 1918)

Scottish novelist, short-story writer, biographer and poet; *The Prime of Miss Jean Brodie* first brought her fame. She became a Roman Catholic in 1954; since 1960 has lived mainly in Rome and New York. Created a Dame of the British Empire in 1993.

## SPENCE, Eleanor (b. 1928)

Outstanding Australian children's writer, in 1998 she received an emeritus award, presented to living Australian authors, for her children's writing. Her book *The October Child* was Book of the Year in 1977, an award given by The Children's Book Council of Australia.

## STEAD, Christina (1902–83)

Australian novelist, short-story writer, left Australia in 1928 returning permanently in 1974. She was not published in Australia until 1965. Her autobiographical novel, *The Man Who Loved Children*, is acknowledged as a twentieth-century masterpiece.

## STERNE, Laurence (1713–68)

Irish-born novelist, became prebendary of York in 1741 and later perpetual curate of Coxwold, in Yorkshire. His best-known novel, *Tristram Shandy*, was enthusiastically received in his lifetime, in spite of its highly idiosyncratic style.

## STEVENSON, Robert Louis (1850–94)

Scottish writer trained in law; he travelled widely, married Fanny Osbourne, an older, divorced woman and settled – with her son Lloyd – in Samoa, for Stevenson's health. He died young, from tuberculosis. Fame first came with *Treasure Island*.

*STOWE, Harriet (Elizabeth) Beecher (1811–96)*
American novelist with a strict puritanical upbringing, later married to a theology professor; best known for her anti-slavery novels, especially *Uncle Tom's Cabin*, she was very popular in Britain; she also wrote about New England life.

*SWIFT, Jonathan (1667–1745)*
Irish writer, satirist and cleric, dean of St Patrick's Cathedral, Dublin. An ardent pacifist who hated cruelty, he wrote many pamphlets and articles on religion and war. *Gulliver's Travels* is a biting satire on society and the 'Age of Reason'.

*TAYLOR, Jeremy (1613–67)*
English theologian and writer, best known for his treatises *Holy Living* and *Holy Dying*, widely read and prized; chaplain to Archbishop Laud and royal army chaplain in the Civil War; after the Restoration became bishop of Down and Connor.

*TERESA of Avila (1515–82)*
Spanish religious, born into a large and wealthy Spanish family; at twenty she ran away to join an order of nuns. She later reformed the Carmelite order, imposing a simple, more disciplined life-style; she founded other convents, combining mysticism with shrewd common sense, administrative skill and a fine sense of humour.

*THACKERAY, William Makepeace (1811–63)*
British writer and novelist, born in India, brought up by his great-grandmother and great-aunt in England. After Cambridge and travel on the Continent, he became a journalist in London. His masterpiece, *Vanity Fair*, is satirical but full of human warmth.

*TOLKIEN, J.R.R. (John Ronald Reuel) (1892–1973)*
South African-born philologist and writer, friend of C.S. Lewis at Oxford and fellow member of the 'Inklings' literary club. He constructed his own language and cosmography for the imaginary world of *The Hobbit* and *Lord of the Rings*; both reflect the author's Christian beliefs.

*TOLSTOY, Leo (1828–1910)*
Russian writer, philosopher, moralist and mystic. After serving in the army he lived on his Volga estate; his wife bore him thirteen children. He tried to put the Sermon on the Mount into practice, giving away his fortune and living as a peasant. *War and Peace* and *Anna Karenina* are among the greatest novels.

*TROLLOPE, Anthony (1815–82)*
English writer whose mother maintained the family by her writing. He became a

civil servant (he introduced the pillar-box for letters in Britain) and stood unsuccessfully for parliament. The Barchester novels, with their cathedral setting, brought him fame.

### TURGENEV, Ivan (1818–83)
Russian writer and playwright, grew up on the family estate. In 1850 he inherited his mother's fortune. *A Month in the Country* (his most highly acclaimed play) was published that year. He was briefly banished to his estate on political grounds and left Russia in 1863.

### TWAIN, Mark (Samuel Langhorne Clemens) (1835–1910)
American writer with a varied career. As a Mississippi steam-boat pilot, he met 'all the... types of human nature... to be found in fiction, biography or history'. Best remembered are *The Adventures of Tom Sawyer* and *The Adventures of Huckleberry Finn*.

### TYLER, Anne (b. 1941)
Born in Minneapolis, she has lived for many years with her family in Baltimore, where her novels are set. She is one of America's leading novelists and has been acclaimed as the 'greatest living novelist writing in English'. *Breathing Lessons* won the Pulitzer Prize and *The Accidental Tourist* was made into a major film.

### UPDIKE, John (b. 1932)
American novelist, poet and critic; studied at Harvard and the Ruskin School of Fine Art at Oxford and worked on the staff of the *New Yorker*. He won the Pulitzer Prize for fiction for two of his Rabbit novels.

### WALTON, Izaak (1593–1683)
English writer born in Stafford; he lived in London and became a close friend of John Donne. His best-known work, *The Compleat Angler*, extols the joys and virtues of fishing. First published in 1653, it has had lasting appeal.

### WAUGH, Evelyn (1903–66)
English novelist, travel writer and biographer, younger brother of Alec Waugh. In 1930 he became a Roman Catholic. His comic wit is brilliantly seen in *Vile Bodies*, *Scoop* and *The Loved One*, a satire on the American way of death.

### WEIL, Simone (1909–43)
French Jewish writer, published posthumously, interspersed a brilliant academic career with manual work, to experience its conditions first-hand. Drawn to Catholicism, she hesitated to join any organised religion. She worked for the French resistance in 1942 but died of tuberculosis, refusing to eat while victims of the Second World War still suffered.

### WHITE, Gilbert (1720–93)
English cleric and naturalist, lived most of his life in Selborne, Hampshire, later as curate at the church. He used close observation and experiment to investigate and record details of local flora and fauna, published in his *Natural History of Selborne*.

### WHYTE, Alexander (1836–1921)
Scottish writer, described as 'the last of the Puritans'. Minister of an Edinburgh church for forty years, he had a reputation for graphic and compelling preaching. He wrote a number of books, including studies of Bible – and Bunyan – characters.

### WILDE, Oscar (1854–1900)
Irish playwright, novelist and poet, best remembered for his lifestyle and his wit; he also wrote delightful children's stories, for his own sons. A tragic and brilliant man, the subject of scandal and imprisoned for homosexual practices, he died in exile in France.

### WILDER, Laura Ingalls (1867–1957)
American writer, who was in her sixties when, at her daughter's suggestion, she began to write down her childhood memories in what have become the widely known *Little House* series of children's books.

### WINTON, Tim (b. 1960)
Australian novelist, full-time writer since the age of twenty-two, winning an award with his first book, and the youngest winner of the Miles Franklin Award. Described as depicting 'the concrete, physical world with an optimism and a belief in goodness that is becoming increasingly rare'.

### WOLFE, Tom (b. 1931)
American journalist, pop-critic and novelist, gained a doctorate in American studies at Yale, then went into journalism. Probably best known for *The Bonfire of the Vanities*, his best-seller published in 1987, which satirises the New York of the 1980s.

### WORDSWORTH, Dorothy (1771–1855)
Sister of the poet William Wordsworth, lived with William at Dove Cottage at Grasmere in the Lake District. She kept a journal, intended for his eyes only; her description of some of the things they saw on their walks is echoed in his poems.

# Index of Authors

**A**

Peter Ackroyd 268, 374
Louisa May Alcott 116
Dante Alighieri 159
Hans Christian Andersen 32
Maya Angelou (Marguerite Johnson) 218, 263
Daisy Ashford 343
Jane Austen 168, 292

**B**

Francis Bacon 369
Beryl Bainbridge 243
Richard Baxter 239, 330
The Venerable Bede 115, 277
Alan Bennett 79
Arnold Bennett 297
John Betjeman 328
George Borrow 54
James Boswell 37, 370
Melvyn Bragg 258
Walter Brueggemann 64
John Bunyan 177, 200, 237, 244, 367
Samuel Butler 254, 301

**C**

Lewis Carroll (Charles Dodgson) 61, 310
Miguel de Cervantes 100
Geoffrey Chaucer 273
Anton Chekhov 345
G.K. (Gilbert Keith) Chesterton 73, 93, 197
Winston Churchill 326
J.M. (John Michael) Coetzee 23
Joseph Conrad 248
William Cowper 92
Cuthbert, Abbot of Wearmouth and Jarrow 365

**D**

Daniel Defoe 136, 285
Charles Dickens 21, 38, 59, 106, 118, 147, 199, 282
Isak Dinesen (Karen Blixen) 227

John Donne 211, 234, 381
Fyodor Dostoevsky 170

**E**

George Eliot (Mary Ann Evans) 161, 266, 299
T.S. (Thomas Stearns) Eliot 317

**F**

Sebastian Faulks 324
E.M. (Edward Morgan) Forster 337
Margaret Forster 359
John Foxe 120

**G**

Elizabeth Gaskell 98, 111, 287
William Golding 75
Maxim Gorky (Aleksei Maximovich Peshkov) 341
Elizabeth Goudge 87
Kenneth Grahame 18, 52, 108, 347
Thomas Gray 157
Graham Greene 230
Jacob Ludwig Carl Grimm 238, 356, 377
Wilhelm Carl Grimm 238, 356, 377
John Grisham 185

**H**

Thomas Hardy 103
L.P. (Leslie Poles) Hartley 339
O. Henry (William Sydney Porter) 122
Susan Hill 152
Susan Howatch 134
Aldous Huxley 34, 162, 196

**I**

John Irving 192

**J**

P.D. (Phyllis Dorothy) James 81
Pope John XXIII (Angelo Roncalli) 382
Samuel Johnson 221
Julian of Norwich 224

**K**

Margery Kempe   220
Thomas à Kempis   181
Francis Kilvert   26, 70, 105, 151
Charles Kingsley   279
Rudyard Kipling   40

**L**

Charles Lamb   138, 253
William Langland   225, 303
William Law   91, 209
Doris Lessing   53
C.S. (Clive Staples) Lewis   20, 149, 175, 236, 246, 250
Abraham Lincoln   321
Penelope Lively   155
Hugh Lofting   44

**M**

Rose Macaulay   305
George MacDonald   30
Herman Melville   202
A.A. (Alan Alexander) Milne   113
Lady Mary Wortley Montagu   289
Thomas More   137
Malcolm Muggeridge   77, 187
Iris Murdoch   85, 96
Les Murray   201

**N**

John Newton   132

**O**

George Orwell (Eric Arthur Blair)   283
Wilfred Owen   320

**P**

Blaise Pascal   131
Alan Paton   125
Thomas Love Peacock   63
William Penn   183
Samuel Pepys   56, 295
Ellis Peters (Edith Pargeter)   31, 269
J.B. (John Bertram) Phillips   83
Alexander Pope   68
(Helen) Beatrix Potter   294, 314
Dennis Potter   350
Marcel Proust   97, 166
Barbara Pym   352

**R**

Piers Paul Read   190
Henry Handel Richardson (Ethel Robertson)   57

**S**

Dorothy L. (Leigh) Sayers   179, 316, 349
Paul Scott   204
Anna Sewell   46
William Shakespeare   154
George Bernard Shaw   164
Alexander Solzhenitsyn   216
Muriel Spark   354, 379
Eleanor Spence   140
Christina Stead   361
Laurence Sterne   94, 146
Robert Louis Stevenson   42
Harriet (Elizabeth) Beecher Stowe   280
Jonathan Swift   71, 322

**T**

Jeremy Taylor   260
Teresa of Avila   214, 219
William Makepeace Thackeray   308
J.R.R. (John Ronald Reuel) Tolkien   17
Leo Tolstoy   188, 212, 331
Anthony Trollope   261
Ivan Turgenev   357
Mark Twain (Samuel Langhorne Clemens)   255
Anne Tyler   363

**U**

John Updike   372

**W**

Izaak Walton   102
Evelyn Waugh   48, 375
Simone Weil   226
Gilbert White   36
Alexander Whyte   142
Oscar Wilde   256
Laura Ingalls Wilder   271
Tim Winton   335
Tom Wolfe   312
Dorothy Wordsworth   28

# Index of Book Titles

## A

*Absolute Truths*   134–35
*Adventures of Huckleberry Finn, The*   255
*Ah, But Your Land is Beautiful*   125–26
*Alice's Adventures in Wonderland*   61–62
*All Things Considered*   93
*Anecdotes of Destiny*   227–28
*Argument Against Abolishing Christianity, An*
   71–72

## B

*Bell, The*   85–86, 96
*Bible Characters: Adam to Achan*   142–43
*Bible in Spain, The*   54–55
*Birdsong*   324–25
*Birthday Boys, The*   243
*Black Beauty*   46–47
*Bonfire of the Vanities, The*   312–13
*Book of Margery Kempe, The*   220
*Brave New World*   34–35

## C

*Childhood, Boyhood and Youth*   212–13
*Christmas Carol, A*   59–60
*Chronicles of Wasted Time*   77–78
*Cloud of Unknowing, The*   229
*Compleat Angler, The*   102
*Complete Fairy Tales of Hans Christian
  Andersen, The*   32–33
*Cranford*   98–99, 111–12
*Credo*   258–59
*Crime and Punishment*   170–71

## D

*David Copperfield*   147–48
*Dialogue of Comfort Against Tribulation, A*
  137
*Diaries of Jane Somers, The*   53
*Don Quixote*   100–101
*Down and Out in Paris and London*   283–84

## E

*Ecclesiastical History of the English People*
   115, 277–78
*Emma*   292–93
*End of a Childhood and Other Stories, The*
   57–58
*Essays* (of Francis Bacon)   369
*Essays of Elia*   253
*Eyeless in Gaza*   162–63

## F

*Fathers and Sons*   357–58
*Foxe's Book of Martyrs*   120–21

## G

*George MacDonald: An Anthology: 365
  Readings*   30
*Gift of the Magi, The*   122–24
*Golden Age, The*   347–48
*Grace Abounding to the Chief of Sinners; or, a
  Brief Revelation of the Exceeding Mercy of
  God in Christ, to His Poor Servant, John
  Bunyan*   200
*Grasmere Journals, The*   28–29
*Gravity and Grace*   226
*Great Contemporaries*   326–27
*Great Expectations*   21–22, 199
*Green Stick, The* see *Chronicles of Wasted Time*
*Grief Observed, A*   149–150
*Grimm's Fairy Tales*   238, 356, 377–78
*Gryll Grange*   63
*Gulliver's Travels*   322–323

## H

*Happy Prince and Other Stories, The*   256–57
*Hard Times*   282
*Have the Men Had Enough?*   359–60
*Heart of Darkness*   248–49
*Hobbit, The*   17

**I**

*I Know Why the Caged Bird Sings* 218, 263–65
*Imitation of Christ, The* 181–82
*In the Springtime of the Year* 152–53
*Innocence of Father Brown, The* 73–74, 197–98

**J**

*Jewel in the Crown, The* 204–206
*Journal of the Plague Year, A* 136
*Just So Stories* 40–41

**K**

*Kilvert's Diary* 26–27, 70, 105, 151

**L**

*Life and Times of Michael K* 23–24
*Life of Saint Teresa of Avila* 219
*Life of Samuel Johnson, The* 37, 370–71
*Life of Thomas More, The* 268, 374
*Lion, the Witch and the Wardrobe, The* 20, 175–76
*Little House on the Prairie, The* 271–72
*Little White Horse, The* 87
*Little Women* 117
*Loved One, The* 48–49, 375–76

**M**

*Man Born to Be King, The* 179–80
*Memento Mori* 354–55, 379–80
*Middlemarch* 266–67
*Moby Dick* 203
*Monk's Hood* 31, 269–70
*Murder in the Cathedral* 317
*Murder Must Advertise* 316
*My Childhood* 341–42

**N**

*Natural History of Selborne, The* 36
*No Cross, No Crown* 183–84
*North and South* 287–88

**O**

*October Child, The* 140–41
*Oliver Twist* 38–39
*On the Third Day* 190–91
*One Day in the Life of Ivan Denisovich* 216–17

**P**

*Patchwork Planet, A* 363
*Pensées* 131
*Perelandra* (renamed *Voyage to Venus*) 250–51
*Perennial Philosophy, The* 196
*Perfect Happiness* 155–56
*Persuasion* 168–69
*Pickwick Papers, The* 106–107
*Piers the Ploughman* 225, 303–304
*Pilgrim's Progress* 177–78, 237, 244–45
*Poems* (of Wilfred Owen) 320
*Power and the Glory, The* 230–31
*Prayer for Owen Meany, A* 192–93
*Problem of Pain, The* 236
*Prologue to the Canterbury Tales, The* 273–74

**Q**

*Quality of Sprawl, The: Thoughts About Australia* 201
*Quartet in Autumn* 352–53

**R**

*Rabbit, Run* 372–73
*Remembrance of Things Past* 97, 166–67
*Resurrection* 188–89
*Revelations of Divine Love* 224
*Riceyman Steps* 297–98
*Rites of Passage* 75–76
*Robinson Crusoe* 285–86

**S**

*Saints' Everlasting Rest, The* 239, 330
*Scission and Other Stories* 335–36
*Screwtape Letters, The* 246–47
*Serious Call to a Devout and Holy Life, A* 91, 209–210
*Shrimp and the Anemone, The* 339–40
*Silas Marner* 161, 299–300
*Stories of Russian Life* 345–46
*Story of Doctor Doolittle, The* 44–45
*Strong Meat* 349
*Swann's Way* see *Remembrance of Things Past*

## T

*Tale of Jemima Puddle-Duck, The*   314–15
*Tale of Peter Rabbit, The*   294
*Tale of Two Cities, A*   118–19
*Talking Heads*   79–80
*Taste for Death, A*   81–82
*Testament, The*   185–86
*Threat of Life, The: Sermons on Pain, Power and Weakness*   64–65
*Three Plays for Puritans*   164–65
*Through the Looking-Glass, and What Alice Found There*   310–11
*Towers of Trebizond, The*   306
*Tragedy of Othello, the Moor of Venice, The*   154
*Treasure Island*   42–43
*Tristram Shandy*   94–95, 146

## U

*Uncle Tom's Cabin*   280–81
*Under the Greenwood Tree*   103–104

## V

*Vanity Fair*   308–309
*Vita Nuova*   159–60
*Voyage to Venus* see *Perelandra*

## W

*War and Peace*   331–32
*Warden, The*   261–62
*Water Babies, The*   279
*Way of All Flesh, The*   254, 301–302
*Way of Perfection, The*   214–15
*Where Angels Fear to Tread*   337–38
*Wind in the Willows, The*   18–19, 52, 108–109
*Winnie-the-Pooh*   114

## Y

*Young Visiters* [sic], *The*   343–44
*Your God is Too Small*   83–84

# Acknowledgements

We would like to thank all who have given us permission to include extracts in this book, as indicated on the list below. Every effort has been made to trace and acknowledge copyright holders of all the relevant extracts included in this anthology. We apologize for any inadvertent errors or omissions that may remain, and would ask those concerned to contact the publishers, who will ensure that full acknowledgment is made in the future.

pp. 16, 25, 128–29, 222, 252, 275–76, 291: Scripture quotations are from the Good News Bible published by The Bible Societies/HarperCollins Publishers, copyright © 1966, 1971, 1976, 1992 American Bible Society.

pp. 25, 127–28, 233, 252, 318, 334: Scripture quotations are from the New Revised Standard Version published by HarperCollins Publishers, copyright © 1989 by the Division of Christian Education of the National Council of the Churches of Christ in the USA, and are used by permission. All rights reserved.

pp. 12, 50, 50–51, 232, 307: Reprinted with the permission of Scribner, an imprint of Simon & Schuster Adult Publishing Group, from The New Testament in Modern English, Revised Edition, translated by J.B. Phillips. Copyright © 1958, 1960, 1972 by J.B. Phillips. Published by HarperCollins Publishers Ltd. (UK).

pp. 66–67, 207, 208, 242, 334: Scripture quotations are from the Contemporary English Version published by The Bible Societies/HarperCollins Publishers, copyright © 1991, 1992, 1995 American Bible Society.

pp. 90, 144–45, 158, 174, 194–95, 223, 319, 351: Extracts from the Authorized Version of the Bible (The King James Bible), the rights in which are vested in the Crown, are reproduced by permission of the Crown's Patentee, Cambridge University Press.

pp. 90, 110, 129–30: Scripture quotations are taken from the Holy Bible, New Living Translation, copyright © 1996. Used by permission of Tyndale House Publishers, Inc., Wheaton, Illinois 60189. All rights reserved.

pp. 242, 364: Revised English Bible with the Apocrypha copyright © 1989 by Oxford University Press and Cambridge University Press.

ACKROYD, Peter: from The Life of Thomas More, Chatto and Windus, 1998.

ALCOTT, Louisa May: from Little Women, Penguin Popular Classics, 1994.

ALIGHIERI, Dante: from Vita Nuova, translated by Mark Musa, Oxford World's Classics, 1992.

ANDERSEN, Hans Christian: from The Complete Fairy Tales, Wordsworth Editions Ltd, 1997.

ANGELOU, Maya: from I Know Why the Caged Bird Sings by Maya Angelou, copyright © 1969 and renewed 1997 by Maya Angelou. Used by permission of Random House, Inc. Published by Time Warner Books UK and used by permission.

ASHFORD, Daisy: from *The Young Visiters* by Daisy Ashford published by Chatto & Windus. Used by permission of The Random House Group Limited.

AUSTEN, Jane: from *Emma*, Penguin Popular Classics, 1994, and from *Persuasion*, Penguin Popular Classics, 1994.

BACON, Francis: from *Essays*, Wordsworth Editions Ltd, 1997.

BAINBRIDGE, Beryl: from *The Birthday Boys*, Penguin Books, 1993.

BAXTER, Richard: from *The Saints' Everlasting Rest*, Evangelical Press, 1978.

BEDE: from *Ecclesiastical History of the English People*, translated by Leo Sherley-Price, edited by D.H. Farmer, Penguin Classics, 1990.

BENNETT, Alan: from 'Bed Among the Lentils' from *Talking Heads*, BBC Consumer Publishing, 1988.

BENNETT, Arnold: from *Riceyman Steps*, Pan Books, 1964.

BETJEMAN, John: from *Coming Home*, edited by Candida Lycett Green, Vintage, 1998.

BORROW, George: from *The Bible in Spain*, Pimlico, 1985.

BOSWELL, James: from *The Life of Samuel Johnson*, edited by Christopher Hibbert, Penguin Classics, 1979.

BRAGG, Melvyn: from *Credo*, Sceptre, 1996.

BRUEGGEMANN, Walter: reprinted by permission from *The Threat of Life* by Walter Brueggemann, copyright © 1996 Augsburg Fortress.

BUNYAN, John: from *The Pilgrim's Progress*, edited by Roger Sharrock, Penguin Classics, 1984, and from *Grace Abounding*, Everyman's Library, 1928.

BUTLER, Samuel: from *The Way of All Flesh*, Penguin Books, 1947.

CARROLL, Lewis: from *Through the Looking-Glass, and What Alice Found There*, Collins, 1954, and from *Alice's Adventures in Wonderland*, Macmillan, 1938.

CERVANTES, Miguel de: extract from *Don Quixote* by Miguel de Cervantes, translated by P. A. Motteux. Used by permission of Wordsworth Editions Ltd and Everyman's Library.

CHAUCER, Geoffrey: from *The Prologue to the Canterbury Tales*, OUP, 1946.

CHEKHOV, Anton: from 'Little Jack' from *Selected Stories* by Anton Chekhov, 1996 Wordsworth Classics. Used by permission of Wordsworth Editions Ltd.

CHESTERTON, G.K.: from *Father Brown Stories* by G.K. Chesterton. Reprinted by permission of A.P. Watt Ltd on behalf of The Royal Literary Fund. Extract from *All Things Considered* from *Selected Essays*, Collins, 1939.

CHURCHILL, Winston: from *Great Contemporaries*, Fontana/Collins, 1962. Copyright the Estate of Winston Churchill.

*The Cloud of Unknowing: A New Paraphrase*, edited by Halcyon Backhouse, Hodder and Stoughton Religious, 1985.

COETZEE, J.M.: from *Life and Times of Michael K* by J.M. Coetzee, copyright © 1983 by J.M. Coetzee published by Secker &Warburg. Used by permission of The Random House Group Limited and of Viking Penguin, a division of Penguin Group (USA) Inc.

CONRAD, Joseph: from *Heart of Darkness*, Oxford World's Classics, 1998.

COWPER, William: from *English Letters of the XVIII Century*, edited by James Aitken, Pelican, 1946.

CUTHBERT, Abbot of Wearmouth and Jarrow: from 'Letter on the Death of Bede', translated by D.H. Farmer and included in *Ecclesiastical History of the English People*, Penguin Classics, 1990.

DEFOE, Daniel: from *Robinson Crusoe*, Penguin Popular Classics, 1994, and from *A Journal of the Plague Year*, Oxford World's Classics, 1998.

DICKENS, Charles: extracts from *The Christmas Books*, volume 1, Penguin Classics, 1985; *David Copperfield*, Penguin Popular Classics, 1994; *Great Expectations*, Wordsworth Editions Ltd, 2000; *Hard Times*, Penguin Classics, 1969; *Oliver Twist*, Nelson – New Century; *A Tale of Two Cities*, Penguin Popular Classics, 1994.

DINESEN, Isak: from *Anecdotes of Destiny* by Isak Dinesen, copyright © 1958 by Isak Dinesen. Used by permission of Random House, Inc., and the Rungstedlund Foundation.

DONNE, John: extracts from *Sermons*, edited by John Hayward, Nonesuch Press, 1946.

DOSTOEVSKY, Fyodor: from *Crime and Punishment*, Oxford World's Classics, 1998.

ELIOT, George: from *Middlemarch*, Zodiac Press/Chatto and Windus, 1950, and from *Silas Marner*, Penguin Popular Classics, 1994.

ELIOT, T.S.: from 'Murder in the Cathedral' from *Collected Poems*, Faber and Faber Ltd.

FAULKS, Sebastian: from *Birdsong*, Vintage/Random House, 1994.

FORSTER, E.M.: from *Where Angels Fear to Tread* by E.M. Forster. Used by permission of The Provost and Scholars of King's College, Cambridge and the Society of Authors as the Literary Representative of the E.M. Forster Estate. Published by Random House, Inc. in the USA.

FORSTER, Margaret: from *Have the Men Had Enough?* by Margaret Forster published by Chatto & Windus. Used by permission of The Random House Group Limited. Copyright © Margaret Forster, 1989 by kind permission of the author and The Sayle Literary Agency.

FOXE, John: from *Book of Martyrs*, Zondervan (Clarion Classics).

GASKELL, Elizabeth: from *Cranford*, Dent/Everyman's Library, 1940, and from *North and South*, Penguin Popular Classics, 1994.

GOLDING, William: Excerpt from *Rites of Passage* by William Golding. Copyright © 1980 by William Golding. Reprinted by permission of Farrar, Straus and Giroux, LLC, and Faber and Faber Limited.

GORKY, Maxim: from *My Childhood* by Maxim Gorky, translated by Ronald Wilks (Penguin Classics, UK, 1966). Translation copyright © Ronald Wilks, 1966. Reproduced by permission of Penguin Books Ltd.

GOUDGE, Elizabeth: from *The Little White Horse*, Lion Publishing.

GRAHAME, Kenneth: from *The Wind in the Willows* and *The Golden Age*.

GRAY, Thomas: from 'Letter to William Mason' taken from *All in the End Is Harvest*, Dartman, Longman & Todd, 1991.

GREENE, Graham: extract from *The Power and the Glory* by Graham Greene. Published by Random House. Reprinted by permission.

GRIMM, Brothers: from *Complete Fairy Tales*, Wordsworth Editions Ltd, 1997.

GRISHAM, John: extract from *The Testament* by John Grisham, copyright © 1999 by Belfry Holding, Inc. and published by Century (UK). Used by permission of Doubleday, a division of Random House, Inc. (US), and The Random House Group Limited (UK).

HARDY, Thomas: from *Under the Greenwood Tree*, Macmillan, 1950.

HARTLEY, L.P.: from *The Shrimp and the Anemone*, Faber and Faber Ltd, 1975.

HENRY, O.: from *The Gift of the Magi and Other Short Stories*, Dover Publications, 1992.

HILL, Susan: from *In the Springtime of the Year*, Penguin Books, 1977.

HOWATCH, Susan: from *Absolute Truths* by Susan Howatch, copyright © 1995 by Susan Howatch. Used by permission of Alfred A. Knopf, a division of Random House, Inc. (US), and HarperCollins Publishers Ltd (UK).

HUXLEY, Aldous: extracts from *Brave New World* and *Eyeless in Gaza* by Aldous Huxley, copyright © Huxley Literary Estate (Laura Archera Huxley and Matthew Huxley). Used by permission. Extract from *The Perennial Philosophy* taken from *A Book of Faith*, Hodder, 1989. Used in that work by permission of Chatto and Windus and Mrs Laura Huxley.

IRVING, John: from *A Prayer for Owen Meany*, Ballantine Books, 1989.

JAMES, P.D.: from *A Taste for Death* by P.D. James, copyright © 1986 by P.D. James. Used by permission of Alfred A. Knopf, a division of Random House, Inc. (US), and Greene & Heaton Ltd (UK).

JOHN XXIII, Pope: from *In My Own Words*, edited by A.F. Chiffolo, Hodder, 1999.

JOHNSON, Samuel: taken from *English Letters of the XVIII Century*, edited by James Aitken, Pelican, 1946.

JULIAN OF NORWICH: from *Revelations of Divine Love*, edited by Grace Warrack, Methuen, 1920.

KEMPE, Margery: from *The Book of Margery Kempe*, translated by B.A. Windeatt, Penguin Classics, 1994.

KEMPIS, Thomas à: from *Imitation of Christ* by Thomas à Kempis, trs. Ronald Knox and Michael Oakley, Burns & Oates 1959. Reprinted by permission of The Continuum International Publishing Group.

KILVERT, Francis: from *Kilvert's Diary*, edited by William Plomer, Penguin, 1982.

KINGSLEY, Charles: from *The Water Babies*, Penguin Popular Classics, 1995.

KIPLING, Rudyard: from *How the Rhinoceros Got his Skin* from *Just So Stories*, by Rudyard Kipling, 1902. Reprinted by permission of A.P. Watt Ltd on behalf of The National Trust for Places of Historical Interest or Natural Beauty.

LAMB, Charles: extracts taken from *Essays of Elia* and *English Letters of the XVIII Century*, edited by James Aitken, Pelican, 1946.

LANGLAND, William: from *Piers the Ploughman* by William Langland, translated by J.F. Goodridge (Penguin Classics 1959, Revised Edition 1966) copyright © J.F. Goodridge, 1959, 1966. Reproduced by permission of Penguin Books Ltd.

LAW, William: from *A Serious Call to a Devout and Holy Life* by William Law. Reproduced by permission of Hodder and Stoughton Limited.

LESSING, Doris: from *Diaries of Jane Somers*, Penguin, 1985. Copyright © Doris Lessing 2002.

LEWIS, C.S.: extracts from *The Lion, the Witch and the Wardrobe* by C.S. Lewis copyright © C.S. Lewis Pte. Ltd. 1950; *A Grief Observed* by C.S. Lewis, published by Faber and Faber Ltd, copyright © C.S. Lewis Pte. Ltd. 1961; *The Problem of Pain* by C.S. Lewis copyright © C.S. Lewis Pte. Ltd. 1940; *Perelandra* by C.S. Lewis copyright © C.S. Lewis Pte. Ltd. 1944. Extracts reprinted by permission. Extract from *The Screwtape Letters*, Fontana, 1959.

LINCOLN, Abraham: from 'The Gettysburg Address', 1863.

LIVELY, Penelope: extract from *Perfect Happiness* by Penelope Lively. Published by Penguin Books Ltd, 1985. Reprinted by permission.

LOFTING, Hugh: from *Doctor Doolittle*, Puffin/Penguin, 1985.

MACAULAY, Rose: extract from *Towers of Trebizond* by Rose Macaulay. Reprinted by permission of PFD on behalf of: The Estate of Rose Macaulay. Reprinted by permission of HarperCollins Publishers Ltd. Copyright © 1956 Rose Macaulay.

MACDONALD, George: from *George MacDonald: An Anthology: 365 Readings*, edited by C.S. Lewis, Bles, 1946.

MELVILLE, Herman: from *Moby Dick*, Penguin Popular Classics, 1994.

MILNE, A.A.: from *Winnie the Pooh* © A.A. Milne. Copyright under the Berne Convention. Published by Egmont Books Limited and used with permission (UK and Commonwealth). From *Winnie-the-Pooh* by A.A. Milne, illustrated by E.H. Shepard, copyright 1926 by E.P. Dutton, renewed 1954 by A.A. Milne. Used by permission of Dutton Children's Books, A division of Penguin Young Readers Group, A Member of Penguin Group (USA) Inc., 345 Hudson St., New York, NY 10014. All rights reserved.

MONTAGU, Lady Mary Wortley: from *English Letters of the XVIII Century*, edited by James Aitken, Pelican, 1946.

MORE, Thomas: from *A Dialogue of Comfort Against Tribulation*, 1534.

MUGGERIDGE, Malcolm: from *The Green Stick*, volume 1 of *Chronicles of Wasted Time*, Fontana/Collins, 1972, and from an article in *The Observer*, 26 March 1967.

MURDOCH, Iris: extract from *The Bell* by Iris Murdoch published by Chatto & Windus. Used by permission of The Random House Group Limited. Copyright © 1958, renewed 1986 by Iris Murdoch. Used by permission of Viking Penguin, a division of Penguin Group (USA) Inc.

MURRAY, Les: from *The Quality of Sprawl*, Duffy and Snelgrove, 1999.

NEWTON, John: from *Letters of John Newton*, Banner of Truth Trust, 1960.

ORWELL, George: extract from *Down and Out in Paris and London* by George Orwell (Copyright © George Orwell, 1933) by permission of Bill Hamilton as the Literary Executor of the Estate of the Late Sonia Brownell Orwell and Secker and Warburg Ltd. Copyright 1933 by George Orwell and renewed 1961 by Sonia Pitt-Rivers, reprinted by permission of Harcourt, Inc. (USA).

OWEN, Wilfred: from Letter/Preface to *Poems*, Chatto and Windus, 1946.

PASCAL, Blaise: from *Pensées*, 1669.

PATON, Alan: extract from *Ah, But Your Land is Beautiful* by Alan Paton published by JonathanCape. Used by permission of The Random House Group Limited (UK). Copyright © Anne Paton. Used by permission.

PEACOCK, Thomas Love: from *Gryll Grange*, OUP, 1987.

PENN, William: from the preface to *No Cross, No Crown*, 1682.

PEPYS, Samuel: from *The Diary of Samuel Pepys: A Pepys Anthology*, edited by Robert Latham and Linnet Latham, HarperCollins, 2000.

PETERS, Ellis: extract from *Monk's Hood*, reprinted by permission of PFD on behalf of: The Estate of Edith Pargeter.. Copyright © 1980 Edith Pargeter.

PHILLIPS, J.B.: extract from *Your God is Too Small* by J.B. Phillips. Copyright © Trustees for Methodist Church Purposes. Used by permission of Methodist Publishing House.

POPE, Alexander: from *English Letters of the XVIII Century*, edited by James Aitken, Pelican, 1946.

POTTER, Beatrix: from *The Tale of Peter Rabbit* and *The Tale of Jemima Puddle-Duck*, F Warne and Co Ltd.

POTTER, Dennis: from an edited transcript of Melvyn Bragg's interview on Channel 4, 5 April 1994.

PROUST, Marcel: extracts from 'Swann's Way', translated by C.K. Scott Moncrieff, from *Remembrance of Things Past: Volume I* by Marcel Proust, translated by C.K. Scott Moncrieff and Terence Kilmartin, copyright © 1981 by Random House, Inc. and Chatto & Windus. Used by permission of the Estate of Marcel Proust, the Estate of Terence Kilmartin and The Random House Group Limited and Random House, Inc.

PYM, Barbara: extract from *Quartet in Autumn* by Barbara Pym. Published by Macmillan Publishers Ltd. Used by permission.

READ, Piers Paul: Extract from *On the Third Day* by Piers Paul Read published by Secker & Warburg.

RICHARDSON, Henry Handel: from 'Conversation in a Pantry', *The End of a Childhood and Other Stories*, 1934.

SAYERS, Dorothy L.: extract from *Man Born to be King* by Dorothy L Sayers, published by Gollancz. Used by permission. Other extracts from *Murder Must Advertise*, New English Library, 1981, and *Strong Meat*, Hodder and Stoughton, 1939.

SCOTT, Paul: from *The Jewel in the Crown*, Panther Granada, 1973, 1978.

SEWELL, Anna: from *Black Beauty*, Blackie and Son Ltd.

SHAKESPEARE, William: from *Othello*, Arden Shakespeare – Methuen, 1941.

SHAW, George Bernard: from the Preface to *Three Plays for Puritans*, Penguin Books, 1946.

SOLZHENITSYN, Alexander: from *One Day in the Life of Ivan Denisovich*, Penguin Books, 1963.

SPARK, Muriel: extracts from *Memento Mori* by Muriel Spark, published by Penguin. Used by permission.

SPENCE, Eleanor: extract from *The October Child* by Eleanor Spence. Copyright © 1976 Eleanor Spence.

STEAD, Christina: from *Penguin Best Australian Short Stories*, taken from *Festival and Other Stories*, edited by Brian Buckley and Jim Hamilton, Wren, 1974.

STERNE, Laurence: from *Tristram Shandy*, Everyman, 1946.

STEVENSON, Robert Louis: from *Treasure Island*, Penguin Popular Classics, 1994.

STOWE, Harriet Beecher: from *Uncle Tom's Cabin*, Penguin Classics, 1986.

SWIFT, Jonathan: from *A Modest Proposal and Other Satirical Works*, Dover Publications Inc., 1996, and from *Gulliver's Travels*, Penguin Classics, 1985.

TAYLOR, Jeremy: from a sermon preached in Dublin between 1651 and 1653.

TERESA OF AVILA: from *A Life of Prayer*, translated from the Spanish by David Lewis, edited by James Houston, Bethany House Publishers, 1998.

THACKERAY, William Makepeace: from *Vanity Fair*, Wordsworth Editions Ltd, 1993.

TOLKIEN, J.R.R.: from *The Hobbit*, Unwin, 1971.

TOLSTOY, Leo: from *Childhood, Boyhood and Youth*, Everyman's Library, 1933, from *Resurrection*, translated by Rosemary Edmonds, Penguin Classics, 1966, and from *War and Peace*, translated by Louise and Aylmer Maude, Wordsworth Editions Ltd, 1993.

TROLLOPE, Anthony: from *The Warden*, 1855.

TURGENEV, Ivan: from *Fathers and Sons*, Wordsworth Editions Ltd, 1966.

TWAIN, Mark: from *The Adventures of Huckleberry Finn*, Penguin Popular Classics, 1994.

TYLER, Anne: from *A Patchwork Planet*, Alfred Knopf, 1998.

UPDIKE, John: from *Rabbit, Run* by John Updike, copyright © 1960 and renewed 1988 by John Updike. Used by permission of Alfred A. Knopf, a division of Random House, Inc. Also published by Penguin Books, 1964, copyright © John Updike, 1960, 1964. Used by permission.

WALTON, Izaak: from *The Compleat Angler*, Wordsworth Editions Ltd, 1996.

WAUGH, Evelyn: extract reproduced from *The Loved One* by Evelyn Waugh (Copyright © Evelyn Waugh 1948) by permission of PFD on behalf of the Evelyn Waugh Trust.

WEIL, Simone: from *Gravity and Grace*, Routledge, 1953, 1997.

WHITE, Gilbert: from *The Natural History of Selborne*, 1788–89.

WHYTE, Alexander: from *Bible Characters: Adam to Achan*, 1896.

WILDE, Oscar: from *The Happy Prince and Other Stories*, 1888.

WILDER, Laura Ingalls: Extract from *Little House on the Prairie* © 1935 by Laura Ingalls Wilder. Published by Egmont Books Limited and used with permission.

WINTON, Tim: Extract from *Scission and Other Stories* by Tim Winton, 1987. Copyright © Tim Winton 1985, 1987. Published by Weidenfield and Nicolson.

WOLFE, Tom: from *The Bonfire of the Vanities*, Picador, 1987.

WORDSWORTH, Dorothy: from *The Grasmere Journals*, edited by Pamela Woof, OUP, 1993.